EDUCATION RECONFIGURED

D1611592

As philosophers throughout the ages have asked: What is justice? What is truth? What is art? What is law? In *Education Reconfigured*, the internationally acclaimed philosopher of education, Jane Roland Martin, now asks: What is education? In answer, she puts forward a unified theory that casts education in a brand new light. Martin's "theory of education as encounter" places culture alongside the individual at the heart of the educational process, thus responding to the call John Dewey made over a century ago for an enlarged outlook on education. Look through her theory's lens and you can see that education takes place not only in school but at home, on the street, in the mall—everywhere and all the time. Look through that lens and you can see that education does not always spell improvement; rather, it can be for the better or the worse. Indeed, you can see that education is inevitably a maker and shaper of both individuals and cultures.

Above all, Martin's new educational paradigm reveals that education is too important to be left solely to the professionals; that it is one of the great forces in human society and, as such, deserves the attention and demands the vigilance of every thoughtful person.

Jane Roland Martin is Professor of Philosophy, Emerita, University of Massachusetts Boston.

EDUCATION RECONFIGURED

Culture, Encounter, and Change

Jane Roland Martin

Routledge
Taylor & Francis Group

NEW YORK AND LONDON

KH

First published 2011
by Routledge
711 Third Avenue, New York, NY 10017

Simultaneously published in the UK
by Routledge
2 Park Square, Milton Park, Abingdon, Oxon OX14 4RN

Routledge is an imprint of the Taylor & Francis Group, an informa business

© 2011 Taylor & Francis

The right of Jane Roland Martin to be identified as author of this work
has been asserted by her in accordance with sections 77 and 78 of the
Copyright, Designs and Patents Act 1988.

Typeset in Bembo and Stone Sans by
Florence Production Ltd, Stoodleigh, Devon
Printed and bound in the United States of America on acid-free paper by
Walsworth Publishing Company, Marceline, MO

Library of Congress Cataloging in Publication Data
Martin, Jane Roland, 1929–.
  Education reconfigured: culture, encounter, and change/
  Jane Roland Martin.
      p. cm.
  1. Educational change.   2. Progressive education.   3. Educational
  sociology.   4. School management and organization—Social aspects.
  5. Education—Philosophy.   I. Title.
  LC199.M37 2011
  370.1—dc22   2011000555

ISBN: 978–0–415–88962–9 (hbk)
ISBN: 978–0–415–88963–6 (pbk)
ISBN: 978–0–203–82914–1 (ebk)

SUSTAINABLE
FORESTRY
INITIATIVE

Certified Sourcing
www.sfiprogram.org

The SFI label applies to the text stock.

3/19/10

To Michael Lou Martin

Education is too important to be left solely to the professionals.
Francis Keppel, 1916–1990

CONTENTS

ACKNOWLEDGMENTS

I am indebted to Lydia Hurd Smith for her careful reading of an early draft of Part I of this volume; Ann Diller, Susan Franzosa, Barbara Houston, Beebe Nelson, Jennifer Radden, and Janet Farrell Smith for their helpful extended discussions and critiques of early drafts of all but one chapter; Susan Laird for feedback on the last draft of the book and for passing down to the next generation of scholars my earlier work; and Maurice Stein for reading the completed manuscript several times over and giving it his whole-hearted support. I also owe special thanks to Peter Singer for looking over the sections of this book that pertain to non-human animals; Ted Stein, whose perceptive comments about the talk entitled "Education is Everywhere" I gave in the Brookhaven at Lexington Semafor Lecture Series in January 2009 made me realize that the theory I present here reclaims the broad sense of "education;" Lucy Townsend, whose comments on a revised version of that Semafor Lecture led me back to Bernard Bailyn's *Education in the Forming of American Society*, a book I had read many times but whose relevance to this project I had not yet fully understood; Janet Giele for our many fruitful talks about her sociological research on the family and my philosophical study of education; and Hilde Hein for our ongoing conversation about how to be a philosopher and stay in touch with the world. Finally and above all, I wish to thank Michael Martin, to whom this book is dedicated, for being willing to discuss every issue with me and for giving me good advice even in the hardest of times.

INTRODUCTION

No matter how the Western world's philosophical theories of education have differed from one another across the ages, they have all taken it for granted that whenever education occurs an individual has some sort of encounter, and that in this encounter the individual changes. I present here a theory of education that gives these basic insights of the past brand new form. Pulling together and carrying forward the philosophical ideas I have developed over several decades, "the theory of education as encounter," as I call it, reconfigures its subject.[1]

Whether every culture has a favored conception of what education is and what it can and cannot do, I am not able to say. Certainly Western culture does. Long ago John Dewey challenged a number of the assumptions that comprise the West's prevailing educational paradigm: most notably its divorce of mind from body, thought from action, and reason from feeling and emotion; but also its radical separation of school and society. However, one of the first discoveries I made when, in the early 1980s, I began to study the place of women in educational thought was that there was far more wrong with the dominant mode of educational thinking than even Dewey perhaps realized.

By 1980 feminist scholars in many fields had shown that women's works and deeds were missing from the historical record. The research I then undertook established that the insights of women educational thinkers had also been lost to history. Perhaps the greater significance of my investigations was, however, the revelation that a huge amount of human learning—the portion associated both historically and culturally with the world of the private home and family, and consequently with girls and women—had gone missing from educational thought. The theory of education as encounter seeks to rectify that error along with many others.[2]

My research on women also delivered me from my dogmatic attachment to the canons of the analytic philosophy in which I was trained. In particular, my discovery of the exclusion of the world of the private home and family from educational thought made me realize that, if I wanted to understand my subject, it would not be enough to analyze language, concepts, and arguments. I would also have to dig up the culture's fundamental, largely unspoken assumptions about education. What I here call "the deep structure of educational thought" is a systematic rendering of the findings I unearthed on my many archeological expeditions. Drawing the boundaries of the educational realm so as to give pride of place to human rationality, this tacit belief system excludes the greater part of human learning from education's purview. It is this unduly narrow conception of what education is that the theory of education as encounter seeks to replace.

As my work on women prompted my search for the assumptions by which a culture defines and delimits education, those archeological ventures opened my eyes to the limitations of the standpoint from which my colleagues in the philosophy of education and I tended to view education. My decision to develop an alternative "cultural wealth perspective" on education provided what turned out to be the immediate impetus for this book. For having distinguished between the dominant standpoint of the individual and the oft forgotten standpoint of the culture, I felt compelled to determine if it was possible to join the two perspectives together. I am able to call the theory of education as encounter "unified" because it combines the two very different standpoints from which education has historically been viewed—that of the individual and that of the culture.[3]

The consequences of synthesizing the two perspectives are much greater than anyone could have anticipated. It was perhaps to be expected that whatever theory I developed would reject definitions that reduce education to an activity that is always and everywhere voluntary and intentional, whose sole object is the development of rational mind, and whose methods are invariably moral. Reclaiming the broad sense of education—the sense that includes all learning within its scope—was, so to speak, the end to which my previous writings tended. I did not foresee, however, that my theory would challenge one of the fundamental assumptions of Western educational thought, namely that only human beings are the subjects and objects of education. Yet it does.[4] Nor did I dream that it would make plain for all to see that the processes of cultural transmission and individual learning are the two sides of a single coin. Yet this is quite possibly its greatest strength.

Had I not, over the course of some 30 years, rather haphazardly collected case studies of whole person transformations, I might never have understood how to join the two perspectives.[5] Thanks to my realization that the educational journeys the cases described were culture crossings, I was eventually able to see that culture stands alongside the individual at the very heart of the educational process. It has often been observed that culture and education are closely connected, but the assumption that the individual is *the* fundamental educational unit has seldom been challenged. Putting culture on an equal footing with the individual, the theory of education as encounter represents education as an interaction between an individual and a culture in which both parties change. In the one instance, the change is what is commonly called individual learning; in the other, the change goes by the name of cultural transmission.

To this sketch of the origins of the theory of education as encounter, let me add that, at the time of this writing, studies of education are apt to treat a single aspect of their subject—be it higher education, charter schools, national standards, the science curriculum, the teaching of reading, the education of gifted children, or something else entirely. In contrast, as philosophers throughout the ages have asked "what is justice?", "what is truth?", "what is art?", and "what is law?": this book asks "what is education?" and then spells out the far reaching implications of its findings.

Do not most people already know what education is? Do they not intuitively recognize it when they see it? People's intuitions about education are not always consistent and do not necessarily correspond with the facts of the matter. In consequence, we all are likely to make false assumptions about what can and should be done. Besides, the pithy definitions of education that immediately leap to mind are likely to be either misleading or uninformative. Thus the dictionary definition, "Education is the act or process of educating a person," is no help whatsoever.[6] On the other hand, "Education is what takes place in school" overlooks the vast amount of learning that occurs at home, on the streets, and in the workplace; and "Education develops the faculties and powers of a person by teaching" leaves no room for the learning that occurs without teaching, ignores education's cultural component, and begs the question of whether humans are the only individuals who are subject to education.

The purpose of this investigation is not to formulate a rule by which to test whether the word "education" is being used correctly. Rather it is to provide a theoretical framework that furthers educational thought. Responding to the call Dewey made over a century ago for an enlarged outlook on education,[7] it offers, at a relatively high level of abstraction, a synthesis that overcomes deficiencies in past accounts of education, illuminates pressing educational issues of the present, and opens up future paths of inquiry.

Readers may wonder why a book intended to shed light on education today and tomorrow so often cites ideas from the past. My references to earlier thinkers are meant to show, on the one hand, that educational thought has a vibrant history; and, on the other, that, although the theory of education as encounter reconfigures education, it is not some alien construct imported from a science fiction universe but emerges, as it were, out of the philosophies that preceded it. This is not to say that a person must know all there is to know about Plato, Rousseau, Dewey, Montessori, and the rest in order to understand the theory of education as encounter. On the contrary, no prior acquaintance with the historical "greats" is required. Because this theory is also intended to encourage the systematic treatment of particular issues by providing the basis for a deeper understanding of them, I should add that it is not imperative to read the chapters of this book in the order in which they are presented. Indeed, those who are mainly interested in the theory's applicability to actual educational problems may want to begin at the back of the book.

Whatever starting point is chosen, my hope is that, as readers encounter *Education Reconfigured*, they will be moved to ask questions they have not heretofore entertained. Above all, by showing that education is a much more fundamental, pervasive, ubiquitous,[8] and unruly phenomenon than is commonly acknowledged, I hope to convince readers that former U.S. Commissioner of Education, Francis Keppel, was right when he said that education is too important to be left solely to the professionals. Keppel was giving voice to the oft forgotten truth that education is one of the great forces in human society; and that, as such, it deserves the attention and demands the vigilance of every thoughtful person.

PART I

A Unified Theory of Education

1

EDUCATION AS ENCOUNTER

Theorists and philosophers in the Western tradition tend to look at education today from the standpoint of the individual. There is, however, another equally valid point of view to take—that of the culture. Keeping in mind the basic insights of the past that education involves an encounter between an individual and something external and that this encounter brings about change, I will sketch in here a theory that combines the two perspectives that seldom, if ever, have been joined. Illuminating the fundamental structure of each and every educational encounter, the theory of education as encounter makes it clear that whenever and wherever education occurs, it is at one and the same time an instance of individual learning and a case of cultural transmission.

1. Two Perspectives on Education

At present, the standpoint of the individual—that is to say, the individual human being—dominates Western educational thought. I do not mean that those who are concerned with education tend to embrace the ideology of individualism, although many do. Rather, I draw attention to the widely held assumption—one shared not only by traditionalists and progressives but also by most of those who have taken note of the cultural aspects of education—that a human individual is the basic educational unit. Thus, parents ask: Is my child learning in school what she (or he) needs to know? Psychologists ask: How does a child construct knowledge? What forms of intelligence does he or she possess? Philosophers ask: What is an educated person? What does a citizen of a democracy need to know? To be sure, it may sometimes be asked: What does my dog need to learn to be a cooperative member of this household? What training does my horse need to be able to pull this cart? But these latter questions are seldom, if ever, thought to be about education; and in any event, they too adopt the standpoint of the individual—albeit a non-human individual.

Sometimes the scope of the educational question is broadened to address the classroom, the school, the community, or even the nation. Thus, concerned citizens and educational researchers ask: How do girls experience the co-educational classroom climate? What do high school graduates need to know? Which school in a given region ranks first on reading proficiency? Which country ranks last? But in the final analysis these queries are fueled by a concern about the learning of individuals. Indeed, the standpoint of the individual prevails even when education is seen as the solution to a political, economic, or social problem. Whether the issue is taken to be the establishment of a democratic form of government, the maintenance of a strong economy, or the abolition of racial inequality, the educational question is assumed to take the form: What do individual people need to learn so that the problem can be solved?

Historically, the viewpoint of the individual human learner has also prevailed. Saying in Book VIII of his *Politics* that education must be made a public concern, Aristotle proceeded to discuss what free men should and should not learn. Stating in a letter to city officials that a city must have well trained people, Martin Luther wrote, "we must see to it, and spare no trouble or expense *to educate and form them* ourselves."[1] In *Some Thoughts on Education,* John Locke insisted that the welfare and prosperity of a nation depends on parents "well educating" their children.[2] Johann Heinrich Pestalozzi's classic pedagogical novel, *Leonard and Gertrude,* in its turn, described the education a mother gives her children, and his far more technical work, *Gertrude Teaches Her Children,* was intended to codify her pedagogy.

Asking in her groundbreaking 1792 treatise *A Vindication of the Rights of Woman*: What kind of education must women have to become the equals of men? Mary Wollstonecraft broadened the scope of the inquiry but retained the perspective of the individual. And W.E.B. DuBois did the same when, in his 1903 classic *The Souls of Black Folk,* he asked: What does the "Negro race" need to learn to be socially "uplifted"?

When, in the second half of the twentieth century, U.S. philosopher William Frankena isolated the elements of what he took to be a complete philosophy of education, he built the perspective of the human individual into the very concept of education:

> Education is primarily a process in which educators and educated interact, and such a process *is called education if and only if it issues or is intended to issue in the formation, in the one being educated,* of certain desired or desirable abilities, habits, dispositions, skills, character traits, beliefs, or bodies of knowledge.[3]

And American educator Mortimer Adler presupposed the perspective of the human individual when in the last decades of the twentieth century he said, "The ultimate goal of the educational process is to help human beings become educated persons,"[4] as did philosopher Steven Cahn when he wrote:

> Education is the acquisition of knowledge, skills, and values. But what knowledge, skills, and values ought to be acquired? Who ought to acquire them? And how should they be acquired? These highlight the three central concerns of any philosophy of education: the subject matter, the student, and the instructional method. And primary among these is the student, for what is to be learned and how it is to be learned ultimately depend upon who is to do the learning.[5]

In light of comments like these, it is not surprising that past philosophies of education tended to view the elements of encounter and change as one dimensional. The human individual was seen as coming in contact with something external and was therefore taken to be the entity that changed. The idea that the encounter might be a two-way interactive affair and that both parties to it might change was not entertained.

The question of whether education is indeed a human-specific phenomenon will be addressed in Chapter 3. Here the issue is whether there is another way to look at education. In *Democracy and Education*, John Dewey wrote:

> We have seen that a community or social group sustains itself through continuous self-renewal, and that this renewal takes place by means of the educational growth of the immature members of the group. By various agencies, unintentional and designed, a society transforms uninitiated and seemingly alien beings into robust trustees of its own sources and ideals.[6]

Describing education as an initiation into civilization, the twentieth century British philosopher Michael Oakeshott said that some people

> think of education as a stock of things like books, pictures, musical instruments and compositions, buildings, cities, landscapes, inventions, devices, machines and so on—in short, as the results of mankind having impressed itself upon a "natural" world. But this is an unduly restricted (indeed, an exceedingly primitive) understanding of that "second nature" (as Hegel called it) which is the context of our activity. The world into which we are initiated is composed, rather, of a stock of emotions, beliefs, images, ideas, manners of thinking, languages, skills, practices, and manners of activity out of which these "things" are generated.[7]

Pointing out that the cultural processes of diffusion, assimilation, acculturation, and innovation "are the manifestations of education,"[8] the American educational philosopher Theodore Brameld said at approximately the same time, "It is from the stuff of culture that education is directly created and that gives to education not only its own tools and materials but its reason for existing at all."[9]

Brameld no more than Oakeshott or Dewey spelled out the implications of this different standpoint. Historian Bernard Bailyn began to do so, however, in his new interpretation of the transformation that America underwent in its colonial period. "This fundamental change," wrote Bailyn in *Education in the Forming of American Society*, can only be seen when one assumes a broad definition of education

> as the entire process by which a culture transmits itself across the generations; when one is prepared to see great variations in the role of formal institutions of instruction, to see schools and universities fade into relative insignificance next to other social agencies; when one sees education in its elaborate, intricate involvements with the rest of society, and notes its shifting functions, meanings, and purposes.[10]

The issues that emerge when a cultural perspective on education is taken are profound. From this vantage point one can see that groups and institutions of every conceivable sort are the custodians of what Brameld called "the stuff of culture" and I will henceforth call "cultural stock." I should stress that I use the term "cultural stock" rather than "cultural capital" even though the latter has entered the lexicon, because "capital" prejudges the vitally important question of whether the stuff of culture is valuable and "stock" does not.[11]

Schools, of course, fall into the custodian or guardian category and so, too, do libraries and museums. Less obviously, but just as surely, items of cultural stock are also in the keep of churches, synagogues, mosques, businesses, banks, governmental agencies, non-profit organizations, the military, publishing companies, advertising agencies, television networks, Internet websites, and so on. Thus, just as art museums are the custodians of the paintings hanging on their walls and the pieces of sculpture in their gardens, symphony orchestras are the custodians of the music they perform. Just as churches have in their stock portfolios religious doctrines, symbols, rites, and rituals, registries of motor vehicles have traffic rules and regulations, licensing procedures, and bureaucratic red tape in theirs.

Such groups and institutions do not merely preserve the stock in their portfolios. Serving as educational agents of the culture to which they belong, they transmit or pass it along to any number of individuals. Moreover, if one looks closely, one will see that the stock portfolios of these educational agents contain not just the culture's wealth or assets but also what may be considered its liabilities: for instance, violence, hatred, poverty, and greed.

Given how different the sightings are from the cultural vantage point, it is to be expected that questions present themselves that make no sense when the only valid standpoint from which to view education is assumed to be that of the individual. Is the culture preserving its assets for the next generation? Are some educational agents failing to perform their educational functions so that cultural assets—for example, farming skills, native languages and dances, household arts, alternative ways of responding to aggression—are getting lost in transmission? Are cultural liabilities such as racism, misogyny, greed, and mendacity being transmitted? If so, what can be done?

In sum, when the cultural perspective is introduced, a host of new questions acquire legitimacy, among them questions about the kind of change the culture itself is undergoing. Another way to put this is that when the cultural perspective is missing, a significant portion of the educational process is lost to view.

2. Joining the Two Perspectives

The issue here is whether the two perspectives on education can be joined together into a single theory. Now it may be held that such integration is unnecessary. Indeed, some might want to insist that a cultural perspective illuminates the whole range of educational issues so powerfully that it can and should replace the perspective of the individual. Others might argue instead that there are distinct educational contexts to which one and not the other of our perspectives applies. And a third group might hold that every educational issue can be viewed from both an individual and a cultural perspective.

The first two strategies are unsatisfactory ways of handling the two perspectives on education, however. The first is unacceptable for the simple reason that, in education, the standpoint of the individual is too important to forswear. The second alternative is untenable too. It may be tempting to hold that the natural site of the individual perspective is the private home and family whereas the appropriate location of the cultural perspective is the public sphere. Yet a town, a city, a state, a nation, has as much interest in the education of the individuals within its boundaries as do home and family, and home and family have at least as much reason to be concerned about the assets and liabilities that their culture is passing down to the next generation as do those larger socio-political units.

The third alternative of leaving both perspectives intact and letting people decide which one to adopt might seem an acceptable fallback position. Before I consider it, however, another possibility must be explored, this one suggested by Albert Einstein's search in the last decades of his life for a unified field theory.

For many years, Einstein's dream of finding a theory that would show that gravity and electromagnetism, then thought to be distinct forces, were really manifestations of one underlying principle was considered delusional. As I write, however, there are those who believe that his dream has become reality.[12] One does not have to take sides in this dispute to wonder if our two perspectives on education are manifestations of a single underlying approach.

At present, perhaps the most promising candidate for an approach to education that underlies our two perspectives is meme theory, or mimetics—a theory of cultural evolution developed by Susan Blackmore from an idea put forward by scientist Richard Dawkins and elaborated by philosopher Daniel Dennett.[13] As a gene is the basic unit of genetics, a meme is the basic unit of meme theory. As genes are replicators that drive biological evolution, memes are replicators that drive cultural evolution.

What counts as a meme? Beethoven's Fifth Symphony is a meme and so is that work's first four notes. Other examples adduced by Blackmore are vocabulary words, stories, songs, skills, habits, recipes, clothes fashions, interior designs, architectural trends, rules of political correctness, and the recycling of glass bottles. Not everything is a meme, however. Perceptions, emotions, and thoughts that belong to a single person and that are never passed on do not qualify, for a meme "is a replicator that jumps from one brain to another"[14] and the process of replication is imitation.

Like genes, memes are often found grouped together in what Blackmore calls "memeplexes." Memes also resemble genes in being "selfish," but this is to say nothing more than that successful memes are the ones that get copied and spread. Memes have no foresight or intentions. They just get copied through the process of imitation—indeed, if they are not copied, they are not memes—and some do this better than others.

At first glance a meme might seem to be identical with what from a cultural perspective constitutes an item of cultural stock. The concept of cultural stock is broader than that of memes, however, in that it includes, for example, not just architectural designs but the buildings themselves. Yet this divergence scarcely matters, for the problem mimetics presents to any search for an underlying perspective on education is not primarily a function of the concept of a meme. It is, rather, that in focusing on brains and imitation, meme theory renders education's function as a preserver and transmitter of culture invisible; indeed, meme theory gives the impression that education plays no role in cultural evolution.

Meme theory does not make the mistake of reducing human beings to non-material minds as educational thinkers of the past were wont to do. It tends instead to treat us as nothing but brains. Getting rid of the hearts and lungs, muscles and ligaments, arms and legs that we need if we are to be the beneficiaries and custodians of our culture's stock, it reduces even such sophisticated memes as piano playing to sets of instructions. Then, assuming without argument that for every skill, habit, and social practice to be passed down there is a recipe or algorithm that, if followed, will yield the desired result, meme theory reduces the learning that is required in order to follow a set of instructions to one of its many forms—imitation.

Simplicity is widely thought to be a mark of a good scientific theory, and meme theory is admirable for its simplicity. Says Blackmore, "Memes are instructions for carrying out behaviour, stored in brains (or other objects) and passed on by imitation."[15] Yet the notion that, for example, the instructions for playing a late Beethoven piano sonata can be passed on by imitation alone, as opposed to deliberate teaching and extensive practice, or that Kant's Categorical Imperative will jump without assistance from one brain to another holds good at best for those few individuals who possess prodigious musical or philosophical gifts. In portraying cultural transmission as a simple, straightforward, all but automatic process of following instructions, meme theory drops out of the picture the educational labor of musicians and artists, athletes and dancers, doctors and lawyers, architects and engineers. In meme theory the work and accomplishments of mothers and their newborns, teachers and their students, the U.S. Marine Corps and its recruits come to naught.

In view of meme theory's neglect of the educational processes and agencies that loom large when the cultural standpoint is adopted, it cannot provide the underlying perspective on education we seek. I do not want to rule out the possibility that it might, in the future, be appropriately modified and amended or that a more promising candidate might one day present itself. I do, however, conclude that what, at present, appears to be the best candidate for the role of underlying perspective is sadly wanting.

In light of this finding, should we not acknowledge that both perspectives on education apply to all contexts, encourage interested parties to adopt whichever one they wish, and leave it at that? The problem with this fallback position is that it presupposes the validity of precisely what a unified theory of education must question—namely, a radical divide between individuals and cultures.

Try the following experiment in imagination. Picture a world filled with individual capacities but devoid of cultural stock; in other words, one in which every individual has a number of capacities but not one of them attaches to an item of cultural stock. This is a world of know-nothings, do-nothings, and be-nothings. Immanuel Kant said that concepts without percepts are blind and that percepts without concepts are empty. As percepts need concepts, individual capacities need cultural stock. Otherwise they will be empty vessels.

Now imagine an opposite world, one in which cultural stock abounds but no individual has the capacity to use or understand or appreciate or adapt or modify any of it; in other words, a world in which there are no capacities to which items of culture can attach. Actually, if there were no capacities, there would be no cultural stock at all, for the assets and liabilities that comprise a culture's stock are the creations of individuals, whether acting singly or collectively. But assuming for the sake of the thought experiment that cultural stock can exist without there being the capacities of individuals for them to attach to, in such a case the items of stock would be nothing more than unactualized ideas or, if you prefer, mere potentialities. Or they might be thought of as analogous to scripts that have no actors or to musical scores for which there are no performers. As concepts without percepts are blind, cultural stock without individual capacities is inert, lifeless, without meaning.

3. Education as the Coupling and Uncoupling of Individual Capacities and Cultural Stock

Case studies of educational metamorphoses—that is, whole person transformations that are due to education—confirm that individual learning and cultural transmission are inextricably bound together.[16] They show education to be a process of change in which the capacities of an individual and the stock of a culture become yoked together.

In human lives, cultural stock and individual capacities initially meet in the newborn child.[17] They meet in the gestures babies learn to make and in the particular ways in which they learn to walk, talk, and relate to the world. Whatever doubts one may have that these earliest attainments represent a joining together of human capacities and items of human culture are put to rest by the case of Victor, the Wild Boy of Aveyron.[18]

In 1797 Victor first came out of the woods where, presumably, he had been abandoned as an infant, but it was not until 1800 that he willingly stayed in "civilization." From letters and other documents written after he was taken in charge by a French government official and sent to an orphanage, we know that this boy, who then appeared to be about 12 years old, ran on all fours, trotted when he walked, did not speak, tore off his clothes and slept on the floor, defecated wherever he happened to be, and ate only potatoes, raw chestnuts, and acorns. One year later, and by now under the guardianship of physician Jean-Marc-Gaspard Itard, he still spent his days squatting in the corner of a garden or hiding in an attic.

By negative example, as it were, Victor's case reveals that practically every human being undergoes a radical transformation that turns us from creatures of nature into inhabitants of human culture. In so doing, it shatters the illusion that the walking and talking, the eating and dressing, the manners and the judgments of hot and cold or far and near we call "second nature" spring up automatically when we are very young. It demonstrates that this great change is brought about not by the wave of a wand or the simple maturation of human capacities but by education in the broadest sense of the term.

Victor's case serves as a window through which one can see the yoking together of individual capacities and items of cultural stock. Other case histories of educational metamorphoses reveal that, although the first great educational transformation that almost all humans undergo—the one Victor missed out on when he lived in the woods—is the occasion on which cultural stock and human capacities initially meet and join together, it is by no means the only time they do.[19]

Consider Minik, a six-year-old Inuit child who was taken to New York City by Artic explorer Robert Peary exactly 100 years after Victor emerged from the woods.[20] Given a home by the family of the custodian of the Museum of Natural History, Minik quickly turned into an all-American boy. In just a few years, he was speaking English, dressing like the other boys his age, attending the local public school, playing football, saying "Now I lay me down to sleep" before going to bed every night, and telling people he wanted to be a New York State farmer when he grew up.

Dramatic as this transformation was, it was not Minik's first metamorphosis. He had already undergone a radical transformation from being a creature of nature to an Inuit child. Like that earlier metamorphosis, this one was brought about not by drugs, a sudden insight, or the wave of a wand but by education broadly defined. And this second metamorphosis also involved the linking of an individual's capacities to items of cultural stock. The difference between the two is that Minik's second metamorphosis constituted a culture crossing. When it began he was a member of the Inuit culture. By its end he was an American. This is not to say that he applied for U.S. citizenship. He was too young for that. He had, however, made the culture of his new country his own.

Now compare Minik's case to that of Richard Rodriguez, who was born in Sacramento, California to Mexican immigrants.[21] As a result of his first great metamorphosis, the young boy was steeped in Mexican customs, could speak only a few words of English, and had next to no experience of mainstream American culture. Once Rodriguez started attending parochial school and the nuns persuaded his parents to stop speaking Spanish at home, however, he began to experience a thoroughgoing transformation that eventually culminated in his writing a Ph.D. dissertation in English literature.

As surely as Minik's metamorphosis into an all-American boy was a culture crossing, so was Rodriguez's transformation into an educated man, American style. The difference was that, whereas Minik can be said to have crossed from one cultural whole to another, Rodriguez crossed from one cultural group to another within the same cultural whole.[22]

These and other case studies of whole person transformations strongly suggest that every human being undergoes a number of educational metamorphoses in a lifetime after the first great one. We are transformed by, among many other things, going to school, coming of age, military service, professional training, political movements, marriage, parenthood, divorce, artistic endeavors, and higher education. Moreover, all but the first great metamorphosis constitute culture crossings.[23] When the subject is education it is therefore a recipe for disaster to abstract individuals from culture. And it is all the more self-defeating because the yoking together of cultural stock and capacities does not only take place when transformational change occurs. Even the smallest changes that education produces involve encounters between capacities and cultural stock.

An individual's capacities can of course link up with cultural stock without benefit of education, for instance by dint of dreams, drugs, or disease. The question is whether both capacities and cultural stock are implicated in every instance of education. I answer this affirmatively but, even if genuine exceptions to the rule that education involves the linkage of capacities and stock are adduced, they will present no serious challenge to the theory under development here. The cases of Victor, Minik, Rodriguez, and countless others bear witness to the fact that culture, encounter, and change are implicated in education from the start.

4. The Element of Encounter

Some clarification of the element of encounter is required here. Rousseau said, "education comes to us from nature or from men or from things."[24] Although this remark would seem to be unexceptionable, the presence of nature on his list of education's sources appears to cast doubt on the thesis that the encounters that occur in every educational event or episode are necessarily between some individual and some portion of culture.

To settle the question, compare two cases, one real and the other imaginary. In the imaginary case, a seven-year-old boy is standing in the shallows off Paradise Beach on the Gulf of Mexico and meets up with a jellyfish. This child does not know what he is looking at and, for one reason or another, does not find it interesting. An instant later, when his mother calls to him that it is time to go for ice cream, he runs off without a further thought about what he has just seen. Here we have an encounter, but it is not an *educational* encounter.

Consider now the meeting between seven-year-old Ed Wilson and a jellyfish when, in 1936, he was standing in the shallows off Paradise Beach on the Gulf of Mexico.[25] In contrast to our imaginary boy, Ed had some idea of what he was looking at. Moreover, he was so fascinated by the creature that he watched it for hours, during which time he acquired a burning desire to know more about jellyfish and other living things. Here we have an educational encounter. The desire for knowledge about jellyfish and other creatures is not something human beings are born with or that automatically develops as we mature. It is an item of cultural stock and in Ed Wilson's case it became yoked to his already existing capacity of wonder.

The theory of education as encounter recognizes that large-scale changes can have small beginnings. As it happened, one outcome of the haphazard coupling of an item of cultural stock and Ed Wilson's capacities was that more such yokings occurred: at that same Paradise Beach; at Pensacola and Orlando; at the National Zoo and the National Museum of Natural History in Washington D.C.; at the University of Alabama, the University of Tennessee, and Harvard; in Cuba, Mexico, and New Guinea; and everywhere else he went. Ultimately, the sum total of yokings of stock and capacities to which his encounter with the jellyfish led transformed a young child of the southern U.S. into the world-renowned Harvard University scientist and naturalist, E.O. Wilson.

The fact that a scientific career can, in a sense, be attributed to an encounter with a jellyfish is not really the issue here, however. For now, the relevant point of Wilson's story is that, although there are all kinds of encounters in this world, only some of them are educational encounters. The existence of an encounter—

be it between an individual and a jellyfish, a mountain, an animal, a book, another person, the square root of two, or the idea of God—is no guarantee, therefore, that an educational event has occurred. Our theory holds that education only occurs if there is an encounter between an individual and a culture in which one or more of the individual's capacities and one or more items of a culture's stock become yoked together; or, if they do not in fact become yoked together, it is intended that they do.

Furthermore, our theory affirms that, whenever capacities and stock meet and become attached to one another, education occurs. In other words, there does not have to be a prior encounter such as that between Wilson and the jellyfish. For example, one can imagine the belief that Santa Claus exists attaching to a very young child's capacities simply because the child has overheard someone say so.

At this point three caveats are necessary. The first is that I am not suggesting that, whenever there is education, a human capacity becomes yoked to what, from its point of view, is a brand new item of stock. On many occasions an existing linkage between a given capacity of an individual and a particular item of cultural stock is simply being reinforced. My second caution is that there is no one-to-one correspondence between human capacities and cultural stock. A given item of stock can be yoked to more than one of an individual's capacities: for example, the song "Twinkle, Twinkle, Little Star" can become coupled with a person's capacities to hear and to sing. And, conversely, a given capacity can become yoked to more than one item of stock; indeed, an individual's capacity to sing will normally attach to many pieces of music. The third reminder is that it is an oversimplification to characterize education solely in terms of the yoking together of human capacities and cultural stock, for case studies reveal that educational metamorphoses involve losses as well as gains, unyokings as well as yokings.

In the terminology of the theory of education as encounter, a loss occurs when stock and capacities become uncoupled as well as coupled. Actually, the term "loss" is ambiguous in that it can signify either a mere disappearance or a deficit. I do not mean to suggest that the weakening of the linkages between capacities and stock or the uncoupling of cultural stock from an individual's capacities necessarily entails that something of value has gone missing. Think of the cultural practice of smoking, an item of stock that medical evidence has shown to be a huge liability. If this cultural liability becomes uncoupled from an individual's capacities, the loss can be judged a definite gain to both the individual and the culture.

On the other hand, items of cultural stock that are not obvious liabilities can get lost in the course of educational metamorphoses. As Minik turned into an all-American boy, the ability to speak the Inuit language that had been part of his first curriculum disappeared. Similarly, Rodriquez lost the ability to speak Spanish. And Heidi Bud, a Vietnamese child who was brought to the United States under the auspices of a government-sponsored program called "Orphan

Airlift," lost her ability to speak Vietnamese as she was transformed into an American girl.[26]

Does an individual's loss of a first language really matter? In the case of Rodriguez, his forgetting his first language was not merely a loss in the removal or disappearance sense of that term. To the extent that it distanced him from his parents and his Mexican roots, it can also be considered a loss in the value or deficit sense. And although his loss of the Spanish language would not seem to have been a loss for either the U.S. or the Mexican culture, it might have been one for the Mexican community to which his family belonged in Sacramento. On the other hand, once in the U.S., Minik had no parents or Inuit community to whom he might have stayed connected. Moreover, when he returned to Greenland, he quickly learned the adult variety of the language he had forgotten and adapted quite easily, if not altogether happily, to the Polar North culture. It is less obvious in his case, therefore, that the uncoupling of his first language from his capacities amounted to the disappearance of something of value.

Like Minik, Heidi Bud had no one among her acquaintances in the U.S. from whom to become alienated; however her language loss as a child created barriers between her and her birth family when she later returned to Vietnam to see her mother. Still, her basic problem when she went back to Vietnam seems to have been her total loss of a Vietnamese identity rather than her language loss. Minik may have forgotten his mother tongue, but from what one can tell he never stopped thinking of himself as an Eskimo—which is what others then called him. When Heidi Bud first arrived in San Francisco, a Vietnamese journalist living in the area told her and the other young children that it was important to understand who they are. As Heidi permed her hair, ate bologna, and told people that she was born in South Carolina, the cultural stock that, in infancy, had made her a Vietnamese child became uncoupled from her developing capacities.

Whether the uncoupling of cultural stock and individual capacities in the disappearance sense is a loss in the deficit sense can only be decided on a case-by-case basis, on the one hand because individual circumstances vary and, on the other, because the value to a culture of any given item of cultural stock can vary. Suppose that Minik had been the last speaker on earth of his native tongue.[27] Then, even if the uncoupling of that cultural stock from his capacities was not a loss in the deficit sense for him, it would have been one for his culture.

5. Individual Change

In sum, when an item of cultural stock becomes yoked to or unyoked from an individual's capacities, the change that occurs can be a loss in the deficit sense to an individual, a culture, or both. The question remains of the kind of change that education involves and here some conceptual clarification is necessary.

The term "change" refers to both a process that takes place over time and a result, and the two senses of "change" are independent of one another. To say that something is in the process of change is not necessarily to say that a change has yet occurred. Moreover, to say that a change has taken place does not entail that a change process has occurred, for something can change instantaneously. Think of Cinderella: a fairy godmother waves her wand and she is instantly transformed. Think of what psychologists call "quantum changes": an individual has a sudden insight or an epiphany and almost instantly becomes a different person.[28] But whether or not a change in the result sense is the product of a change process, in all such cases of change the condition or state that something has attained differs from that thing's initial condition or state.

The theory of education as encounter takes both aspects of change into account, but this is not to say that every change is an instance of education. Think of a man who, like his father and grandfather before him, becomes bald. In his case, the change is not the result of the yoking together of some capacity of his and an item of cultural stock; rather, it is due to his genetic endowment. Think now of a woman whose health is considerably improved by surgery. She too has undergone change, but it is not the kind that is normally considered to be an instance of learning.

Just as the term "change" can refer to a process or a result, so can the term "learning." As in the case of "change," the process sense of "learning" is independent of the product sense, for someone can be in the process of learning something without having yet learned it. Similarly, to say that someone has learned something is not necessarily to say that he or she has undergone the process of learning, for learning, like change, can occur instantaneously. In the theory of education as encounter, the change process that an individual undergoes when his or her capacities and cultural stock become yoked together is what is called learning. The change in that individual's end state is, in turn, what has been learned.

Granted, the woman who has had surgery may learn a thing or two from undergoing the operation—for instance, that her surgeon is a highly skilled person. If one or more items of cultural stock do attach to her capacities in the course of the surgery, then that treatment can be considered an educational encounter. But, although the change in her health is brought about by the surgery and the ability to perform the surgery is a result of the surgeon's education, the change she undergoes will not itself be an instance of education.

To this point, the discussion has focused mainly on large-scale changes of the individual—transformational changes of the self—because they allow one to see the yoking of individual capacities and cultural stock. However, small changes are also important, both in their own right and because they enter into transformational change.

Consider George Bernard Shaw's Eliza Doolittle. When the curtain rises on his play *Pygmalion*, Eliza is a flower girl. By the end of the play she is a lady. For Eliza there is no fairy godmother or mystical experience that instantly transforms her. Her metamorphosis is due to education. Eliza's transformation takes a fairly long time—six months, to be exact—and the change process she undergoes includes a number of relatively small changes: for example, she learns how to say her "a's," her "o's," and her "h's;" how to incorporate new pitches and rhythms in her speech; and how to sit, stand, walk, and behave like a lady.

Whether or not small changes like these belong to a whole person metamorphosis as they do in Eliza's case, they are staples of education. We humans learn to name the colors, to recite the alphabet, to recognize the letter "a" when we see it, to write our names, to read words, to add 2 + 2, to sing songs, and so on. In every such instance of learning, our capacities become yoked together with, yoked in some different way to, and in many instances unyoked from some item or items of cultural stock; hence each instance represents a change in us.

The question of whether large-scale transformations of the self are reducible to a set or series of small changes is not easily answered. Perhaps the only reason why Eliza's educational metamorphosis from a cockney flower girl to a lady, and Minik's from an Inuit to an all-American boy, appear to be more than the sum of their parts is that we lack the relevant knowledge. Were it possible to escape the finite human condition and look at whole person transformations from an all-seeing standpoint, we might be able to specify enough small changes to satisfy ourselves that they are reducible to these. Or, for that matter, were the human sciences more advanced than they now are, they might tell us all we need to know to reduce educational metamorphoses to a set or series of small changes.[29] On the other hand, there is the possibility that, in a far more radical sense,[30] educational metamorphoses defy analysis into component changes.

There is no need to decide this issue here. For our purposes it is sufficient to point out that there is, at present, a great gap between the small changes a transformed individual undergoes and what he or she becomes; and that the theory of education as encounter is in no way committed to a simple linear or sequential model of mind, cognition, learning, or anything else. In so saying, I do not mean to minimize the importance of small changes. Education is composed of both small- and large-scale changes, and of the many intermediary degrees of change as well. I do, however, wish to highlight the inadequacy of a largely unacknowledged yet widely held model of education that treats learning as a matter of small discrete changes in an individual.

This "incremental model" of education makes educational assessment relatively easy. It encourages the belief in the predictability of educational outcomes. And it offers the prospect of managing—indeed, even micromanaging—learning as well as predicting it. Although it is often assumed that prediction and control are the two sides of a coin, predictable events can fall outside human control—just think of the motions of the planets; and unpredictable events such as an epidemic can be brought under control. Be this as it may, the incremental model of education holds out the promise of both.

Small wonder that the incremental model ignores the large-scale changes wrought by education. Educational metamorphoses tend to be unruly, unpredictable affairs. Even if young Ed Wilson's encounter with the jellyfish had been planned, nobody could possibly have predicted where it would lead. The same can be said of the casual encounter reported by Malcolm X in his autobiography. One day, his eighth grade English teacher asked him if he had been thinking about a career. Upon hearing that Malcolm—who happened to be one of the top students in an almost all-white school—would like to be a lawyer, Mr Ostrowski responded: "You've got to be realistic about being a nigger. A lawyer—that's no realistic goal for a nigger. You need to think about something you *can* be. You're good with your hands—making things. Everybody admires your carpentry shop work. Why don't you plan on carpentry? People like you as a person—you'd get all kinds of work."[31]

Malcolm X called this the first major turning point of his life. Although it was not the first time that he had encountered racism, this particular yoking of racist cultural stock to his capacities became the springboard for his dropping out of school. This event led, in turn, to his transformation into a Harlem thief, pimp, and drug dealer; from that low point in his life to his stint in prison; and from there to his metamorphosis into the leader of Black Americans known as Malcolm X. Who could have dreamed that such a small event could have such enormous consequences!

The visit that three nuns made to Richard Rodriguez's family when he was in first grade was also a chance occurrence with huge unpredictable educational consequences. "Do your children speak only Spanish at home, Mrs Rodriguez?" those teachers in the local parochial school asked. "Is it possible for you and your husband to encourage your children to practice their English when they are home?"[32] Who would have anticipated that his parents would then and there have started speaking English at home, let alone that this event would have been the springboard for his metamorphosis into a highly educated man!

Shaw's Professor Higgins thinks of his work with Eliza Doolittle as a scientific experiment in which he has control over the conditions that will bring about her transformation into a lady. Yet, despite his intentions, the new Eliza is the product not merely of his treatment of her, but also of the housekeeper's numerous kindnesses and her daily reminders to Eliza of what to do and say, the positive lessons that Higgins's friend Colonel Pickering unwittingly teaches by his very presence, the negative ones that Eliza's father transmits during his visits to Wimpole Street, the lessons she learns on her forays into "high" society, and the ones she learns from her suitor, Freddy Eynsford-Hill. Over these factors, Higgins is able to exercise little, if any, control.

Unless an individual's entire environment is closed to all outside influences, the ideal of total control over a person's education is an illusion. Even in the simplest cases of learning, ones that seem to conform to the incremental model, unanticipated changes can occur. The child may not heed the teacher's instructions. He or she may have a headache or be dyslexic. A jokester in the classroom may convince the child that $2 + 2 = 5$. Indeed, even when research confirms that the methods of teaching employed are the best way to achieve a given outcome, predictability is not assured for the connection between educational episodes, and their desired end states is probabilistic, not deterministic. But then, although it may be likely that a given participant in a particular educational episode will attain a specified state, this outcome is not certain.

Only if education proceeds under strict laboratory conditions does total control seem possible, and even then unintended end states can occur. In real life, a parent or teacher's walk, talk, dress, and demeanor are apt to send powerful hidden messages, and the setting in which an educational episode occurs can also have unintended consequences. Yet, for simplicity's sake, the incremental model treats both the outside influences on deliberate educational episodes and the unintended learning that occurs within such episodes as fluctuations from the norm that are best ignored.

In truth, the incremental model does scant justice to educational events in the real world. Furthermore, in reducing learning to small changes, the incremental model conceals the fact that educational episodes are likely to have multiple outcomes, some of which are not intended; it thereby renders invisible the radical transformations that give shape to human lives and human cultures. Biologists stress what they call "amplification"—the magnification of a small change in a very few genes. "As a consequence," say Wilson and his colleague Bert Hölldobler, "evolution in the social organization of a species can occur within a few generations."[33] Amplification is as significant a factor in education as it is in evolution: as a small change in a gene can lead to a huge change in the behavior of, for instance, the red imported fire ant (*Solenopsis invicta*), small changes in a capacity of an individual human being can lead to a radical change of self.

And that is not all. Because the incremental model of learning views education solely from the standpoint of individual learning, it loses sight of the fact that education is as much about culture as it is about individuals. It conceals the fundamental truth that each and every educational event involves an encounter between individual capacities and cultural stock; in consequence, each encounter is both a learning event and a cultural transmission event; and that, in these encounters, both individuals and cultures change.

6. Cultural Change

I do not mean to give the impression that everyone ignores the cultural aspect of education. Many educational thinkers agree that culture leaves its fingerprints on education. Among other things, they point out that it influences the way teachers teach and children learn, affects the attitudes and expectations of children in school and family members at home, and enters into decisions about what to teach and to whom. But those who stress education's cultural dimension often give the impression that culture is something separate from education; something external that simply leaves its marks upon it. The theory of education as encounter assumes a far more intimate connection between culture and education. Insisting that culture is an integral element of every educational event or encounter, it represents education as an interactive process in which both individuals and cultures change.

To take a simple example, every time a first language is mapped onto a newborn's capacities, that stock acquires a new lease on life. If the language is later forgotten, the stock is, to that extent, diminished. Just as in a brightly lit room the subtraction of one 60-watt bulb will scarcely make a difference, when a language has millions of native speakers, the loss of one of them may not matter. But when a cultural practice, be it a language or something else, has only a few adherents, the fact that it becomes uncoupled from the capacities of even one person can be momentous. Furthermore, as is made evident by the case of Ed Wilson, even under normal conditions it is possible that the coupling or uncoupling of one person's capacities and an item of cultural stock will have enormous cultural consequences.

Ed Wilson's story contains another important lesson as well, namely that although the initial impact on a culture of the yoking of any given item of stock to a person's capacities may be minimal, that first yoking can eventually result in the creation of new cultural stock. Depending on the individual, the coupling and uncoupling of stock and capacities can lead to that stock or other items of stock being reinterpreted, refigured, reconstructed, or even rejected. And, in the case of exceptional individuals, it can even lead to the creation of brand new cultural practices.[34]

This point is worth stressing, for it is often assumed that someone who expresses concern about the items of cultural stock that are and are not being transmitted to the next generation must be in the grip of a conservative or traditionalist political or social bias. The theory of education as encounter makes no assumption, however, that cultural stock is static and unchanging or that old stock is necessarily more valuable than newly created stock. On the contrary, one premise of this volume is that individuals who are capable of learning are inventive. In consequence, the theory of education as encounter takes it for granted that new items of stock are constantly being produced and that old items undergo modification or even disappear as others are in the process of appearing. In other words, it assumes not only that the yoking of cultural stock to individual capacities changes both individuals and cultures, but also that individuals can create brand new cultural stock. The theory of education as encounter is also compatible with different views regarding the value of old and new stock.

The changes education produces in cultures, like those it produces in individuals, can be great or small. When one or a few capacities of an individual become yoked to one or a few items of cultural stock, the individual is to that degree changed, but the change is not a whole-person transformation. For this to occur, a significant number of capacities must become coupled with a significant portion of cultural stock. So too, a cultural part—be it a group, institution, practice, or process—may change without the culture as a whole undergoing a radical transformation.

Nevertheless, as speculative thinkers such as Karl Marx, Oswald Spengler, and Arnold Toynbee have pointed out, and as anthropologists and historians with more modest agendas have also shown, whole-culture transformations do occur. Consider, for example, the Tanala culture of western Madagascar.[35] Over an extended period of time, the introduction of the cultivation of wet rice in addition to that of dry rice led to a large-scale transformation. This agricultural innovation initially produced small-scale change, but over time it led to the rise of a class of landholders. The landless eventually had to go further and further afield, villages became split into the landless who needed to move and the landowners who were unwilling to move, intermarriages grew in importance, the nature of warfare changed radically, a system of slavery was instituted, and eventually a kingdom developed.

Think now of the great changes that occurred in the U.S. and many other Western nations in the last three decades of the twentieth century. If a latter day Rip Van Winkle had gone to bed in the wee hours of January 1, 1965 and had awakened in the year 2000, would he have recognized New York's culture? During that period, the economy became global, communications became electronic, popular culture became sexualized, the population of his country became much more diversified, gender roles became unmoored, and family structures were transformed. Just as Minik suffered from culture shock when he arrived in New York harbor, so Rip would have experienced cultural dislocation when he awakened in the twenty-first century.

Temporal culture crossings are not merely the stuff of fiction. Think of a latter day Paul Gaughin leaving Paris in 1965 to live in a relatively isolated community for over three decades and then returning home. He would very likely have to undergo a whole-person transformation in order to fit back in.

It must be asked, however, if education really has a role to play in the changes a culture undergoes. Are not these shifts strictly economic, political, or technological in nature? Of course these factors produce cultural changes, but the changes they produce require the cooperation of education.

Think, for example, of the telephone when it emerged in the 1870s.[36] Although its invention was obviously a technological feat, it was accomplished by people who possessed the relevant know-how, vision, and perseverance—attributes that do not "just emerge" as human beings mature. That is to say, it was accomplished by individuals whose capacities had already been yoked by education to certain scientific and technical portions of the culture's stock as well as to certain cultural dispositions or traits of character. Education had then to attach the new invention—aka the new item of cultural stock—to the capacities of at least some individuals. In other words, through education, one or a few people had to become acquainted with the telephone and acquire the skills needed to use it. These few yokings modified the individuals in question and gave a lease on life to the relevant cultural stock, although the resultant change in the culture was doubtless too small to detect. However, by 1900 the telephone was being used by millions of people in small towns and rural areas across the U.S., which is to say that the capacities of millions had, by then, become yoked through education to this stock.

The sociologist who traced the origins of modern communications did not give education credit for the cultural changes that occurred. Yet, imagine how different our culture would have been had people not learned to love and use the telephone and it becomes clear that the great cultural change that the telephone represented was a function of education as well as technology. To be sure, people did not, for the most part, learn how to use the telephone in school. But education never was and is not now confined to the classroom.

Think now of the late twentieth-century invention of email. Although email is a product of technology, it was developed in the first place by people with the relevant know-how; that is, by individuals whose capacities had already been yoked to certain technological portions of the culture's stock. Equally importantly, email would not—and could not—have become widespread had the capacities of countless other individuals not become attached to this new item of stock. Thus, the cultural change that email represents is as much a function of education as it is of technology. True, most people who learn how to use this cultural stock do not do so in school. But once again, education is not reducible to schooling.

The theory of education as encounter does not rule out the possibility that cultural change can occur without the coupling and uncoupling of human capacities and cultural stock; that is, without learning. It holds that education entails change, not that change entails education. In other words, just as our theory allows for encounters that are not instances of education, it allows for change that occurs without benefit of education. It is worth noting, however, that cultural changes that might initially be thought to be due to nature alone may actually have an educational component. Thus, for example, when a cultural change follows upon a natural disaster such as an earthquake, knowledge and beliefs about the changed environment and new patterns of behavior will no doubt have become yoked to individual capacities.

2

THE DEEP STRUCTURE OF EDUCATIONAL THOUGHT

It has yet to be established whose capacities become yoked to cultural stock, which capacities and which items of cultural stock these are, who the agents are that yoke capacities and stock together, and by what means the yokings are accomplished. To answer these questions it is necessary to determine the extent of the educational realm. Inquiring into that area's dimensions, I find that its boundaries place an enormous amount of learning off limits. Rejecting the deeply entrenched cultural belief system that drastically restricts the scope of education, I reclaim the broad sense of the term and redraw the boundaries of the educational realm accordingly.

This project is the culmination of the cultural archeology I have been engaged in for many years. Parents, teachers, school administrators, citizens, politicians, philosophers: almost all in the West who talk, write, or think about education tend to take for granted a number of fundamental beliefs about the social order. On the basis of these, they draw conclusions about the scope of education. With the help of some additional premises they then formulate claims about what education is and is not, what it can and cannot do, and the way it can and cannot proceed. It is necessary that the beliefs constituting what may be called the "deep structure" of educational thought be identified and their failings exposed, for the view of education they provide is the very one that the theory of education as encounter challenges.

1. Preliminary Notes

Several preliminary cautions are in order. The first is that, in the interests of determining why it is so difficult to effect school reform, a number of perceptive analysts have isolated what they have taken to be the deep structure of schooling, although they have not always called it by this name.[1] The widely accepted, taken-for-granted school practices that they have pinpointed include such matters as the use of time and space, age grading, ability grouping, and the like. The deep structure under discussion here belongs, in contrast, to the culture's very general and fundamental habits of thought about education rather than to specific practices of schooling.

A second caveat is that, in calling the beliefs under discussion "fundamental," I do not imply that they are wired or programmed into the members of Western culture from birth. Positing the existence of innate ideas and capacities, contemporary linguistic and psychological theories have compelled scholars to revisit the age-old question of whether the human mind is a blank slate or a repository of inborn ideas. Quite clearly, these debates bear on the subject of education. The beliefs about education to be discussed in what follows are so basic that they can be said to constitute the "deep structure" of Western culture's educational thought, yet they are far too sophisticated and complex to be considered innate. Although it may sound paradoxical to insist that the deep structure of education is learned, and hence is acquired through education, the truth is that education's reach is much larger and the scope of what it transmits is much broader than most of us who have internalized its deep structure imagine.

A third caveat is that, despite the "deep structure" label, the assumptions at issue are not universally held. This study of deep structure focuses only on the thought of the West, and even so it makes no claim that every member of Western culture subscribes to all of the deep structure's beliefs. The deep structure label is meant to suggest, however, that like the generative grammar posited by linguists, the West's most basic beliefs about education are tacit rather than explicit. The label is also intended to indicate that, as the deep structure of language serves to generate sentences, the deep structure of education serves as a set of rules for generating ideas about education; that, as the former places limits on what can be said in a language, the latter constrains what can be thought about education. Thus, as the one is compatible with different languages, the other is compatible with different proposals regarding the way education *should* proceed.

A fourth caveat is made necessary by the analogy to linguistics. However fixed and unchanging the deep structure of language is thought to be, no assumption is being made here that the beliefs belonging to the deep structure of education are immutable. To be sure, as the philosopher W.V.O. Quine once said, "Any statement can be held true come what may, if we make drastic enough adjustments elsewhere in the system."[2] Nonetheless, in what follows it is taken for granted that, no matter how deeply embedded the beliefs under discussion here may be, they have changed in the past and will continue to do so in the future.

This is not to say that all the beliefs at issue are equally amenable to revision. Picturing the totality of human beliefs as "a man-made fabric which impinges on experience only along the edges,"[3] Quine pointed out that a conflict with experience may occasion readjustments somewhere in the fabric, but he added that there is always latitude as to which statements will be re-evaluated. Just as centrally located beliefs such as the highly theoretical statements of physics and logic are less apt to be disturbed by conflicts with experience than those at the fabric's edges, statements belonging to education's deep structure may be more resistant to change than more peripheral beliefs. But also, just as some statements of physics are closer to the border of the fabric than others and, consequently, easier to dislodge, so—to revert to the imagery of the linguists—some elements of education's deep structure are closer to the surface than others.

Granted, it is naïve to think that the modification, let alone the outright rejection, of any of these beliefs can be quickly achieved. Indeed, the fact that someone may at one moment publicly affirm that one or another of these deeply held assumptions is unfounded and at the next moment presuppose its truth indicates just how tightly yoked to individual capacities this set of beliefs is and, therefore, how difficult it is for a person to give any one of them up. Nonetheless, another working assumption of this volume is that structural change is possible, and one of its major conclusions is that such change is of the greatest urgency.

As will soon be made clear, one reason why structural change is sorely needed is that the beliefs constituting the deep structure of educational thought clash with twenty-first-century realities. Another reason is that education's realm includes far more territory and its reach is far more extensive than is allowed for by its deep structure. In brief, the fundamental beliefs of education's deep structure systematically narrow down our thinking about education and ruthlessly cut off our options.

2. Two Rock-Bottom Dichotomies

Two dichotomies—the nature/culture split with its attendant mind/body dualism and the two-sphere analysis of society with its accompanying gender divide— may be said to constitute the rock bottom of the deep structure of Western culture's educational thought. Their uncritical acceptance is not in itself remarkable, for they have long informed Western thought quite generally; indeed, their connection to educational thought is, as it were, extra-systemic. What is noteworthy is that these dichotomies yield a corollary that serves to shrink the boundaries of the educational realm.

The Nature/Culture Divide

The separation of man from the animals represents one of Western culture's major projects. Some philosophers—Plato and Aristotle, for instance—have said that man is distinct by virtue of his rationality. Some, such as Karl Marx, have said that he is distinct because he is a toolmaker. Christian theologians, among others, have said that he is distinct because he is formed in God's image. The reasons differ according to the thinker but the motive is usually the same: "separate from" signifies "superior to."[4]

Our separation from the animals has been achieved by the positing of two distinct domains, namely nature and culture; the conceptualization of these as polar opposites; and the placing of animals in nature and humans in culture. Volumes have been written about the history of the nature/culture divide in Western thought and any number of treatises have challenged definitions that represent nature and culture as polar opposites. Yet, notwithstanding the cogent critiques, the sharp nature/culture dichotomy informs Western culture's idea of education at the deepest level. Quite simply, in envisioning culture as a realm of mind and reason, and nature as a kingdom of bodies and instincts, it provides the justification for reserving the educational realm for ourselves. Indeed, even those who acknowledge that we humans belong to the animal kingdom are apt to cling to the idea of the sharp divide by the simple expedient of assigning our bodies and animal-like instincts to the natural world and locating our minds, and more particularly our reason, in the domain of culture.

In principle, a sharp nature/culture divide does not have to entail a divorce of mind and body; nor is this divorce required by the project of separating us from the animals. In all consistency one can hold: that nature and culture are two distinct realms, that non-human animals belong in the one and human animals in the other, and that both sorts of creatures have minds and bodies that are, in one or another way, inseparable. Conversely, one can embrace the divorce of mind from body while rejecting any sharp separation between nature and culture.

Furthermore, it should be noted that philosophers in the Western tradition have long debated the relationship between mind and body, and that not all of them have been dualists. To be sure, many have argued for a sharp separation of the two on the ground that they are irreducibly different substances—the one material and the other immaterial. Some, however, have claimed that the two substances are really one: that mental phenomena reduce to physical phenomena or else that physical phenomena reduce to mental phenomena. And some have maintained that the important question is not whether mind and body are a single substance or two different ones, but what kind of correspondence there is between mental and physical states.

It is not necessary to take sides here in the still-ongoing arguments about the relationship between mind and body. Their significance for us lies not in what yesterday's or today's participants in the discussion may have concluded. It stems from the fact that, although philosophers in the Western tradition have not all taken for granted a sharp divide between the mind and the body or between mental and physical states, that divorce is built into the nature/culture split that is deeply embedded in the West's educational thought.[5]

The Two-Sphere Split

To be precise, even as the deep structure of educational thought takes culture to be the domain of mind, it considers only one part of culture to be the domain of reason and rationality. For after drawing a sharp line between nature and culture, Western thought divides culture into two separate "spheres" or "realms" that are also defined as polar opposites.

Here, another caveat is needed, for the names that have been assigned the two spheres or realms tend to be misleading. Sometimes the one sphere or realm is called "public" and the other "private," and sometimes the one is called "civic" and the other "domestic." Either way, the labeling is problematic. The term "civic" tends to focus attention on the tasks and duties of citizenship at the expense of economic- and work-related processes and activities. On the other hand, the point of the two-sphere divide is not to protect the human spirit or conscience from the intrusions of others, as the term "private" may suggest. Nor is the object of the distinction to carve out an area in which political discussion can thrive, as the term "public" is sometimes meant to do. Rather, the two-sphere analysis is intended to mark a sharp separation between what Virginia Woolf called the world of the private house and the world of professional or public life.[6]

I will use labels resembling Woolf's here, but it must be understood that the two-sphere analysis does not merely signal an institutional divide. Rather, it draws a line of demarcation between the activities, processes, tasks, duties, responsibilities, knowledge, skill, attitudes, values, and worldviews associated with home and family on the one hand, and with work, politics, and the professions on the other. And now another caveat is required, for it should not be supposed that the two worlds are at present, or ever were, as sharply divided as the deep structure of educational thought seems to imply. Think, for example, of the ways in which marriage, an act that would seem to belong solely to the private sphere, is regulated by laws enacted in the so-called public arena. Think of the fact that births must be publicly recorded. Think of the respects in which governments try to regulate sexuality. The two-sphere dichotomy encapsulates a perception—an ideological representation, if you will—of the social order rather than an accurate account of it.

The line of demarcation between the two spheres also represents a gender divide. Historically, women have, for the most part, performed the activities and processes of the world of the private home and men have, for the most part, performed those belonging to the world of work, politics, and the professions. And, culturally speaking, the latter sphere is considered to be the domain of men and the former the domain of women.

Throughout history, Western culture has placed a far higher value on men than on women, and the question of whether or not the different valuations of the two genders is due to their association with the different spheres has been hotly debated. It is not necessary to repeat the arguments here, however. For the present purpose it is enough to know that, in educational thought, one sphere is considered to be the domain of women and the other of men. Nor is it necessary to include here the arguments against dividing humankind into two genders or the ones challenging the very category of women.[7] It suffices to say that the existence of these discussions serves to confirm the presence of the gender dichotomy in Western thinking.

Given that most men in the West grow up in the world of the private home and continue to spend many hours of each day there in adulthood, it may be wondered how the deep structure of educational thought could possibly consider the realm of the private home to be women's sphere. The assumption is especially puzzling because, according to the West's gender role stereotypes, men are the masters of their homes and families. The puzzlement is somewhat alleviated, however, when it is understood that, while the West's stereotypical men were in the past expected to rule the roost, their stereotypical wives, mothers, sisters, and daughters were expected to do whatever was needed to perform the everyday chores, tasks, duties, and responsibilities these institutions involve. These women were expected to make the roost a haven for men whose days were, presumably, spent in the hectic and heartless public world.[8]

Just as the two-sphere analysis of society represents the two worlds as polar opposites, so it views males and females. Thus, it does not simply assign men and women to different spheres. It attributes distinctly different kinds of knowledge, skill, attitudes, values, and the like to males and females and also assigns the two supposedly opposite sexes responsibility for carrying out different societal tasks and processes. In other words, it views the cultural stock that it locates in the so-called public world—the activities and responsibilities, the traits and dispositions— as male or masculine; and it views the stock it locates in the world of the private home and family as female or feminine.

Here, again, a caveat is necessary. To say that the two-sphere ideology assigns a gender to various items of cultural stock is not to endorse biological determinism or to embrace essentialism. On the contrary, the theory of education as encounter makes no assumption whatsoever that the traits or other items that a culture considers masculine or feminine are biologically determined or, for that matter, universally distributed according to sex or gender. Insofar as any implications of biological determinism and essentialism exist, they inhere in the deep structure of educational thought and not in this analysis of it.

Now it is logically possible for society or culture to be divided into two spheres without one of them being considered superior to the other. However, just as the assignment of mind to culture is thought to demonstrate its superiority over nature, the assignment of reason to the world of work, politics, and the professions is viewed as demonstrating its superiority over the world of home and family. In the two-sphere ideology, the public world is portrayed as the arena where intellect, theoretical knowledge, and rationality hold sway. In contrast, the world of the private home is the place where childrearing, nursing the sick, and caring for the elderly are located. Given that tending to bodily functions is a central component of these activities and that whatever knowledge and skill is required to do this work is believed to be instinctual, the inferiority of the world of the private home is thought to be assured.

Actually, there is a logical glitch here. The two-sphere analysis locates the world of the private family squarely within human culture, yet by virtue of that world's concern with bodily functions the nature/culture divide places it within nature. In other words, the deep structure of educational thought situates the world of the private home and family both inside and outside the domain of human culture. As might be expected, it also places women both inside and outside human culture. In designating the world of the private home and family as their domain, the two-sphere analysis places them within human culture; yet insofar as women are thought to lack reason and rationality by their very nature, it would seem to disqualify women as members of human culture.

The woman problem can be avoided if culture is held to be the domain of mind in a very general sense and only the public world is held to be the sphere of reason and rationality. The contradiction regarding the world of home and family can, in turn, be circumvented if the nature/culture distinction is conceptualized as a continuum rather than a sharp dichotomy. Then the world of home and family would simply fall closer to the nature end of the world of work, politics, and the professions, and so would the women who inhabit it. When anthropologists say that, because of women's association with childbearing and childrearing, they are cross-culturally seen as being closer to nature than men are; they are presumably interpreting the distinction in just this way.[9] But supposing that the nature/culture distinction is reinterpreted, the fact remains that the two-sphere analysis attaches a much higher value to the one world and everything associated with it than to the other.

Needless to say, the two-sphere analysis of society does not now correspond with historical or sociological realities and very likely never did. Just as most men in the past lived a good part of each day in the world of the private home, many women left home to go out to work—be it as domestic servants in other women's homes, as factory workers, or as teachers and nurses. It may be protested that this lack of match between the real world and the belief system embedded in educational thought means that the various elements of education's deep structure can safely be ignored. However, to ignore this belief system is tantamount to leaving it in place. When the objective is to develop a unified theory of education, it is far more productive to isolate the several premises of this belief system, determine how they function, assess the damage they do, and then proceed to dismantle it.

3. Additional Assumptions

One corollary of the two dichotomies that constitute the rock bottom of educational thought's deep structure radically restricts the scope of education. A false equation that limits educational agency to one of its myriad forms and an unduly narrow definition of education then contribute to the process of containment.

The Educational Corollary

Picturing nature as the realm of instinct and representing culture as such a highly sophisticated and complex human creation that participation in it requires extensive learning, the nature/culture divide places education squarely outside nature and inside culture. The two-sphere ideology then replicates that divide within human society by portraying the world of the private home and family as a stand in, as it were, for nature. Representing the activities and processes of what it considers to be women's sphere as natural, it would have us believe that the learning that occurs there is instinctual; that which Victor missed out on, as well as all the other learning that takes place at home, will emerge in the course of maturation or else be acquired automatically at a mother's knee. In contrast, it takes it for granted that the activities and processes belonging to what it considers to be men's sphere—that is, the world of work, politics, and the professions—are so complex that their learning requires education.

In sum, it follows from the nature/culture divide and the two-sphere ideology that education is a public world process whose function is to prepare those destined to inhabit that world for membership therein. To the extent that the two realms are thought to represent a gender divide, it also follows that education is a gendered process: one whose function is to prepare boys to take their places in men's world.

In an age and culture in which co-education prevails and women attain university degrees, the gendered implications of the educational corollary will appear to many to be hopelessly out of date. And so, of course, they are. Nevertheless, and as the case of home economics illustrates, the deep structure of educational thought turns education into a single-sphere process.

Although home economics education has sometimes focused on preparing both male and female students for careers in the public world, it was originally intended to prepare girls to be homemakers.[10] As such, it represents a genuine exception to the single-sphere corollary. Its status in the school curriculum as the only school subject to acknowledge explicitly the importance of learning the activities and acquiring the knowledge and skills traditionally associated with home and family is itself evidence, however, that educational thought's deep structure assumes that education is a single-sphere process.

That this corollary greatly reduces the scope of education is undeniable. On the one hand, it makes the public world of work, politics, and the professions the sole arena of educational activity; on the other, it makes preparing people for life in that sphere education's primary responsibility.

I say "primary" rather than "sole" responsibility because the educational corollary contains an "other things being equal" clause. When things are not equal—or at least are perceived as not being equal—this corollary leaves open the possibility that a certain amount of education for life in the private home will be necessary. Consider the early twentieth-century efforts by the U.S. government to teach immigrant parents how to keep their house and raise their children.

Rather than contradicting the rule that education is for life in the public world, they represent the belief that the traditional approach had failed in the case of immigrants. The *ceteris paribus* clause also allows for exceptions to the rule that the things one learns at home are not acquired through education; for example, that differently abled children may need instruction in the very things that "normal" children presumably do not.

Be this as it may, some readers will perhaps object to my thesis that the deep structure represents all education as preparation for membership in the public world on the grounds that liberal education has no external function or purpose, but is an end in itself. This, however, is one of the many illusions that the deep structure of educational thought generates in those who internalize it. To be sure, liberal education is regularly contrasted with vocational education, and vocational education is conceived of as preparation for the workplace. But once it is understood that the nature/culture divide, together with the two-sphere analysis, entails the restriction of education's domain to just one of those spheres, all of education can be seen to constitute preparation for membership in the world of work, politics, and the professions, and not the world of the private home and family.

A Narrow One-Sided Definition of Education

If the deep structure of educational thought consisted solely of the nature/culture divide, the two-sphere ideology, and the educational corollary, there would be no grounds for saying that it adopts one perspective on education to the exclusion of the other. To be sure, in making the public world the realm of education, the nature/culture divide and the two-sphere split effectively assign education the function of preparing the individual for life in that one sphere. But it can equally be said that they assign it the function of transmitting the cultural stock that belongs to that sphere to the next generation. However, the definition of education embedded in the deep structure delivers the *coup de grâce* to the cultural perspective by portraying education as a voluntary, intentional, and witting process whose aim is the acquisition by human individuals of knowledge and intellectual understanding, and whose methods and outcomes are morally acceptable.

As it happens, this definition does not only ignore education's cultural dimension. It also excludes an enormous amount of individual learning. It is generally agreed that education can be unintended and involuntary, although this is then often forgotten. Thus, for example, the author of the classic educational autobiography *The Education of Henry Adams* repeatedly referred to his "accidental education."[11] Malcolm X, in turn, said in his autobiography that his college was in the streets of Harlem.[12] Similarly, it is widely recognized that education extends beyond the getting of knowledge. Consider, for example, the sentiment that you have to be taught to hate, or the belief that love of country and the desire to improve the lives of others are learned affairs. It is also well known, if not always remembered, that education can employ morally questionable means and can be turned to immoral ends. Thus, the hero of Dickens's *David Copperfield* attends a school that indulges in brutal educational practices and the villain of Dickens's *Oliver Twist* teaches his boys to steal. Nonetheless, the definition of education embedded in the deep structure of educational thought disregards cases such as these.

The deep structure's narrow conception of education follows from a nature/culture divide and an accompanying divorce of mind and body that seeks to separate us from the animals. Only we humans possess minds and are rational animals, or so the story goes: thus, only we have intentions and act wittingly, only we are capable of intellectual achievements, and only we are moral beings; and therefore, only we are qualified to be the objects of education.

Perhaps nowhere has this rationalistic sense of education been stated so clearly and embraced so openly as in the writings of the influential twentieth-century British philosopher R.S. Peters.[13] After distinguishing two concepts of education —a broad and a narrow one—neither of which incorporates a cultural perspective, Peters opted for the narrow concept. Originally, he said, the term "had a very generalized meaning"[14] in that it "indiscriminately" marked out "any process of rearing, bringing up, instructing, etc."[15] But he maintained that, with the rise of industrialism and the development of compulsory schooling, the term "education" was increasingly used in connection with "the development of knowledge and understanding"—or, as Peters put it, with "the ideal of an educated man."[16] In the broad sense, said Peters, education "must have included passing on things that were thought valuable, but probably also included a lot of other things that were of little importance."[17] He held, however, that a value condition "is indissolubly connected" to the narrower sense that he said was associated with "special institutions"[18]—in other words, with schools.

Actually, the value condition Peters placed on education was two-fold: what is transmitted must be—or at least must be thought to be—worthwhile; and the procedures used must be "morally legitimate."[19] Peters' school-related concept of education also presupposed intent on the part of both the educator and the educatee: for the educational procedures to be morally legitimate, the pupil must undergo them willingly and voluntarily; and, although it is not necessary that the learner acquire the knowledge being transmitted, the educator must be trying to produce this happy state.

Peters did not merely assert that the intentional, knowledge-based, moralistic concept of education was school-related. He considered only his school-based definition of education to be philosophically interesting and took it for granted that it sufficed. Thus, although he later admitted that in earlier writings he had not perhaps appreciated how widespread the broad sense of education is,[20] he persisted in turning his back on it.

Quite aside from its one-sided perspective, the Peters-like definition of education that is built into the deep structure of educational thought is open to question. For starters, the definition commits the educator's version of the intentional fallacy. In the field of literary criticism, this fallacy is, roughly, the belief that disputes regarding the meaning of a text are definitively decided by appeal to the author's intentions.[21] The fallacy's counterpart in the context of educational thought is the assumption that, in order to know what, if any, education has occurred one must know what, if any, learning was intended. Portraying education as a strictly intellectual affair whose ultimate purpose is the acquisition of knowledge and understanding, the definition's cognitive bias overlooks the fact that education affects practically all aspects of our lives and ourselves, and that physical education is an established subject of the school curriculum. The definition also promotes the myth that education can do no wrong.[22]

The narrow rendering of education has some advantages. In ruling out morally repugnant learning, it absolves education of blame for passing down cultural liabilities such as racism and greed to the next generation. In excluding unintended or involuntary learning, it relieves it of responsibility for whatever unanticipated and undue effects its practices and procedures may have. In limiting education to the getting of knowledge and understanding, it makes the educator's task relatively simple. That a great deal of school learning, as well as much of the learning that takes place outside school, does not begin to conform to this concept of education means, however, that there is an enormous disconnect between it and reality.

The False Equation between Education and Schooling

The vast literature on the unintended learning that occurs in school and the fact that some of it—for instance, cheating and a hatred of learning—can scarcely be called worthwhile cast doubt on Peters' claim that his narrow concept of education accurately reflects what happens in school. Nonetheless, his dismissal of the broad sense of education, and with it home's claims to being an educational agent, is in perfect alignment with the boundaries that the deep structure sets for the educational realm. His preference for a school-based concept of education is matched, in turn, by the deep structure's reduction of education's institutional base to school.

That the equation between education and schooling is false has long been recognized. Deploring "an unduly scholastic and formal notion of education," in *Democracy and Education*, John Dewey remarked that school is only one means "which forms the dispositions of the immature."[23] Identifying the family as the main educational agency in the forming of U.S. society, Bernard Bailyn pointed out that, whatever it left undone, the community undertook, and that what was then left over was undertaken by the church.[24] Historian of American education Lawrence Cremin made it clear that neither Thomas Jefferson nor Horace Mann—both enthusiastic supporters of schools—considered school to have a monopoly over education.[25]

Perhaps the most eloquent critic of the false equation was social theorist Ivan Illich who, in the second half of the twentieth century, compared the reduction of education to schooling to the reduction of religion to churchgoing. Both school and church divide social reality into two realms, Illich said in *Deschooling Society*. As one distinguishes between the sacred and the profane, the other separates out the educational from the non-educational. As the church names itself the sole guardian of the sacred, the school appoints itself keeper of the educational.[26]

Despite the protests of Dewey, Illich, and the historians, the false equation has proven to be difficult to uncouple from people's capacities.[27] In the nineteenth and twentieth centuries, school gradually became, and in the twenty-first century it continues to be, Western culture's designated educator. Thus, to the extent that those guided by the deep structure acknowledge the educational role of home, religious institutions, libraries, museums, television, and the like—and they often do not—they have tended to view these institutions as school's helpers rather than as educational agents in their own right.

To be sure, museums have educational departments, newspapers and magazines have education editors, and television networks have some educational programming. However, the very fact that an institution allocates one small portion of its resources to education signifies that it does not consider itself, and is not considered by others, to be an educator in its own right. After all, schools do not have separate departments whose business is education and school buildings do not have separate education corners. Indeed, it makes no sense for an educational agent to contain a special educational section or division.

In reducing education to schooling, the deep structure of educational thought causes us to lose sight not only of the culture's vast array of educational agents but also of the vast amount of cultural stock that is not in school's portfolio. In consequence, we will not know if the culture's assets are being transmitted to the next generation or if some agents are failing to fulfill their educational functions. Nor will we know if some of them are transmitting cultural liabilities in addition to—or perhaps instead of—cultural assets, let alone if any of them are working at cross-purposes with school.[28]

4. Some Gaps in the Education Text

Do the dichotomies and assumptions matter? From a logical point of view, the nature/culture split and the bifurcation of culture mandated by the deep structure of educational thought pose no threat to the theory of education as encounter. Neither do the contraction of the educational realm that these entail, the narrow individual-based definition of education, or the reduction of education to schooling. There is no formal contradiction in saying that education is an encounter between individual capacities and cultural stock in which an educational agent yokes the two together, and both parties to the encounter change, and also maintaining that the stock belongs to only one portion of a culture's entire stock. Nor does a formal contradiction arise when it is maintained that that education only occurs in schools and is necessarily a voluntary, intentional, conscious, morally correct process. Nonetheless, the restrictions that the deep structure places on the scope of education have a number of untoward consequences.

Three gaps in the educational text that follow directly from education's deep structure are particularly telling. As the verification of the implications of a scientific theory contributes to the theory's confirmation, the existence of these lends credence to the hypothesis that the fundamental beliefs isolated here are embedded in educational thought.

The Missing Perspective

The most important gap in the educational text is the absence of discussion about education "writ large." As I write, those whose concern is education talk a great deal about individual learning and relatively little about cultural transmission. They pay a vast amount of attention to the ways in which school can be improved so as to enhance individual achievement and virtually none to the strengths and weaknesses of the culture's other educational agents. Are the old established educational agents doing their jobs well? Are any of them transmitting the culture's liabilities rather than its assets? How are the culture's various educational agents dividing up the labor? Do new agents need to be created?

When, in the *Republic*, Socrates was trying to discern the nature of justice, he said that the search requires keen eyesight. Drawing an analogy to trying to read small letters at a distance and finding them easier to see when written large, he suggested that he and his companions look for justice in the city-state before attempting to observe it in the actions of individuals. The deep structure of educational thought is one step ahead of Socrates and his friends in that it recognizes from the very start that education is part of culture. But forgetting that education is the process by which individuals become members of culture and remain so throughout their lives, it then loses sight of the big picture.

As a case in point, consider the lack of attention paid to the great changes in home and family that occurred in the last decades of the twentieth century and the failure to recognize that these were placing children's domestic curriculum at risk. At the end of the nineteenth century, John Dewey told a Chicago audience that the Industrial Revolution had irrevocably transformed the American home by removing manufacture from the household and he went on to say that, when home changes radically, school must also change.[29] A century later, home again underwent a radical change. With women as well as men making the daily trek from their private homes into the workplace, a domestic vacuum cutting across class, race, and ethnic lines was created in the lives of many children.[30]

Why did educators ignore Dewey's insight that home's history has educational ramifications? Concealing the vast array of the culture's educational agents, the deep structure's embrace of the standpoint of the individual made it—and continues to make it—difficult to see that the very discernible changes in the home might have educational consequences. Moreover, the assumption that education has no role to play in the world of the private home and family made the neglect of this historic trend all but inevitable. A realm from which education is banished is, by definition, a realm that has no curriculum, let alone one that could be at risk.

The Missing Educational Aim

A related gap in the educational text occurs in discussions of the general aims of education in modern democratic societies. These goals are commonly said to include the development of each person as a worker, a citizen, and an individual. Conspicuously absent from this list is the preparation or development of each person as a member of a home and family. In consequence, most reports on the condition of the American educational system fail to ask if children are being prepared for life at home.

Given the deep structure of educational thought, it comes as no surprise that the goal of preparing children for life in the arena of the private home is missing from discussions of education's purposes or aims. With culture divided into two spheres and education restricted to preparation for life in just one of them, it cannot be otherwise.

The Neglected Educational Issue

The silence surrounding the topic of violence represents another gap in the text of education. Despite the fact that the twentieth century was an extraordinarily violent age and that violence at home, in local neighborhoods, in schools, and in the world at large persists in the twenty-first century, violent behavior is rarely, if ever, thought of as an educational issue. The perpetrators of violent deeds are considered to be bad seeds or rotten apples—the victims of bad genes, child-hood abuse, or drugs. That violent behavior might be a learned affair is seldom considered.[31]

Insofar as violent behavior is thought to bespeak our "bestial" as opposed to our human nature, the primary responsibility for the "violence gap" in the education text can be said to rest with the nature/culture divide. Both the mind/body split accompanying the nature/culture divide and the rationalistic, moralistic definition of education embedded in the deep structure of educational thought also more or less insure this gap in the text. For violence is ordinarily expressed in action, whereas the divorce of mind from body effectively splits off thought from action, and the narrow definition makes the acquisition of knowledge and understanding the sole object of education.

To be sure, human actions ordinarily have a cognitive component. Nevertheless, knowledge does not translate directly into action. A man who believes that world peace is the highest good is perfectly capable of beating his wife and children. A woman who has read and understood Aristotle's *Nicomachean Ethics* and John Stuart Mill's *Utilitarianism* is quite capable of shooting her colleagues. Furthermore, the received definition banishes unintended learning from education's realm and many—perhaps most—of the yokings of violent patterns of behavior to individual capacities belong in this category.

The standpoint of the individual and the false equation between education and schooling represent two more reasons for the violence gap in the educational text. They effectively conceal the fact that—wittingly or not—many of the dominant groups and institutions in children's lives yoke both a belief in the efficacy of violence and violent patterns of behavior to their capacities.

Every group and institution of a society is the custodian or guardian of some portion of cultural stock. Like it or not, since some of the items of cultural stock in the keep of each custodian become yoked to the capacities of individuals, each custodian is an educational agent. And like it or not, the stock in the various portfolios includes cultural liabilities such as violent behavior. No one knows how many educational agents at any given time in a given culture are glorifying violence and making it appear fatally attractive, and no one knows how many children are learning to admire and emulate the practices they experience vicariously or first-hand. By dropping out the cultural perspective, defining education very narrowly, and reducing it to schooling, the deep structure of educational thought makes it difficult, if not absolutely impossible, to find this out.

5. Do the Gaps Matter?

The question remains of whether the gaps in the education text are so serious that an adequate theory of education must reject the assumptions responsible for them. Cannot the theory of education as encounter simply acknowledge that the deep structure of educational thought has these implications, and leave it at that?

Would that we could sweep educational thought's deep structure under the rug and go about our business with impunity. However, the elements of deep structure that have thus far been unearthed are themselves items of cultural stock. A theory of education that accepts them does not merely preserve these dubious items for the next generation. It transmits the message that the gaps are unimportant.

Think, however, about the missing perspective. Bemoaning the then standard interpretation of education in American history, whose leading characteristic was its separateness as a branch of history, Bernard Bailyn said of his fellow historians, "by limiting education to formal instruction they lost the capacity to see it in its full context and hence to assess the variety and magnitude of the burdens it had borne and to judge its historical importance."[32] By limiting the perspective from which to see education, the deep structure of education thought sacrifices the capacity of parents and teachers, citizens and politicians, scholars and lay people: to see at work the full range of agents; to assess how well they are transmitting the culture's stock; to decide if any educational tasks need to be reassigned or if new educational agents should be created; and, above all, to understand that education is one of the basic forces of life on earth.

Think now about the lack of concern regarding home's curriculum. The fact that the great changes in home and family may adversely affect children's first great metamorphosis from creatures of nature into inhabitants of human culture renders this oversight bad enough, but the domestic vacuum in children's lives also means that they may not be receiving the preparation for living at home with others that, in the past, they were expected to learn at their mother's knee. In addition, the vacuum places at risk of extinction that portion of cultural stock that home has, in the past, been expected to pass down to the next generation, included in which are the three Cs of care, concern, and connection to others.[33] We can scarcely expect adults whose capacities never became coupled with this stock to transmit it, in turn, to their children. So again, the consequences of holding onto the deep structure of educational thought are too important for us to ignore with impunity.

Consider the missing educational aim. Statistics regarding divorce, desertion, child negligence, domestic violence, and child sexual abuse leave little doubt that the world of the private home and family is not the safe, peaceful, happy sanctuary it was once thought to be. Whether educational programs for life at home would significantly improve the situation cannot be decided in advance of the facts, but they are certainly worth a try, and the gap in the text is certainly worthy of attention. Indeed, a belief system that, by fiat, precludes this kind of education, as the deep structure of educational thought does, is a belief system whose premises cry out for questioning.

Finally, think about the refusal to treat violence as an educational issue. If a theory of education were to ignore this gap in the text, the false illusion would be created that learning guarantees improvement of the individual, and the culture's many educational agents would also be absolved of all responsibility for passing down vices as well as virtues. For a group or institution to be considered *mis*educative, it must first be seen to be an educational agent. Because the false equation admits only school into this category, this necessary step cannot be taken.

It is impossible to exaggerate the harm done to the next generation by the miseducation that is brought about by contemporary culture's non-school educational agents. For the present purpose, however, let it suffice to say that racial and gender stereotypes, hatred, greed, consumerism, a high tolerance of mendacity, and a scorn of intellectuals are among the cultural liabilities that are being passed down along with the violence.

Besides concealing the miseducation of our young by the myriad non-school agencies, the reduction of education to schooling places an undue burden on schools. School people frequently complain that school is continually and unfairly asked to do more than any single institution possibly can, yet small wonder the demands on school keep growing. With only the one educational agent to call upon, the culture has no choice but to demand that school should do it all.

In truth, no culture whose institutions include the private home and family can afford a theory of education that makes school its sole educational agent, if only because these play such a crucial role in the education of each new generation. But the false equation also means that we lose sight of the many occasions in which school and other educational agents can work together cooperatively to educate our young.

Home is, after all, but one of a multitude of non-school educators that inhabit contemporary society. Only if church, neighborhood, police and fire departments, TV, the Internet, and all the rest are officially acknowledged to be educational agents can they be expected to share the culture's educational responsibilities with school constructively. It is utopian thinking at its worst to suppose that education by itself can staunch the flow of even one of the cultural liabilities listed above, let alone of all. But it is equally mistaken to think that education plays no part in the passing along of a culture's liabilities and can do nothing at all to prevent their transmission.

6. Rejecting the Deep Structure

The deep structure of educational thought does not only lose sight of the full context of education. In embracing the two-sphere split, it endorses an outmoded ideology. Even if the so-called public and private spheres were sharply divided in the past—and the historical record suggests otherwise—in the twenty-first century they are not. Even if women and men used to inhabit different spheres, now women as well as men perform the tasks and responsibilities traditionally associated with the world of work, politics, and the professions, and men as well as women perform those traditionally associated with the world of the private home. It is, of course, possible to revise the two-sphere analysis and the traditional gender stereotypes so as to allow for some of the changes that have occurred. But altering the details of the two-sphere ideology does not address the fact that the ideology unduly narrows down the educational realm.[34]

A pressing issue remains, however. Rousseau, who is considered to be one of the founding fathers of democracy, wrote in *Emile* that it is "by means of the small fatherland which is the family that the heart attaches itself to the large one."[35] In a similar vein, a turn-of-the-twenty-first-century political theorist commented, "The development of character at home . . . is, of course, a *sine qua non* of long-term democratic institutions."[36] Does rejection of education's deep structure entail rejecting the institution of private home and family? If so, does it court totalitarianism?

The answer to both questions is "No." In the first place, private homes and families can exist without a polarized split between the public and private worlds and without a polarized conception of gender. Indeed, these institutions are compatible with a wide range of gender ideologies and conceptions of the public and private spheres. Furthermore, they need not entail any shrinking of education's domain. One can in all consistency advocate that people live in private homes and families while agreeing that education takes place therein.

Thus, in rejecting the rock bottom premises of the deep structure of educational thought, the theory of education as encounter does not reject the institutions of the private home and family. This is not to say that the theory of education as encounter actively endorses the latter. Going on the assumption that every culture must decide for itself whether or not people should live in private homes as members of private families—and also what form or forms those homes and families should take—our theory leaves these normative questions open.

In sum, then, the thesis that democracy relies on the learning that occurs in the private home and family does not mandate retention of the public/private split and the accompanying gender dichotomy. It must be understood, however, that claims that one or another portion of the cultural stock that is required by democracy is necessarily learned at home are open to debate. Indeed, in light of the vast array of educational agents, it is far from obvious that any given item of stock—be it love of country, a certain kind of character, or something else entirely—can only be attached to the capacities of individuals by the private home and family. Is someone who grows up in a loveless home so maimed or undeveloped that he or she can never develop a love of country? Are there really no other educational agents—for instance, school, the scouts, a community organization, the military—that can step into the breach? And what about those who grow up in an institution other than the private home and family? Is it really impossible for an orphanage or a kibbutz to yoke the requisite cultural stock to individual capacities?

In other words, although the theory of education as encounter does not reject the private home and family, the case has not been made that democracy requires this institution. Nor, for that matter, can a case be made that its existence will guarantee democracy. Think of Nazi Germany. Think of the Soviet Union. Think of groups whose private homes actively seek to promote a love of God or of their own community in lieu of love of country. Think also of all those private homes in democratic societies that instill character traits antithetical to democracy.

At this point it may be objected that, although the private home and family are neither necessary nor sufficient for democracy, the idea that education encompasses preparation for life in the private home smacks of totalitarianism. Is it not a mark of a totalitarian regime that it would, if it could, dictate every facet of life? To jettison the two-sphere ideology and the traditional gender stereotypes and say that education takes place at home, as well as in the world, and includes preparation for life in both arenas is not to take a stand on what that education should be. It need hardly be said that education for living at home does not have to be dictatorial. The teaching of cooking, bed making, simple housekeeping rules, and basic infant care has not made society totalitarian. Media portrayals of different kinds of living arrangements and balanced discussions of alternative childrearing practices do not betoken totalitarianism either.

To be sure, if the deep structure of educational thought is renounced, governments can dictate behavior in the private home and terrorize those who flaunt the edicts. But they can do this now. The belief that the two-sphere ideology represents a barrier to totalitarianism flies in the face of history and so does the belief that any efforts to yoke individual capacities to items of home-related cultural stock are in themselves authoritarian.

It is safe to conclude, then, that it is foolhardy for the theory of education as encounter to try to draw new boundaries for the educational realm and leave it at that. Even as it seeks to unify the standpoints of the individual and the culture, it needs to reject unequivocally the obsolete bifurcations that have far too long been embedded in educational thought.

Here, two more cautionary notes are in order. The first is that to reject the two-sphere analysis and replace it with a unified conception of culture does not mean that in all contexts human culture must be regarded as an indivisible whole. To be sure, cultures have sometimes been thought of as unitary entities, yet no one has suggested that a culture lacks subdivisions. Anthropologists are apt to divide cultures into systems of, for example, kinship, language, economics, childrearing. Others might instead cite the scouts, the Roman Catholic Church, the middle class family, the public school system, and commercial television as some of the parts or units of a given contemporary culture. Furthermore, it is commonplace today to treat at least some of the parts of a cultural whole as cultures in their own right. Thus, we speak of the culture of the scouts, the Roman Catholic Church, the middle class family, and a particular school system. In sum, a theory of education that rejects the two-sphere analysis and its assumption of polar opposite domains can still take account of cultural subdivisions, including that of the private home and family.

The second proviso is that rejection of the traditional gender stereotypes does not mean that the theory of education as encounter must eschew all reference to gender. It simply means that the traditional stereotypes will no longer define the boundaries and the norms of the educational realm.

Once education's realm is seen to include the whole of human culture, is there any need to abandon the narrow rationalistic and moralistic definition of education? Provided it is understood that this definition merely applies to a limited form or special case of education, there is no reason for the theory of education as encounter to reject it altogether. Our theory cannot, however, accept it as a general definition of education. In building intentionality into the very nature of education, this element of education's deep structure casts the hidden curriculum of school and society outside the educational realm. In requiring voluntariness on the part of learners, it rules out the first great metamorphosis, for newborns are not in a position to choose to be inducted into human culture. In confining education to the achievement of knowledge and understanding, it excludes the acquisition of feelings and emotions, passions and actions. In limiting the intended outcomes of education to ones that are worthwhile, it places vices and other undesirable qualities beyond the pale. And, of course, in viewing education solely from the standpoint of the individual, it loses sight of education writ large.

Logically speaking, the theory of education as encounter could restrict its subject matter in these ways, but there are excellent pragmatic reasons for preferring a broad definition of education to the narrow one. On the intentional/knowledge-based/moralistic sense of the term "education," so much yoking together of human capacities and cultural stock falls outside education's domain that a realistic estimate cannot be gotten of the changes that learning brings about in both individuals and cultures. In addition, because it focuses solely on what an educational agent intends that people learn, the narrow sense of "education" renders invisible all those unintended outcomes that may conflict with an educator's expressed aims.

Suppose, for example, that a given culture's schools have made universal literacy one basic educational aim and critical thinking another objective. Suppose also that many other educational agents of that culture are yoking to the capacities of the next generation the belief that literacy is unimportant and that independent thinking is to be avoided. A theory of education whose definition of its subject matter refuses to recognize the unintended and undesirable outcomes of learning conceals problems of this sort. Failing to acknowledge conflicts between intentions and the learning that is actually taking place, it is unable to devise ways of resolving them.

Finally, the narrow sense of education robs the subject of education of its significance for both the individual and the culture. Actually, responsibility for doing this rests with the deep structure of educational thought more generally. Just as the incremental model of learning trivializes education by cutting if off from culture, so does the deep structure of educational thought. Shrinking education's realm to a fraction of its rightful size, discounting the culture's wide range of educational agents, concealing the learning that takes place in every nook and cranny of the social order, ignoring the transformation of each one of us from a creature of nature to an inhabitant of culture, and ruling out of court the enormous harm that education can do, it turns education into a rather tedious enterprise.

Refusing to trivialize its subject matter, the theory of education as encounter rejects the deep structure's construction of the educational realm. Abandoning the tacitly held beliefs that have been isolated here, it reclaims the whole of culture as education's domain and portrays education as both a cultural and an individual process. In other words, it assumes that education ranges over all cultural contexts rather than only over those located in the public sphere. Our theory also defines the educational process broadly enough to encompass all learning. In particular, it makes no assumption that education is necessarily an intentional, voluntary activity whose procedures always accord with morality and whose outcomes are always worthwhile cognitive attainments. To be sure, it does not deny the existence of education in the narrow sense of the term. Rather, it affirms that what the narrow definition takes to be the whole of education is merely one small part of that complex enterprise. And finally, it acknowledges the whole wide range of a culture's groups and institutions, as well as the whole culture itself, as educational agents and treats the transmission of culture and individual learning as the two sides of a single coin.

3

REPOPULATING THE EDUCATIONAL REALM

When a realm's boundaries are redrawn, its population changes. With the whole of culture reclaimed for education, it is necessary, therefore, to identify the inhabitants of the area. I do so here by taking special note of populations that the deep structure of educational thought has excluded from the educational realm.

1. The Missing Women

In the latter part of the twentieth century, a body of literature known as "the new scholarship on women" documented the ways in which intellectual disciplines such as history and psychology, literature and the arts, sociology and biology were biased according to sex—or gender, as it would now be said. My research on education showed, in turn, that, although throughout history women had reared and taught their young, had themselves been educated, and had also formulated educational theories and philosophies, they had officially been excluded from the educational realm. The textbooks and anthologies in the field almost totally ignored philosophical works about education written by women and also the very topic of the education of girls and women.[1]

Writing in 1976 about political theory, one scholar said that, from that discipline's standpoint, women, children, and the family dwelt in the "ontological basement." She pointed out that their apolitical status was due not to historical accident or necessity, but to arbitrary definition. The "reproductive processes" of society—processes in which she included creation and birth and the rearing of children to "more or less independence"—were, by fiat, excluded from the political domain, which was defined in relation to the public world of "productive processes."[2] As it happens, these and all the cultural stock associated with them are precisely what the deep structure of educational thought excludes from the educational domain. In defining education in relation to the public world of "productive processes," it renders the status of women and the family "a-educational," as well as apolitical. Lest there be any doubt, this "a-educational" status extends to women of all races, classes, and ethnicities.

When the new scholarship on women was introduced into undergraduate studies, feminist educators distinguished between simply adding women to the curriculum and genuinely integrating the study of women. The texts and anthologies in the field of educational thought admit of a similar distinction. As a lecture on women poets can be inserted into a poetry course without affecting the rest of the course content, and a class in women's history can be added to a school curriculum without materially affecting the content of the other history courses that are offered, a chapter on a woman's educational philosophy can be added to a text without educational thought being otherwise affected.

By the start of the twenty-first century, some simple addition had taken place in educational thought, but very little integration had occurred.[3] The practice of adding without integrating women is to be expected so long as the field of educational thought retains the beliefs that constitute its deep structure. An example provides insight into why this is so.[4]

According to the received reading of *Emile*, Rousseau put forward in that work an ideal of a self-sufficient, self-governing, autonomous man and accordingly designed the educational program for boys that he described in Books I–IV. On this reading, his discussion of the education of girls in Book V represents an afterthought. Yet, if from the start one reads Book V in conjunction with Books I–IV, one realizes that Sophie's education is no postscript to *Emile*; on the contrary, Rousseau's program for the boy Emile's education only makes sense in relation to the one he formulates for the girl that Emile is to marry.

Look at Sophie and Emile separately and one sees an utterly dependent woman and an equally independent man. Look at the two together and one sees a man who is not nearly as self-sufficient or self-governing as Rousseau's interpreters have claimed. As an adult, he will be as dependent on his wife as she is on him—not just for creature comforts but also for loving, living, and morality itself. Sophie will make a home for him. She will bear and raise his children and even teach him to love them. Furthermore, she will make it possible for him to be a complete moral person, for Rousseau makes it clear that neither Sophie nor Emile taken alone is a fully moral individual: only the two together comprise a truly moral being.

In other words, when Sophie is integrated into the interpretation of Rousseau's educational philosophy, it becomes apparent that, contrary to accepted opinion, Rousseau designed a two-track educational system for the production of an interdependent heterosexual couple—not a one-track program for the development of an autonomous man. For this integration to be carried through, however, the world of the private home and family must be seen as Rousseau saw it—namely, as part of the educational realm—and Sophie's virtues of caring for her family and loving her children must also be acknowledged. Both measures are precluded by the deep structure of educational thought's presumption that education begins and ends in the world of work, politics, and the professions.

Although this example of failed integration involves the interpretation of just one man's philosophy, its echoes are far reaching. Consider the worldwide co-education movement. In effect, its strategy has been to extend Emile's education to Sophie; that is, to give girls and women an education originally designed for boys and men and intended to prepare them for membership in the world of work, politics, and the professions. This movement could also have tried to extend to boys and men the education of girls and women—one whose function was to prepare students for living in the world of the private home and family. But, instead of attempting this, it turned its back on the kind of education that Rousseau, however imperfectly, designed for Sophie.

Had Western culture chosen to follow Plato's recommendations in the *Republic* and abolish the institutions of private home, family, and childrearing, it might make no difference that education in the societal tasks and duties, knowledge and skills, and the three Cs of care, concern, and connection traditionally associated with women and the world of the private home has been allowed to drop out of the picture.[5] But the West has rejected Plato's scenario. Along with Aristotle, Rousseau, and most of the other great Western philosophers, it has embraced the private home and family. In light of the West's continued allegiance to these institutions and the fact that the values and virtues, traits and dispositions required for membership in them are not innate, the neglect is serious indeed. This is not to say that the historical, gender-based two-track educational system, with one track designed for boys and the other for girls, should have been retained. It is simply to point out that, when women are not integrated into educational thought, it is all too easy to overlook the importance of preparing young people of both sexes for life in the world of the private home and family.

The deep structure of educational thought mandates this amnesia. So long as the educational realm is assumed to be coextensive with the world of work, politics, and the professions, the fact that the education historically intended for boys is incomplete cannot be acknowledged. So long as the world of the private home is considered to be closer to nature than to culture, it will not be granted that at least some cultural stock associated with girls and women may have great worth.

It is true that women in the twenty-first century have, to some extent, been brought into the texts and curricula of educational thought even as the two-sphere analysis and the traditional gender dichotomy have been retained. Their entrance has, however, been conditional—the condition being that women's presence should make no significant difference to the field of education. Rejecting education's deep structure, the theory of education as encounter brings the missing women into the educational realm unconditionally as both participants in the educational process and educational thinkers. Indeed, it brings into education's domain not only women but also the cultural stock that the West has long considered to be in women's keep—the functions and institutions, tasks and responsibilities, knowledge and skills, attitudes and values, virtues and vices, ideologies and worldviews, ways of thinking and modes of action long associated with the world of the private home.

Once again, some caveats are needed. One is that to draw the boundaries of the educational realm so as to include the cultural stock that tradition associates with women is *not* in and of itself to validate these items. When the educational realm is defined as coextensive with the whole of culture, it necessarily encompasses the whole range of activities, traits, and so on—which means vices as well as virtues, activities that do harm as well as ones that do good, and the trivial as well as the momentous. Thus, to the extent that the cultural stock traditionally associated with women includes liabilities as well as assets, these too fall within education's domain.

The second caveat is that the inclusion in the educational realm of cultural stock associated with women is neutral regarding *whose* capacities should be yoked to the various items that comprise it. It is *not* to say that this stock can or should attach only to the capacities of women. To be sure, if childrearing, family living, the three Cs of care, concern, and connection, and the like were in some absolute sense denied men by nature, they could not become yoked to the capacities of boys as well as girls, and men as well as women. But this contrary to fact assumption is not being made here.

This leads directly to a third caveat. It is well known that many items of cultural stock are assigned to one or another gender. Clothing is an obvious example of this phenomenon, but many careers, hobbies, toys, books, films, colors, foods, drinks, musical instruments, types of knowledge, individual traits, and innumerable other types of stock are also genderized. These attributions of gender are not rooted in biology; indeed, anthropologists inform us that the gender designations of particular items of stock often vary from one culture to another. Such variation does not, however, render the cultural practice of stock genderization innocuous. On the contrary, where education is concerned, the fact that knowledge, skills, attitudes, values, character traits, and other items of cultural stock are classified as male or female is of prime importance.

Because gender designations of stock are culturally based and not determined by nature, an item of stock that is classified as male or masculine can become yoked to the capacities of biological females, and an item classified as female or feminine can become yoked to the capacities of biological males. Evaluations of the yoking of any given item of cultural stock to an individual's capacities tend to differ, however, according to whether there is a match or a mismatch between the gender assignment of the stock and the individual.

Consider, for example, the traits of competitiveness and aggressiveness. In the U.S. and other Western societies, these two items of cultural stock have tended to be seen as male or masculine while caring and empathy have been assumed to be female or feminine. It should again be stressed that this is a cultural perception, not a biological fact. It is not the case that all men in the U.S. are competitive and that all women are empathetic: women, as well as men, can be aggressive and men, as well as women, can be caring; indeed, men can excel at childcare and women at aggressive sports. But because these items of stock are genderized in favor of males, a woman is likely to be disparaged for displaying the very kind of aggressive behavior that is praised in a man. Similarly, a man risks denigration for exemplifying caring behavior that is deemed a virtue in a woman.

In including cultural stock in the educational realm that is associated with women and the world of the private home and family, the theory of education as encounter brings in stock that is genderized in favor of women. But it no more endorses the conventional labeling of this stock as female or feminine than it endorses the conventional labeling of stock associated with men and the public world as male or masculine.

Some may be inclined to protest that to bring both women and the stock that has been culturally associated with them into the educational realm will inevitably reinforce the association between the two, and that women will, in consequence, once again be expected to do all the cooking, cleaning, and childrearing. They may propose, therefore, that the theory of education as encounter welcome the missing women but ban the stock. Since, however, childrearing practices and the like are learned affairs and not merely instinctual acquisitions, there is no justification for excluding this stock from the realm of education. Moreover, the association of women with homemaking, childrearing, and related activities is itself an item of cultural stock, one that continues to be passed down even though women have entered the workforce in record numbers. To ignore its existence is, in effect, to sanction its continuation.

2. The Missing Minorities

No sooner was the absence of women from the disciplines of knowledge documented than scholars began to voice the objection that the category "women" obscures the differences between and among women. In particular, they held that the terms "woman" and "women" should be eschewed because they imply—or else those who use them tend to assume—that all women are white, middle class, and heterosexual.

It may well be the case that some of the authors of the new scholarship on women were thinking only of white, middle class, heterosexual women.[6] It may also be true that some findings that were based on samples of white, middle class, heterosexual women were presented as if they were about women of all races, classes, and sexual orientations. To equate the whole category or class of women with one small group of women is no more legitimate than it is to equate the whole of culture with one small part of culture, and to draw conclusions about all women from a sample of one small group of women is to generalize falsely. But, serious as these errors are, they do not warrant the exclusion of the category or concept or term "women" from the realm of education.

To be sure, there is justice to the complaint that the category "women" calls attention to similarities rather than differences. However, since every general term—be it "chair," "table," "virtue," "women," "men"—does this, the fact does not militate against the use of the category "women." On the contrary, if the theory of education as encounter were to ban the concept or term "women," in the name of consistency it would have to avoid all general categories. Instead of adopting this self-defeating policy, let us simply acknowledge that the masking of difference or diversity is built into language itself.

Those who argued against the general category of women suggested using in its stead particularistic categories such as African-American women and Asian-American women. But, of course, these also obscure diversity: in the one case, the differences between Japanese-American, Chinese-American, Vietnamese-American, Cambodian-American women, and so on are overlooked; in the other, those between, for instance, South African-American, Sudanese-American, Ethiopian-American, and Nigerian-American women. Furthermore, each of these more limited categories itself obscures diversity: thus, for example, the category Chinese-American obscures class differences, religious differences, linguistic differences, regional differences, and so on. And so too would an even more particularistic category. Indeed, taken to its logical conclusion, the ban on the category, concept, or term "women" would mean the end of all theorizing, indeed of almost all language-based communication.

Advocates of the use of categories such as Asian-American women and African-American women might reply to this line of argument that there are good pragmatic reasons for employing them, even though they too mask diversity. However, there may also be good practical reasons for retaining the more general term "women." In light of this possibility, it is appropriate for a general theory of education to make room for discourse about women at all levels of specificity and generality. Let it be understood, however, that, while welcoming all the missing women and the category or concept "women" into the educational realm, the theory of education as encounter rejects any a priori assumption of the uniformity of women.

Since men, as well as women, come in all races, classes, ethnicities, and sexual orientations, let it also be understood that the theory of education as encounter rejects any a priori assumption of the uniformity of men. As it happens, although men as a category or class have never been missing from the texts and anthologies of Western educational thought, men's diversity has not generally been acknowledged. Thus, for example, African-American men were seldom to be found there in the past, and the topics of "Negro" rights and education that Booker T. Washington and W.E.B. DuBois so hotly debated in *Up From Slavery* and *The Souls of Black Folk* were rarely mentioned.[7]

Studies documenting the racial prejudice in Western thought have revealed that even the heroes of the eighteenth-century European Enlightenment and the American Revolution devoutly believed in white superiority.[8] Echoing the sentiments of the General Assembly of Virginia, which in 1705 proclaimed: "That from and after the passing of this act, all negro, mulatto, and Indian slaves, in all courts of judicature, and other places, within this dominion, shall be held, taken, and adjudged, to be real estate," the nineteenth century's leading European naturalists consistently portrayed black Africans as approaching the beasts in form.[9] Conjoin Western culture's longstanding racial stereotypes with the sharp nature/culture divide embedded in the deep structure of educational thought, and the exclusion of African-American men from the educational realm is to be expected. When people who are not white are likened to the animals that fall within nature as opposed to culture, and when education's domain is restricted to one part of culture, those people necessarily fall outside education's boundaries.

In the theory of education as encounter, the realm of education is coextensive with the realm of culture. Moreover, this theory rejects the traditional racial and gender stereotypes that place groups of people outside culture. Indeed, it rejects stereotypical thinking altogether.

Some today condemn all use of the concept of race on the grounds that it presupposes that races are biological entities whereas they are in fact cultural constructs.[10] It is not necessary, however, to ban the use of a concept or term because beliefs about its referent are mistaken. Think of the sun. It used to be assumed that it travels around the earth but now we know that the reverse is true. This fundamental change in the West's belief system involved the rejection of many deep-seated assumptions but it did not require that all talk of the sun be eschewed. Similarly, it is possible to reject the belief in separate and distinct biologically based races while continuing to use the concept or term "race." Making no such assumption, indeed abandoning the old racial stereotypes and the fallacious science on which they were often based, the theory of education as encounter does just this.

Refusing to embrace the West's traditional stereotypical thinking about race, gender, class, disabilities,[11] or any other category, the theory of education as encounter also rejects the hierarchies that the stereotypes entail. It does this without, however, rejecting the concepts of gender, race, class, disabilities, and so on. In the first place, as items of cultural stock, these concepts belong in the educational realm. In addition, so long as the culture employs them, it is foolhardy to eschew them. To be sure, race, class, gender, and disabilities are social or cultural constructions. But this fact makes these more, not less, relevant to a theory of education that views both cultural and individual change as the product of the coupling and uncoupling of individual capacities and cultural stock.

Our theory's refusal to bar all talk of race, gender, and the like should not be construed as approval for race-bound, gender-bound, or otherwise-bound theories of education. Affirming in *Emile* that gender is a difference that makes all the difference, Rousseau designed separate unequal educations for boys and girls in order to prepare them for different and unequal societal roles. South Africa under apartheid and the United States under segregation did the same for blacks and whites, and many social orders have done as much for upper and lower socio-economic classes. Although the theory of education as encounter does not banish cultural categories such as race and gender, it makes no assumption that an individual's education or place in society should be determined by his or her race, gender, or class. Nor does it assume that an individual's education or place in society should be determined by his or her ethnicity, religion, or the like.

It is often taken for granted that the only alternative to a race or gender "bound" educational theory is a race or gender "free" one. The roots of this position can be traced back to Book V of Plato's *Republic* where, after saying that sex is a difference that makes no difference in regard to the question of who should rule the Just State, Socrates insisted that it makes no difference either to the kind of education that the rulers should receive. But Plato reported Socrates' remarks more than two millennia ago. Today, empirical research suggests that gender does make a difference to education, and that race, class, ethnicity, sexual orientation, and disabilities do as well. In different ways, and to varying degrees, they affect the way people are portrayed by the media and other educational agents, the way children are treated in school by their teachers and their classmates, the way families and peer groups perceive schooling, and, of course, the way school and college curricula reflect the lives and experiences of students.

We seem to face an unpleasant dilemma: either a theory of education assumes that race, gender, class, and the like determine a person's place in society and make all the difference to education, in which case it is inherently racist, sexist, classist, and so on, as the case may be; or the theory assumes that these make no difference to education, in which case it denies the facts. Fortunately, however, there is no need to choose between the two extremes, for they represent a false dichotomy. There is a middle ground or, if you prefer, a third way between a race/gender/etc. "bound" position and a race/gender/etc. "free" position, namely a race/gender/etc. "sensitive" position that takes these categories into account when they are relevant to education, and ignores them when they are not. This last is, indeed, the position adopted by the theory of education as encounter.[12]

When exactly are race, gender, class, and so on relevant to education and when are they not? If a culture's governing ideology holds race or gender, for example, to be the difference that makes all the difference, race or gender becomes relevant to just about every aspect of education. But it is a mistake to assume that, in cultures that subscribe to the ideal of race or gender equality, race or gender makes no different at all. Is the co-educational classroom climate chilly for girls and women? Would more African-Americans study science if more science professors were black? Empirical research is needed to answer questions such as these. It will be noted that, in principle, the respects in which race, gender, class, and so on can matter to education are countless. Given that new educational ways and means are constantly being introduced and old ones discarded, the research findings of today may, moreover, be overturned tomorrow. Yet, none of this is to say that race, gender, and the rest always and everywhere make a difference to education. The point to be made is, rather, that the sensitivity to race, gender, class, and the rest that marks the theory of education as encounter must be continual.

Finally, it should be stressed that the theory of education as encounter does not seek to place human beings in categories in which they do not comfortably fit. Thus, it does not assume that every individual is a member of one and only one race, one and only one gender, one and only one ethnicity, one and only one sexual orientation, and so on. Let it be understood, therefore, that education as encounter brings into the educational realm all human beings. Hence, it brings in people of all genders, races, classes, ethnicities, religions, and sexual orientations, as well as those who define themselves, or are defined by others, as falling outside these and other rigidly defined categories. It also includes people who differ in their abilities, disabilities, family circumstances, personal preferences, and histories.

3. The Missing Persons

More needs to be said about the people who inhabit the realm of education. In particular, the mind/body split embedded in the deep structure of educational thought makes it necessary to affirm that the men and women, girls and boys included therein are whole persons.

The presence in the school curriculum of a subject called *physical* education is mute testimony to the existence of the deep structure's mind/body split. Why would one particular curriculum subject be called "physical" education if every subject were thought to educate both minds and bodies? Why indeed would only one subject bear the label "physical" and no subject be called "mental" if mental education were not the default position; if, unless otherwise specified, every subject can be assumed to be an instance of mental education?

The late nineteenth-century movement for including manual training in the U.S. school curriculum provides additional evidence for the presence in educational thinking of both the mind/body split and the higher valuation of "mental" education.[13] On the one hand, the label "manual" implies that the established subjects of the school curriculum were expected to train heads, not hands. On the other, a major criticism voiced by opponents of the inclusion of manual training in schools was that it was directed at the development of one of the "lower" faculties. This assessment, it should be noted, was implicit in the movement of that era to make manual training—or industrial education as it came to be called—the curriculum of choice for African-American children.

One of the most unfortunate aspects of education's mind/body dualism is that it separates thought from action. The cognitive bias of the deep structure's definition of education reflects this divide. Whether the aim of education is thought to be the acquisition of knowledge, beliefs, facts, concepts, or ideas, the referents of the various labels are presumed to be cognitive attainments sharply divorced from action.

One consequence of this narrowing down of education's mission is that the "best" students in the "best" school systems are considered to be those who answer the most questions correctly on examinations. Can they apply the factual and theoretical knowledge they have acquired to practical situations? Can they acquire knowledge through practical experience? No one seems to know or care. Yet, think of all the people in the world who know, intellectually, what is the right or moral thing to do but do not do it. Moral behavior aside, think of all the school children who get high scores on paper-and-pencil tests, or their computerized equivalents, but do not know how to bring their intelligence to bear on the activities of living.

Another consequence of the mind/body split and its sharp divide between thought and action is the devaluation of the abilities that people who do not answer the test questions correctly may actually possess. As psychologist Howard Gardner made clear,[14] they may have "intelligences" that are not being developed in school or measured by tests. That they may have learned how to bring those intelligences to bear on real-world problems and situations is not considered. Nor is it acknowledged that the divorce of thought from action may cause them to lose all interest in learning the very subjects that school wants them to learn.

Dewey once said, "It would be impossible to state adequately the evil results which have flowed from this dualism of mind and body, much less to exaggerate them."[15] Agreeing with Dewey, the theory of education as encounter brings into the educational realm whole persons, not disembodied minds and mindless bodies. This does not mean that education cannot aim at the development of mental capacities such as theoretical understanding and critical thought, or physical capacities such as small muscle agility or eye-hand coordination. Of course it can. Rather, it is a reminder that the men, women, and children in the educational realm are people with minds and bodies; or, if you prefer, composites of physical and mental capacities.

In view of the fact that education's deep structure has, in the past, located feelings and emotions in the world of the private home, hence outside the educational realm, it perhaps also needs to be made explicit that the whole persons envisioned by our theory have hearts, as well as heads and hands. Feelings and emotions such as love, hatred, tenderness, callousness, caring, resentment, empathy, and anger may have a biological basis, but the form they take and the manner of their expression make them just as much items of cultural stock as the capitals of countries and the dates of wars, hence just as much learned affairs. As such, they too populate education's domain.

4. The Missing Species

The question remains of whether the educational realm includes non-human animals. Given that jellyfish and ants can lead to educational encounters and can be the objects of human study, one can conclude that, at least in a limited sense, of course it does. But the pertinent issue is whether the fundamental educational unit of analysis that, in these pages, has been called "the individual" can be a non-human animal; in other words, whether members of species other than our own can be the individuals whose capacities become yoked to cultural stock in educational encounters.

The West's philosophers may have disagreed about the importance of culture to education, but they have tended to be of one mind in assuming that we humans are the only individuals who can play the role of educatee. To be sure, Rousseau said in *Emile* that education comes to us from nature, men, and things.[16] Nevertheless, the referent of the "us" to whom education comes was human beings. R.S. Peters, in turn, acknowledged that the English word "education" was originally used to talk about "the bringing up of children and animals" and that, in the nineteenth century, "it was even used of silkworms!"[17] But, of course, Peters rejected this broad sense of the term and, on this subject, the deep structure of educational thought is also unambiguous. It does not bar non-human animals from membership in the class of objects from which we humans may gain knowledge, but in locating them in nature and placing education inside culture, it limits full-fledged membership in the educational realm to humans by fiat.

Once the sharp nature/culture divide is rejected, however; and once it is acknowledged that education embraces more than the getting of knowledge and understanding, and that learning can occur without the learner's awareness or consent, the claims of non-human animals to being one of the two essential parties in education events or encounters become compelling. Arguing, in effect, that animals, as well as humans, are members of the moral realm, philosopher Jeremy Bentham said in his 1789 treatise *An Introduction to the Principles of Morals and Legislation*: "The question is not, Can they *reason*? Nor Can they *talk*? But, Can they *suffer*?"[18] When the subject is the status of animals in the educational realm the question is not, Can they have *language*? Can they have *self-awareness*? Can they have a *sense of human identity*? Nor even, Can they *suffer*? It is, Can they *learn*?

In "the wild," vervet monkeys make different sounds to warn off different predators. Very young vervets appear to have an innate tendency to make different shouts for things in the air such as eagles and things on the ground such as snakes. As they grow older, however, they learn to refine their calls through what seems to be positive reinforcement: for instance, when they make the right call, the adults join in.[19]

In "civilization," we train horses to run races, jump hurdles, and work in the field. We send dogs to obedience schools, teach them to be the eyes of sightless humans, and train them to rescue people, guard property, find bombs, and assist therapists. In addition, the American Kennel Club website tells us, "dogs who have a solid obedience *education* are a joy to live with."[20] How can these animals be legitimately excluded from education's domain? Granted, they do not voluntarily undergo their training, but neither do very young children. True, they are learning behavioral patterns rather than historical facts and spelling rules, but much of human learning also takes this form.

Consider also the experiments whose object is to teach birds or primates human language. Experts debate whether the signs that chimpanzees learn to make and the spoken words that parrots master qualify as language. So far, as the demographics of the educational realm are concerned, however, the relevant point is not that animals can or cannot learn language. It is that efforts to teach them English, French, American Sign Language represent efforts to yoke human cultural stock to animal capacities. In this regard, it should be noted that the skeptics do not deny that the primates and parrots in the language experiments learn to make signs or say words. Their objection is that the animals and birds do not understand what they are signing or saying and are simply mimicking humans.

The theory of education as encounter takes no stand on the kind of learning a participant in an educational event achieves: whether it is automatic, unreflective rote learning, or something far more intellectual, such as learning with understanding, is immaterial. From our theory's point of view, the relevance of these experiments lies in the fact that: the signs and spoken words are items of cultural stock; they are intended to, and sometimes do, become yoked to animals' capacities; as a result of the yokings, the animals change; and by no stretch of the imagination is signing "drink," "banana," "out," "more," and "sorry" purely instinctual as opposed to learned behavior.

Because language has long been thought to separate humans from other animals, the experimenters have tended to underplay, if not entirely ignore, the fact that the capacities of the primates raised in human homes have become yoked to a wide range of human cultural stock. Consider Nim Chimpsky, a chimpanzee who was taken from his mother as a newborn and raised in foster homes in New York City and its environs until he was almost four.[21] During this period, he learned to sleep in a bed, put on pants and a shirt each morning, brush his teeth, sit in a high chair, eat with utensils, watch television, take drives in the family car, and help cook, wash dishes, and do laundry. In other words, Nim was expected to learn—and, indeed, did master—a domestic curriculum very like the one that many human newborns in New York City experience. In some respects, moreover, he went way beyond that curriculum, for he became a whiz at opening locks on doors and cupboards and also greatly enjoyed playing jokes on people.

It may be wondered if Nim and the relatively few other cross-fostered chimpanzees represent exceptions that prove the rule that only humans can be educatees. The subtitle of Nim's biography is "The Chimp That Would Be Human" and some of those closest to him when he was very young speculated that he thought he was a human being. Can we not then reserve that role for ourselves and simply consider Nim and those like him to be honorary humans?

Researchers have discovered that pigs can learn to open and close cages, play video games, and understand mirrors.[22] Who knows what other non-human animals might learn to do if they were raised as Nim was! Moreover, we humans are still in the process of discovering what those raised in the wild learn to do. Furthermore, there would seem to be no reason—other than that of the desire to exclude non-human animals—why members of the educational realm must have self-awareness, let alone identify as human beings. So long as an individual's capacities and cultural stock meet and become yoked together and both parties to the encounter change, an educational event will have occurred. If the individual is a non-human animal, so be it.

That Nim underwent the kind of change we call learning as a result of his encounters with human cultural stock is indisputable. Few chimpanzees go around signing "sorry" to humans and opening doors and cabinets that people have tried to make "chimp-proof," and few, for that matter, sign to other chimpanzees, as Nim did when he was sent back to a cage in Norman, Oklahoma. Besides, the culture underwent at least a modicum of change because of Nim's encounters with its stock. The nature and extent of the cultural change that occurs when one individual's capacities become yoked to an item of culture stock are never easy to determine. In Nim's case, however, one can safely assume that his signing led to an increase in teaching signing to other chimpanzees.[23]

Nim may have been an exceptional chimpanzee, but he is merely one of the untold numbers of non-human animals who have a legitimate claim to being the learner in educational events. Think of dogs, cats, cows, horses, oxen, donkeys, camels, sheep, and goats. Fitting into human culture—and into roles that humans formerly played such as pulling plows, bearing heavy loads, serving as unsighted people's guides, and being companions—is what their breeding, breaking in, and training is intended to achieve. In other words, the general expectation is that the capacities of the world's domestic animals will become yoked to human cultural stock in ways that will enable them to play their designated roles in human society. It is presumably in this spirit that the American Kennel Club promotes its Canine Good Citizen® Program as one "that can help us assure that the dogs we love will always be welcomed and well-respected members of our communities."

It may be suggested that non-human animals deserve, at best, second-class membership in the educational realm because the cultural stock that attaches to their capacities belongs to human culture. Although it was long debated if non-human animals have cultures of their own, that question now seems to be settled: authorities on the subject firmly believe that animal cultures do exist and that at least a portion of non-human animal behavior is culturally transmitted. However, even if the experts are mistaken: so long as a non-human animal can learn—in other words, so long as its capacities can become yoked to cultural stock whatever its origin, and change in the process—there is no reason to exclude it from the realm of education.

Given that a great deal of non-human animal behavior is not purely instinctual, it would be an instance of blatant speciesism for the theory of education as encounter to consider animals anything but full-fledged members of the educational realm.

This is not to say that our theory offers the last word on the education of animals; on the contrary, it represents perhaps the first on this topic. Philosopher Peter Singer has pointed out that, although many thinkers have proposed the principle of equal consideration of interests, few have recognized that it applies to species other than our own.[24] Few, if any, of those who have taken the interests of animals seriously have, in their turn, recognized that an animal can be one of the fundamental parties in an educational event or episode. It would clearly seem to be in the interest of all animals that their membership in the educational realm be explicitly acknowledged.

Here, a caveat is needed. To say that, according to the theory of education as encounter, non-human as well as human animals can be the educatees or learners in educational events is not to say that cultural stock does in fact attach to the capacities of the members of all species so as to bring about change. Which species do and do not function in educational events in this manner is a question to be answered by future investigations. In light of the tremendous variation among species and the documented difficulties in drawing any hard and fast lines between humans and other animals,[25] it would not be surprising, however, to discover that such decisions must be made on a case-by-case basis.

It should also be noted that the role of educatee or learner neither presupposes nor entails the possession of rights.[26] For those who argue in favor of animal rights, however, the acknowledgement that animals are full-fledged members of the educational realm does raise the question of whether there is one among those rights that is not usually considered to apply to animals—namely, the right to education; and, if so, what kind of education.

5. The Missing Cultural Stock

Just as the theory of education as encounter includes humans and other animals in the educational realm, it includes the sum total of cultural stock. Everyone agrees that the culture side of the nature/culture divide encompasses a great deal more than the arts, literature, philosophy, and the sciences. No one doubts that it also includes institutions and practices, rites and rituals, beliefs and skills, attitudes and values, worldviews and localized modes of thinking. When, however, the subject is education, a narrow definition of culture is assumed.

In view of the deep structure's divorce of mind from body and its privileging of mind, the reduction of the whole of human culture to what is often called "high" culture is hardly surprising: it is widely assumed that only the fine arts and the "higher" learning are products of the human mind as such. One unfortunate consequence of educational thought's reduction of culture to high culture, however, is that the significance of the first great metamorphosis of a human life is lost to view. Even when it is granted that education has occurred— and this, frequently, is not acknowledged—the fact that this earliest education represents a bridge between nature and culture remains hidden from view because a newborn is not inducted into high culture. Another untoward result is that Minik's metamorphosis from a child of the Polar North to an all-American boy, and countless educational transformations like his, do not qualify as culture crossings because the items of stock from which the individual's capacities become uncoupled, and those new ones to which they attach, do not belong to high culture either.

It is in the interests of a unified theory of education to reject the reduction of the whole of culture to high culture and embrace a broad conception akin to the sort employed by anthropologists and sociologists.[27] Their definitions of culture differ in detail but whether they call culture "a design for living" or "everything that is learned," they encompass high, popular, and material culture as well as countless other items.

Granted, not everything in a culture's stock counts as wealth or assets for these terms carry a positive assessment. It is a far cry, however, from acknowledging that a culture's stock includes practices that do harm or are otherwise morally suspect to the assumption that high culture and the higher learning exhaust its riches. By ignoring huge portions of cultural stock, the reduction of culture to high culture keeps us from knowing which items of cultural stock are becoming attached to human capacities. In so doing, it keeps us in ignorance of what is being passed down to the next generation and what of value may be getting lost in transmission. As if this were not a serious enough loss, because the evaluative label "high" conceals the fact that a culture's stock includes both assets and liabilities, the reduction of culture to high culture also prevents us from seeing that cultural liabilities, as well as assets, are being handed down to future generations.

It would be unwise for a theory that includes in the educational realm the whole of culture, as the theory of education as encounter does, to dispense with the notion of high culture, but it would be even more imprudent for it to retain the deep structure's reduction of the whole of culture to one of its parts. For then, most of the changes that education produces in human individuals and their cultures would disappear from view.

It must be noted, however, that to say that the educational realm includes the sum total of cultural stock is not to say that all the stock there is—or, rather, all the cultural assets there are—can or should be yoked to the capacities of any given individual. The wealth of cultures is too abundant for this to occur. Furthermore, the sum total of that wealth is so various and there are so many contradictions, inconsistencies, and incompatibilities between and among the myriad items of stock that this would not, in any case, be possible. The most that can be hoped is that some portion of the sum total, although not necessarily the same portion, will become yoked to the capacities of each inhabitant of the educational realm.

On the other hand, the fact that each individual's capacities attach to a portion of stock rather than to all of it does not mean that each person's capacities must attach only to the stock associated with the culture into which he or she is born. When education is viewed as an encounter in which individual capacities and cultural stock become yoked together, there is no assumption that the stock is the property of a single group or culture[28] any more than there is an assumption that the stock is fixed and unchanging.

Think of Minik. As a young child, his capacities attached to the cultural stock of the Inuit. Next, he became yoked to stock belonging to the culture of the United States. When he returned home, as he eventually did, Minik's capacities soon became coupled with more items of the stock belonging to his original culture. Then, when he went back to the U.S. and found work in a lumber camp, he attached to still more items of American stock.

Minik's saga is unique, but its underlying narrative structure is not. When the young Malcolm X underwent a transformation from a model schoolboy into a hustler,[29] his capacities also became coupled with items of stock belonging to a new culture, although in his case the new culture represented a part of the larger U.S. culture. When a young American joins the U.S. Marine Corps, his capacities yoke up with items of stock from the new culture he enters. The same occurs when a young child starts school, a teenager enters college, an adult goes to work for a large corporation, gets married, or becomes a parent.

Where education is concerned, any item of cultural stock, and not just what is commonly known as high culture, can become coupled to the capacities of one or more individuals. Needless to say, this leaves open a host of questions. In addition to the interesting one of how many cultures an individual's capacities become yoked to in a lifetime, there is the supremely important issue of which items of stock ought to be coupled with individual capacities and which ones ought not to be, and there is the equally pressing issue of which items have in the past been, or now are, yoked up to human capacities. Here, however, it suffices to say that the theory of education as encounter brings all the stock of all human cultures into the realm of education.

The question remains of whether our theory brings into the educational realm the stock of whatever non-human animal cultures may exist. Once it is granted that the members of a given species do learn, there would seem to be no good reason why it should not. Indeed, it seems arbitrary to apply the label "education" to yokings of human stock to the capacities of other animals while withholding it from yokings—whether in the wild or in captivity—of the cultural stock of those animals to their own capacities.

It also seems arbitrary for a system of thought to acknowledge that the capacities of non-human animals can become yoked to items of human culture but rule out the possibility that the capacities of humans can become yoked to items of non-human animal cultures. Our theory takes no stand on the present extent and the advisability of cross-species yoking. In the interests of encompassing the full range of learning, it does, however, allow for the possibility of both cross-species as well as intra-species yokings of capacities and cultural stock. Furthermore, it recognizes that, if animals have cultures, as is now generally recognized, then when Victor walked out of the woods in Aveyron, France, it is likely that some of his behavior was the result of inter-species cultural transmission: in other words, that he had already been a participant in educational encounters— ones in which the cultural stock of non-human animals had become yoked to his capacities.[30]

6. The Missing Educational Agents

Insofar as there can be said to be a single tendency that characterizes the deep structure of Western educational thought, it is the narrowing down of the educational realm. Instead of commandeering the whole of culture as education's domain, it lays claim to just one part of human culture—the so-called public world. Instead of pulling the sum total of cultural stock into education's sphere, it appropriates one small portion—human high culture. Instead of including all individuals therein, it has, in the past, allowed in only a select few humans. It is hardly surprising, therefore, that, instead of welcoming into the educational realm the full range of agents that bring about learning, it ignores the claims of all but school.

A theory that encompasses all learners and all cultural stock cannot, in all consistency, give school a monopoly over educational agency or even assume school's primacy. The failure of the deep structure of educational thought to acknowledge the educational contributions of home and family is especially troubling, for it is all but universally assumed that one task of these institutions is cultural transmission: that is, the yoking of the culture's stock to the capacities of newborns. Furthermore, home and family continue to link stock and capacities together throughout the life cycle of most individuals. School, home, and family are not a culture's only educational agents, however. Indeed, when education is understood as an encounter between an individual and some portion of a culture, and when cultural stock is defined broadly, the list of those who do or could do the yoking—which is to say, the list of a culture's educational agents— becomes well nigh endless.

The theory of education as encounter acknowledges the brute fact of multiple educational agency by including in the educational realm all of a culture's groups, institutions, organizations, social movements, and the like. Among the educational agents of human cultures, it should be noted, are ones such as the American Kennel Club, circuses, stables, and farms that bring about animal learning. And, to the extent that non-human animals have cultures, whatever groups and institutions they include will also be on the list.

Recognizing that cultures can have very different educational agents, that educational agents change over time, and that some old educational agents may disappear as new ones emerge, our theory leaves open the question of which agents are most important. It does, however, hold that in every educational event or encounter there is *some* educational agent at work. In Chapter 1, education was described as an encounter in which the capacities of an individual and the stock of a culture become yoked together, and it can now be seen that this characterization was elliptical. To be more precise, education is an encounter in which the capacities of an individual and the stock of a culture become yoked together *by some educational agent.*

When it is granted that the educational realm includes a multiplicity of educational agents that, at one and the same time, transmit the culture and bring about learning, it becomes clear that analyses that make the teacher an essential component of education are restricted in their scope.[31] To be sure, one does not have to work in a school or university to be considered a teacher. Parents teach their children, brothers teach their sisters, wives teach their husbands, bosses teach their employees, and friends teach one another. Nonetheless, a great deal of the education that takes place in school, at home, in the neighborhood, at work, on the Internet, and in front of the television screen does not involve teaching as it is usually understood.

Lest the wisdom of considering groups, institutions, and the like rather than individuals to be the agents that yoke stock and capacities together be doubted, it must be added that our theory does not deny that teachers, parents, and the countless other individuals who make up these groups and institutions often bring about these yokings. It recognizes, however, that other constituents of institutions —for instance, their rules, rituals, architectural forms, and governing structures— also bring about the coupling of individual capacities and cultural stock. Besides, in arenas where specialization, bureaucratization, and advanced technology prevail, it frequently makes no sense to try to trace back responsibility for any given yokings to an individual person.

When, for example, a television program is charged with instilling a tendency toward—or perhaps an affection for—violence in viewers, there is no presumption that an individual is performing the yokings. The cast, the writers, the directors, the producers, the engineers, the advertisers can all be considered participants in the educational event, assuming one has occurred. Yet, it is the institution itself—the television program or perhaps the television network—and not its individual members that must be considered education's agent. Thus, in the interests of inclusion, the theory of education as encounter conceptualizes institutions and the like as a culture's educational agencies or agents.

Once school loses its monopoly over educational agency and all a culture's institutions are acknowledged to be its educational agents, the question arises of how the various agents are to be individuated or identified. Is each TV program an educational agent in its own right or is each network, or perhaps the industry as a whole, one big agent? Is each art museum a separate agent or are art museums as a class a single agent? For that matter, is each schoolroom a separate agent or is each school, or perhaps each school system, a separate agent?

There is no one correct answer to such queries, nor can they be satisfactorily answered in the abstract. The individuation of educational agents will depend on one's interests and the purpose of one's inquiry, which means that it will vary from context to context. If, for example, a person's main concern is whether a particular television program is yoking violent behavior to its viewers' capacities, it will be appropriate to consider that program—or perhaps particular episodes of that program—an educational agent. If, in contrast, someone wants to know what portion of a culture's stock is being passed down by television as opposed, say, to schools, it may be far more appropriate to designate the entire industry as such.[32] Similarly, it is a matter of decision as to whether one judges that there are as many educational encounters as there are distinctly discernible periods in which a given person watches a certain program or network or television in general; or if all that individual's viewing comprise one big encounter.

Considering the parents, teachers, doctors, lawyers, government officials, business executives, airline personnel, and all those other individuals who attempt to yoke or succeed in yoking capacities to cultural stock both educators and transmitters of culture, the theory of education as encounter treats them as members or representatives of educational agencies rather than as educational agents in their own right. It should be noted, moreover, that, in an educational event or encounter, the educator and the learner can be one and the same individual.[33]

The young Ed Wilson would seem to be a prime example of a self-educator, yet is it accurate to portray him as a member or representative of some group or institution? Some boys and girls may watch ants at home as part of a school project, but Wilson's childhood schools seem to have had little desire to yoke cultural stock about the natural world to his capacities. If one thinks of an educational agent as actively seeking to achieve some specified ends, home and family did not do this yoking either. If, however, one rejects this narrow view of educational agency and notes that Wilson's home and family gave the boy remarkable freedom to roam and follow his own devices, it becomes credible to say that these institutions were indeed the educational agents in his encounter with the harvester ants: that in many areas, including this one, they gave him both permission and the opportunity to be his own educator.

Our theory also recognizes that non-human animals, as well as people, can serve as educators/culture transmitters. Thus, for instance, Nim Chimpsky spent the last years of his life on a Texas ranch, where he shared a cage with other chimpanzees who clearly learned some signs from him. What educational agent did Nim represent? Given that he was part of Project Nim and that he was transmitting some of the cultural stock he acquired in that project, he can surely be considered to have been a member or representative of that group. True, his educational contributions to his peers were probably unanticipated. But our theory does not require that the yokings of cultural stock to capacities be done intentionally, let alone that they are all planned or foreseen.

For a very different kind of educational encounter in which non-human animals play the role of educator, consider the harvester ants that Ed Wilson as a boy kept in a jar of sand under his bed.[34] When a chemistry student watches an experiment, we have no qualms about assigning the professor who performs it the role of educator. Can we not also say that, when Ed Wilson watched his ants excavate, they were his educators? To be sure, the professor is deliberately trying to attach some cultural stock having to do with chemistry to his students' capacities, whereas Wilson's ants were simply going about their business of excavation. But, just as the theory of education as encounter rejects the notion that education is necessarily intentional, it dismisses the idea that an educator must be aiming at learning. Assuming that cultural stock having to do with the ants— or perhaps with nature more generally, or with science as a career—became yoked to Wilson's capacities as a result of his watching them excavate, there would seem, then, to be no legitimate basis for ruling them out as the boy's educators in those encounters.

It is a commonplace for people to say that inanimate objects such as books, the paintings in a museum, or a city's streets have been their teachers. Why not harvester ants as well?[35] Depending on the context of the inquiry, the paintings in a museum can be considered, for example, to represent the museum in which they hang, the genre to which they belong, or the school of art to which historians assign them. So too the ants in Wilson's jar can be thought of as members or representatives of his neighborhood or the streets of Orlando, Florida.

It will perhaps be objected that talk of books, paintings, and streets as teachers or educators is metaphorical and that the terms "teacher" and "educator" literally refer to human individuals—or else to those like Nim who resemble us. It is far from obvious, however, that a person who says, "Books were my best teachers" is speaking metaphorically as opposed simply to employing a broad rather than a narrow non-metaphorical sense of the term "teacher." Be this as it may, and remembering that, for us, the relevant term is "educator" not "teacher," the theory of education as encounter acknowledges that people, animals, other forms of life, inanimate objects, ideas, and imaginary entities of all kinds can be educators. This is not to say that they all do, in fact, serve this function but rather that they are not ruled out by fiat.

7. The Missing Educational Processes

The yoking together of cultural stock and capacities that occurs in an educational encounter usually resembles what philosophers call a "non-basic action" in that it is done by doing something else. Compare the action of moving your arm to the action of opening a door by turning the knob. Assuming your arm is not broken or paralyzed, moving your arm is something you just do without having to do something else. In contrast, opening the door is a non-basic action in that you have to do another action, namely turning the knob, in order to do it. Educational agents do not just yoke stock and human capacities together. They normally transmit culture by performing some other action, be it teaching, training, or something else.

Even as the deep structure of educational thought's false equation whittles down educational agency to that thin sliver called "school," its narrow definition of education as a consciously intentional, volitional, rational, and morally acceptable activity yields a correspondingly narrow conception of the actions or processes by which an educational agent yokes stock and capacities together. At first glance, it might seem that the difference between the processes that the reductive definition excludes and the ones it includes represents the difference between so-called informal and formal processes. However, the reductive definition of education rules out formal processes such as the very deliberate and almost ritualistic training in pickpocketing that Charles Dickens's Fagin gives Oliver Twist, and includes in it informal processes such as the give and take of a graduate seminar.

In fact, the deep structure's reductive definition of education causes an enormous number of processes to disappear from the educational realm. Consider its requirement that the educator intend that learning occur. This manages to exclude processes such as the unconscious modeling of good and bad manners and the unwitting reinforcement of harmful and harmless habits. Educational thinkers often draw a sharp distinction between education and socialization and dismiss processes like these as "mere" socialization, yet educational agents manage to yoke together countless individual capacities and cultural stock in such ways. To place an intentionality condition on education is, therefore, to exclude a tremendous amount of learning.

From the standpoint of formulating an adequate general theory of education, it is disastrous to insist that whatever is learned must, by definition, be intended, for it means foregoing the capability to track vast portions of the cultural stock that is being passed down to the next generation. If that stock consisted only of assets, the degree of ignorance this exclusion entails might be acceptable. Since, however, educational agents can yoke liabilities, as well as assets, to individual capacities, it is important to know when miseducation is happening. Only then can appropriate interventions occur should they be deemed necessary.

Consider now the reductive definition's requirement that the learner be aware of the educator's intention and consent to it. This condition effectively keeps very young children and non-human animals out of the educational realm and also excludes processes that some of the greatest educational thinkers of the West have recommended. In *Emile*, Rousseau described a walk the boy Emile takes with his tutor. So far as the lad is concerned, going for a walk is all he is doing. The tutor, on the other hand, uses this occasion to teach him some geography and astronomy. Another time, Emile plays with a stick in a pond. Once again, from his point of view, that is all he is doing. The tutor, however, takes full advantage of the situation to give the boy a lesson in physics. In general, the methods that Rousseau favored and that countless educators have put into practice derive their efficacy from the fact that the learner does not realize that he or she is participating in an educational encounter of the teacher's design.

So too with the educational methods Dewey recommended. When he said that children learn best by doing, he was proposing that schools engage children in genuine occupations: not artificially constructed ones such as the filling in of worksheets and the drilling with flashcards that are to be found in traditional classrooms, but real-life activities such as making a map of the neighborhood, building a clubhouse, or writing and producing a play. To be sure, if school-children are creating a play about Harriet Tubman or making a map of their area they will be conscious of performing that activity. They will not, however, be aware of learning history, geography, arithmetic, and language arts although this learning may be what their teachers anticipate and intend.

On inspection, it turns out that the deep structure's definition of education fails to accord with our considered judgments. Although the pedagogies of Dewey and Rousseau have often been criticized, no one suggests that these men were not talking about education. No one thinks that their radical recommendations for teaching and learning were not educational proposals.

In addition, the deep structure's definition contains a hidden bias. On the one hand, it readily grants educational status to traditional methods of instruction that announce the educator's intent on their sleeves, as it were: ones such as drilling, recitation, lecturing, and the back and forth of an Oxford tutorial or graduate seminar. On the other, it denies educational status to the methods of teaching and learning proposed by critics of traditional education. Since a very general theory of education such as our own is duty bound to leave open value questions, such as the oft-debated one of whether traditional or non-traditional methods of teaching and learning are to be preferred, the conservative pedagogical bias represents one more reason for the theory of education as encounter to adopt a broad conception of educational processes rather than the narrow one that is entailed by the deep structure.

Besides foreclosing the normative issue of whether traditional educational processes are better than progressive ones, the consent clause of the deep structure's reductive definition rules out of the educational realm the processes that bring about the metamorphosis that transforms a human newborn from a creature of nature into a member of human culture. After all, a newborn is unaware of its mother's or father's or some surrogate parent's intent that it learn to walk, talk, distinguish hot from cold, and so forth; hence, it cannot give the requisite consent.

This, in turn, gives the false impression that the women who are the primary caretakers of newborns barely contribute to their charges' learning.

To be sure, many scholars today say that the capacity to acquire a first language is innate[36] and, on the basis of this Innateness Hypothesis, conclude that we humans learn our first language without being taught it; indeed, without the benefit of education. And some might well extend the scope of this hypothesis to include walking, distinguishing hot from cold, and so on. But supposing that the capacity to learn a first language or one of these other traits or dispositions is innate, the fact that it must be learned makes it a part of the educational realm.

Consider, finally, the narrow definition's requirement that educational processes must be morally acceptable. This may seem praiseworthy in that it prohibits the use of unpalatable techniques such as humiliation, brute force, drugs, electric shock, and the like in those processes we call education. The problem is, however, that this requirement does not eradicate these practices; it simply sanitizes the concept of education. In consequence, it puts educators in the enviable position of always doing the morally correct thing and being able to dismiss the brutal methods used outside their narrowly constructed educational realm as none of their business.

The requirement of moral acceptability does not accord with ordinary usage of the term "teach," however, and teaching is usually thought to be a paradigm case of an educational process. When a parent says, "I'm teaching you a lesson you'll never forget" while mercilessly whipping a child for being disobedient or disrespectful, no one accuses him or her of misusing the English language. When authors such as Charlotte Brontë, Charles Dickens, and Louisa May Alcott portray the beatings and humiliations that take place in classrooms, no one thinks they are misrepresenting the nature of teaching.

In the "obedience studies" conducted in the mid-twentieth century by psychologist Stanley Milgram, the subjects of the experiments were told to think of themselves as teachers and instructed to administer electric shocks to a supposed learner whenever he made a mistake.[37] To the dismay of Milgram and the world, the subjects proceeded to follow instructions. Although the experiments were rigged so that no actual shocks were given, Milgram's studies occasioned protests that he had engaged in unethical behavior by deceiving his subjects into believing that they were administering electric shocks when, in fact, they were not. There was, however, no outcry from schoolteachers or anyone else that he had taken the name of teaching in vain.

It may be objected that there is a narrow sense of the term "teach" that does not countenance morally repugnant practices and that a general theory of education should restrict itself to it. But to ignore the broad sense of teaching is to determine, by arbitrary definition, what should be decided by rational discussion. If shame, humiliation, electric shocks, and beatings are practices that ought not to be employed in education, a moral case for excluding them needs to be made.

It may also be objected that if the theory of education as encounter adopts a broad conception of educational processes, then anything goes. But this is a non sequitur. To say that morally unacceptable processes fall within the educational realm is not to say that they *ought* to be employed or practiced. The category or concept of a human being includes both immoral and moral people, but again the two kinds can be differentiated—which is not to say that everyone will agree on particular cases. Of course, judgments about the moral acceptability of educational processes need to be made. But they should be made in the open for all to see and debate, and not be smuggled into seemingly neutral definitions.

Release education from the conditions of intentionality, volition, and moral acceptability that the deep structure of educational thought now imposes and the category of an educational process will include brainwashing, strict conditioning, indoctrination, and propaganda, as well as such techniques as humiliation and the administration of electric shocks. But again, the inclusion of these processes in the educational realm does not mean that they have to or should be engaged in. To acknowledge that they belong inside education's domain is simply to recognize that they can and often do serve the function of linking together individual capacities and cultural stock.

Finally, it may be objected that our theory's permissive stance toward educational processes blurs the distinction between education and socialization. As it happens, this distinction is not one that all educational thinkers have endorsed. Bernard Bailyn, for example, called the family the most important agency of education in the American colonial period, in large part because of its role in the socialization of the child[38] and Dewey said, "Beings who are born not only unaware of, but quite indifferent to, the aims and habits of the social group have to be rendered cognizant of them and actively interested. Education, and education alone, spans the gap."[39]

In reclaiming the broad sense of education, our theory rejects definitions and distinctions that exclude one or another kind of learning from the educational realm. This does not mean that areas inside that realm cannot be differentiated from one another. Those who wish to do so can fence off the yokings of stock and capacities they consider to be socialization inside the new boundaries of the educational realm. Similarly, those who wish to focus exclusively on education in the deep structure's narrow sense of the term are free to cultivate that small patch of the educational terrain. It does, however, mean that the theory of education as encounter takes as large a view of education's processes as it does of the individuals who inhabit the educational realm, the culture's stock, and its educational agents.

The fact that our theory leaves open normative questions that education's deep structure has heretofore foreclosed is a mark in its favor. Is indoctrination ever justified? Are methods that make students aware of the teacher's intentions always to be preferred over those that do not? When unintentional processes are discovered, should intentional ones be substituted for them? Instead of taking sides on these and kindred issues, our theory opens them up for genuine normative debate.

A purist may balk at the idea that processes such as conditioning and propaganda that bypass reason, and ones that cause physical or psychological pain, have anything in common with teaching. But the truth is that they do. They may proceed very differently from the teaching that occurs in model classrooms, but they too yoke together an individual's capacities and a culture's stock. This pulling together of phenomena that are often considered unrelated is, indeed, one of our theory's strengths. In addition to bringing important new questions to the fore, it opens up the possibility of our keeping track of which portions of cultural stock are and are not being passed down, and hence preserved; and to whom they are and are not being given.

PART II
Implications

4

EDUCATION AS A MAKER OF INDIVIDUALS AND CULTURES

One standard against which to measure a general theory of education is whether it accords with and organizes our considered judgments about its subject matter.[1] Because the theory of education as encounter rejects the assumptions presently embedded in educational thought, it might be wondered if it passes this test. However, the sharp nature/culture divide, the two-sphere analysis, and the consequent shrinking of the educational realm run counter to many of our considered convictions. And so do the false equation between education and schooling and definitions of education that commit the intentional fallacy, contain a cognitive bias, and subscribe to the myth of betterment. In shedding the offending beliefs, the theory of education as encounter conforms to what, upon reflection, we take to be true about such basic matters as the nature and function of education, the definition and scope of culture, the nature and societal place of men and women, and the relationship between school and education.

A second standard by which to judge a theory like ours is the extent to which it suggests new lines of inquiry. Reframing old questions and raising new ones, the theory of education as encounter meets this criterion many times over. Thus, for example, its concept of multiple educational agency encourages queries such as: Which educational agent or agents should be responsible for transmitting a given portion of a culture's stock? What can be done if an educational agent fails to yoke the cultural assets in its portfolio to individual capacities? Its recognition that a culture's stock contains liabilities, as well as assets, leads one to ask: Is the agent yoking cultural liabilities to individual capacities instead of, or in addition to, cultural assets? And its inclusion of non-human animals in the educational realm places a host of new items on the culture's educational agenda.

One more standard by which to judge our theory is the extent to which it illuminates its subject. To this end, in this chapter and the two that follow, I draw out the theory's most important implications. Then, in Part III of this volume, I apply the theory of education as encounter to particularly pressing problems.

1. Two Historical Models

Perhaps the most important implication of a theory that represents the process of education as a series of encounters in which cultural stock is yoked to individual capacities is that education is a maker and shaper of both individuals and cultures. It has long been understood that education can have a profound effect on individual people. The theory of education as encounter says a good deal more than this, however. Its inclusion of non-human animals in the educational realm means that education is a maker and shaper of them, as well as of people. Furthermore, its insistence that, in every educational encounter, both the individual and the culture change means that the making of individuals goes hand in hand with the making of cultures.

In Western thought, the idea of education as a maker of human individuals has a distinguished history, one version of which can be traced back to Plato and another to Ovid.[2] Recall the thought experiment that Socrates and his companions perform in Plato's *Republic*. Its starting point is Plato's assumption that each of us is born with more aptitude for one societal task than for others and that, although aptitudes or talents can flourish or be stunted, the one an individual is born with is his or hers for life. This "postulate of specialized natures" is purely formal: it affirms that people have specific aptitudes at birth but it does not specify what these aptitudes are. Socrates proceeds to give it content, not through a close inspection of human nature, but through an examination of the requirements of society. In other words, he first creates an imaginary city-state and then he maps the city's needs onto human nature.

In the state Socrates envisions, there are three general types of jobs to be done—those of ruler, warrior, and artisan. Assuming a one-to-one correspondence between human nature and society's needs, he assigns education the task of producing people who can perform the functions that nature has pre-assigned them. To this "postulate of correspondence" Socrates then adds a "postulate of identity," according to which those who possess the same nature, and are therefore destined to perform the same societal task, should be given the same education. And he joins to this assumption that identical natures require identical educations a "postulate of difference," according to which those who possess different natures, and are therefore destined for different societal roles, require different educations.

In sum, Plato bequeathed to us a model of education that envisions human beings as the raw materials of production. His is not, to be sure, a factory model. It does, however, take us, like other raw materials, to be malleable within fixed limits set by nature. And, as is the case with other forms of production, it views the object of education to be the turning of this raw material into a finished product; actually, for Plato, there were three different kinds of products—the rulers of the state, the warriors, and the artisans.

The theory of education as encounter acknowledges Plato's key insight that education is a process that fashions individuals, but it rejects the four postulates he built into his production model. It is one thing to view education as a maker and shaper of people and quite another to assume that human beings are born with one or another fixed and unchanging nature that corresponds to one or another societal need, let alone that people should be educated to fill the societal role for which their natures presumably suit them.

Our theory does not take sides in the continuing nature/nurture debates. Recognizing that the jury is still out on the question of the specific abilities or competences that individuals have at birth, it leaves open the question of whether the capacities to which cultural stock becomes yoked are part of a person's genetic inheritance. But assuming it to be true that some of us are born with more musical ability than others and some with more linguistic or mathematical or kinesthetic ability, this does not warrant the Platonic claim that we are born with only one special talent or that we are each suited at birth to fill just one societal need. On the one hand, even if humans are born with just one talent— and that they are is far from obvious—there is no reason why they could not acquire new aptitudes through education. And, on the other, the physicians, teachers, architects, engineers, manufacturers, bankers, and so on that society needs must possess a wide range of competences, not one specific competence.

Plato also claimed that a person does best what he or she is suited for at birth. Yet, someone with enormous musical or mathematical talent may, for reasons of individual preference, desire, or prior training, excel in some occupation other than music or mathematics. In addition, Plato attributed specific inborn aptitudes to whole classes of people. However, there are no grounds for the claim that these, if such exist, are linked to the standard categories of race, class, and gender, into which contemporary societies tend to sort people. Plato also made the assumption that people destined to fill the same societal role require the same education. But, despite its plausible ring, his Identity Postulate does not express a necessary truth. Research has long since established that individual differences in, for instance, learning styles, cognitive approaches, physical capacities, and mental abilities can call for different methods of teaching. In addition, because any given societal task or role can be performed in different ways, different educational treatments may well be appropriate.

In the nineteenth and twentieth centuries, Plato's production model was given new life by a factory version that is still implicit in many discussions of schooling and higher education. One early twentieth-century educator in the U.S. wrote, "Our schools are, in a sense, factories in which the raw products (children) are to be shaped and fashioned into products to meet the various demands of life."[3] And, to this day, technical institutes say they "turn out" engineers,[4] liberal arts colleges claim to "produce" well-rounded people, disgruntled department heads say that they have "too many people running through" and that "quality control" isn't there, and boards of education insist that schools tighten their "standards" and hold teachers "accountable" if their students do not perform up to "grade level." Behind comments like these, there lurks a vision of teachers as factory workers who process their students before sending them on to the next station on the school assembly line, and of curriculum as the machinery that, over the span of 12 or so years, forges their nation's young into marketable products. Those who embrace the factory model do not necessarily accept Plato's theory of human nature. Their conception of school as an assembly line that produces different kinds of workers does, however, mistakenly assume that the same task, job, or societal role requires the same education.

Of course, some people may, in fact, subscribe to Plato's four postulates and some may applaud the factory model's conception of teachers as workers on an assembly line. Yet, just as the theory of education as encounter disowns the commonly accepted but invalid assumptions embedded in the deep structure of educational thought, it disavows these false assumptions and the misleading imagery.

The Roman poet Ovid can also be interpreted as having bequeathed to us a conception of education as a creator of something new, albeit a very different one from Plato's. In one of the Greek myths he included in Book Ten of *The Metamorphoses*, a sculptor named Pygmalion took a block of ivory and made of it such a beautiful figure of a woman that he fell in love with his own work of art. So great was his passion that he draped his statue in the robes of a queen and showered it with kisses. Then, when the day of the Feast of Venus arrived, Pygmalion prayed fervently to the gods to give him a wife as lovely as his work of art. Hearing his plea and knowing what Pygmalion really wanted, the goddess Venus intervened. Lo and behold, when the sculptor returned home and once again caressed his ivory statue, she came to life.

Throughout the ages, the Pygmalion story has been read as a love story, and so it is. But it is also a myth of creation. As the god Zeus created the woman Pandora, the man Pygmalion created a statue in the form of a woman called Galatea. And, of course, it is a tale of transformation; or rather, it is a tale of two radical changes of being in that the ivory becomes a statue and the statue then becomes Galatea. Ovid's Pygmalion poem is of interest here, however, because it can be read as a myth about the power of education to form and transform human lives. This, indeed, is the way George Bernard Shaw was interpreting it when he called his play *Pygmalion*.

To this day, and in all corners of the earth, one encounters real-life instances of the Pygmalion story: people such as Shaw's Eliza Doolittle, whose education has produced in them a thoroughgoing change of being. Furthermore, echoes of the language of sculpture reverberate through educational discourse whenever there is talk of "molding" children's characters or "forming" their beliefs. Yet, just as Plato's production model must be divested of his faulty postulates, Ovid's Pygmalion story has to be stripped of its intentional aspect if it is to be compatible with the theory of education as encounter. Sculpture is a deliberate, goal-directed activity or enterprise whose creations are presumed to be the results of intentional action. Our theory acknowledges the key insight of the sculpture metaphor that education is a creative and ultimately transformational process that brings some-thing brand new into existence. But rejecting narrow definitions of education, it ranges over all learning, whether intended or not.

2. The Growth Conception of Education

Over the years, the main alternative to the idea of education as a maker or creator of something new has been the view that historians of educational thought have attributed to Rousseau. According to their readings of *Emile*, its many references to nature add up to a conception of the child as a plant whose develop-ment is determined by nature and of the educator as a gardener whose job it is to follow nature.

When, however, Book V of *Emile* is taken seriously, it becomes evident that, although he spoke the language of nature, his conception of education was, like Plato's, that of production.[5] In that chapter, Rousseau treats the girl Sophie as raw material to be turned, by education, into a finished product. The product—namely, a traditional wife and mother—happens to be one that Plato rejected in the *Republic*, at least for the governing class.[6] Nevertheless, the basic structure of Rousseau's account of the education of Sophie mirrors that of Plato's account of the education of the artisans, warriors, and rulers in his Just State.

Did Rousseau adopt a production model for Sophie while embracing a growth model for Emile, his representation of Every Boy? Sophie's case is so clearly an instance of production that it alerts one to a central tension or ambiguity within the idea of education as growth: that between the activity or practice of gardening on the one hand, and simply following nature on the other. This tension is perhaps best represented by the distinction between growth pure and simple, as when, for instance, a flower or tree springs up in an untouched wilderness; and growth under human guidance, as when a seed is planted and grows in a cultivated garden.

Given the many elaborate recommendations Rousseau made for Emile's education, it is fair to say that he did not embrace a "growth pure and simple, just follow nature" conception of education. Had he done so he would have told Emile's tutor to pursue a policy of non-intervention. But Rousseau did not want just any aspect of Emile's potential to flourish. He knew that Emile had the potential to be a scoundrel, as well as an honest man; a wife beater and child molester, as well as a good husband and father; and a believer in the divine right of kings, as well as an advocate of democratic self-rule. He wanted the boy to be a morally autonomous individual. Indeed, the ideal of an autonomous man that Rousseau held up for Emile matched the definition of a citizen of the ideal city-state that he put forward in *The Social Contract* in the very same year *Emile* was published. And so he insisted that the tutor arrange each detail of Emile's education toward that end.

A dualistic his/her interpretation of *Emile*, according to which the boy Emile's education is an instance of growth and the girl Sophie's is a case of production, does not stand up under examination. On the contrary, Plato's production model underlies the educations of both Sophie and Emile. It may perhaps be wondered how two theories as different as Plato's and Rousseau's can possibly presuppose the same model of education, but one who compares Books V of the *Republic* and *Emile* will discover that these philosophers gave very different content to the Postulate of Special Natures and the Correspondence Postulate. For Plato, sex or gender was a difference that made no difference to a person's nature or societal role. In light of his Identity Postulate, it therefore made no difference to a person's education. For Rousseau, on the other hand, sex or gender was the difference that made all the difference both to an individual's nature and to his or her role in society. In light of the Difference Postulate, it therefore made all the difference to a person's education. And, if one also compares the *Republic* to *The Social Contract*, one realizes that the citizen mold Rousseau imposed on Emile closely resembles the one that Plato envisioned for the rulers of the Just State.

That Rousseau implicitly embraced Plato's production model is noteworthy because he is considered to be a founding father of child-centered educational theory and progressive pedagogy, and the assumption has been that these presuppose the growth model. To do Plato justice, he did not recommend that children sit silently in rows without moving while teachers use external motivation and enforce strict discipline to promote rote learning. Indeed, he went so far as to advocate free play so that adults could discover each child's nature. Nevertheless, the production model has come to be associated with traditional approaches to education and the growth model with child-centered ones.

Yet, although child-centered approaches may seem to casual observers to presuppose the growth model's dictum that education need only follow nature, appearances are deceptive. Consider the open classroom movement that Canada, the U.S., and other countries imported from Great Britain in the second half of the twentieth century.[7] Giving children the freedom to move around the classroom, encouraging them to associate with one another, and helping them pursue their own interests, it can be considered a paradigm case of child-centered pedagogy. However, even though its underlying philosophy barred teachers from standing in the front of the room in traditional fashion and rejected rote methods of learning, it did not allow children to "just grow."

Although open classrooms were filled with what looked like random assortments of materials dragged in from the outside world—such things as rocks, old tires, wallpaper sample books, egg cartons, cooking utensils, books, balance scales, and costumes—the teachers constructed their classroom environments with an eye to the activities the materials might inspire in children and the learning that might thereby be engendered. True, children in open classrooms were given no paper-and-pencil tests and were not expected to compile portfolios of their achievements. But the teachers kept detailed records of each child's activities so as to know what, in fact, their charges had done, what they had learned, and what they had yet to accomplish. They also were expected to intervene in the educational process with a helping hand, a leading question, and a pointed suggestion.

In general, what, on first glance, may look like instances of the growth model's dictate to follow nature turn out, on inspection, to be disguised forms of production.[8] This is not to say that the open-classroom movement presupposed Plato's specific version of the production model, let alone that it underlies all education. Advocates of open classrooms did not assume that children are destined, by nature, to perform one specific societal task. They did, however, reject the laissez-faire approach implicit in the conception of education as growth pure and simple. Rather than allow children to grow and flourish on their own, teachers in the open classroom movement made it their business to see that those in their charge learned the three Rs and whatever else they were expected to learn so that they would become the kind of autonomous people the teachers wanted them to be.

Ironically, the clearest examples we have of human growth pure and simple are those of Victor and the few other "wild" children of history who grew up in the woods. This should not cause surprise. The term "growth" suggests that learning is a biological process and hence a function of nature. However, Victor's case underscores the moral poverty of the non-interventionist "growth pure and simple" model. It demonstrates that to let a human newborn "just grow" is to place in jeopardy the acquisition of the walking, talking, dressing, distinguishing hot from cold, and so on that constitute the basics of human culture.

It will perhaps be objected that any infant who lives inside human culture instead of in the woods, as Victor did, will automatically learn those basics. But the case of Genie, a Los Angeles girl who, in the 1970s, dwelt until about age 12 in a house where her father kept her tied to a potty chair all day in isolation, belies this hypothesis.[9] Genie's behavior eerily mirrored Victor's: her gait and posture were strange, she could not chew solid food, she could barely swallow, she could not focus her eyes beyond twelve feet, she could not distinguish hot and cold, she was incontinent, and, although she understood a few words, she could only say "Stopit" and "Nomore." Furthermore, to say in defense of the growth model that a child's capacities have attached to these cultural "basics" is in effect to acknowledge that, however unwittingly, the culture's educational agents will impose some shape and form on the child.

Victor's plight exposes the immorality of portrayals of education as a simple matter of following nature, and the theory of education as encounter reveals the impossibility underlying that conception. In *The Subjection of Women*, John Stuart Mill wrote, "What is now called the nature of women is an eminently artificial thing—the result of forced repression in some directions, unnatural stimulation in others."[10] His point that we cannot know women's nature holds true quite generally. Because the cultural stock transmitted by the wide array of educational agents attaches to human capacities from birth, if not before, we are all artificial constructs. Thus, it makes no sense to suppose that education simply follows nature.

Did Rousseau realize that a "growth pure and simple" model of education is neither practicable nor moral? Even as he used plant imagery, he made it clear that, in order to grow in accordance with nature, Emile must be protected from harmful outside influences. Thus, just as gardeners try to keep their plants safe from rabbits, foxes, and weeds, Rousseau insisted that the boy be separated at birth from the presumed evils of home and family and be educated in virtual isolation. Furthermore, the pedagogy Rousseau devised for Emile's tutor did not rest solely on a preventive principle of protection from harmful societal influences. As gardeners are expected to promote growth by watering their plants and adding minerals to the soil, Emile's tutor was supposed to further the boy's education by making sure that his environment provided rich learning experiences. Toward this end, he was expected to keep a close watch over the child day and night so that he could intervene at a moment's notice and turn casual encounters and everyday activities into lessons in, for instance, physics, geography, social philosophy, and ethics.

There is good reason to conclude that Rousseau employed the gardening variety of the growth model rather than the "growth pure and simple" variety. Whether or not he realized that what appear to be cases of education as growth almost invariably turn out to be instances of the production model of education is a question that does not have to be answered here. Nor does it have to be decided if Rousseau is responsible for the ambiguity that lies at the very center of the growth model of education or if his interpreters imposed the tension.[11] The issue for us is whether the progressive pedagogy that he unquestionably put forward in *Emile* is consistent with a view of education as a maker of individuals and cultures.

3. Charlotte Perkins Gilman and the Herland Dream

Given that the products of most manufacturing are commodities intended for consumers, it is perhaps predictable that the very idea of education as a producer or maker of individuals has been thought by many to be dehumanizing. Consider, however, the philosophy of education that Charlotte Perkins Gilman placed at the center of her 1915 utopian novel, *Herland*. It uses the language of making, yet it takes children's needs and interests seriously while eschewing traditional methods of teaching.

Written in the form of a report to the outside world by one of three male adventurers who accidentally come upon the country of Herland, *Herland* tells the story of an all-female society in which the birth of a child is a wondrous event. Gilman's book has usually been read as an exposé of traditional sex roles and gender stereotypes, but it is much more than this. Just as Plato inserted an educational theory into his dialogue about justice, and Rousseau did the same in his pedagogical novel about a boy and his tutor, Gilman embedded one in *Herland*.

In Gilman's ideal society, the inhabitants devote their combined intelligence "to making the best kind of people."[12] They do so because, for them, motherhood is a social, as well as a biological, category. It is a social category in actual societies too, but Gilman does not tie its social content to the wife and homemaker role or to specific tasks of childrearing, such as feeding and diapering. In Herland, motherhood constitutes a particular relation of love in which an adult stands to children—one whose overriding concern is children's welfare and development. Indeed, Gilman's concept of motherhood is, in two respects, a universal category: the love it entails is a relation in which *every* adult stands to *all* children.

Because every adult in Herland is, in effect, a surrogate mother to all the nation's children—not in the sense of putting her womb in the service of another, but in the sense of loving and serving children to whom she has not given birth— the Herland dream is to make the best kind of people. This dream implicates education, not by translating into narrow efforts to improve the country's schools, but by instilling in each inhabitant an ever-present desire to make every nook and cranny of Herland a better place in which to live.

It may be wondered what bearing a book about an all-female society can possibly have on a theory of education that applies to male and female human beings, and to non-human animals as well. *Herland* is instructive in the first place because its ideal of making the best kind of people is grounded on both mother love and the belief that every girl is a moral being with needs and interests of her own. Thus, the book's philosophy of education is as far from being dehumanizing as one can imagine.

Gilman's work is also relevant to this discussion because, in addition to conceptualizing education as a maker of people, she embraced Rousseau's Principle of Protection from Harm. As Rousseau's thought experiment in *Emile* removed a male child from what he perceived to be the corrupting influences of French society, Gilman's thought experiment removed the female children of Herland from what she took to be the corrupting influences of the world at large. In this imaginary country that no man has entered for 2,000 years, and where babies are born by asexual reproduction, the land is in a perfect state of cultivation and there is neither strife, war, poverty, nor disease.

Gilman also embraced a pedagogy very like Rousseau's. From the earliest age, the girls of Herland, like the boy Emile, are provided with an environment offering them interesting things to do that engage both their mental and their physical faculties. As Rousseau required Jean-Jacques to turn the country house and grounds where the tutor and his charge live into an environment in which Emile can roam freely, Gilman required the whole community of Herland to turn the entire country into a safe, nurturing environment and to accompany the girls on every step along "the royal road to learning."[13]

The Herland women tend to the physical environment of their children much as gardeners do the soil surrounding their plants. In this country, "where it is all education, but no schooling,"[14] children are born into a carefully prepared world "full of the most fascinating materials and opportunities to learn."[15] Babies are reared "just as young fawns might grow up in dewy forest glades and brookfed meadows." Houses, gardens, and fields have in them "nothing to hurt." "It's an everlasting parlor and nursery," complains one observer. "And workshop," adds another. "And school, and office, and laboratory, and studio, and theater."[16]

In its fundamental opposition to compulsion and its emphasis on activity, Gilman's philosophy of education also resembles Rousseau's. Indeed, as if in echo of *Emile*, most of the learning that occurs in Herland is a by-product of children's self-directed activities, not the result of compulsory school-invented tasks such as reading textbooks, doing problems on worksheets, and studying for tests.

Does acceptance of the Principle of Protection from Harm and a progressive pedagogy conflict with a conception of education as a maker of individuals? On the contrary, *Herland* makes a compelling case that, if the aim of forming a certain kind of person is to prevail, it is vital to fend off whatever outside influences are perceived to be harmful. The book also demonstrates that a progressive pedagogy is perfectly consistent with, although not entailed by, the kind of minimalist production model of education that is assumed by the theory of education as change.

The question remains of whether a philosophy of education for an all-female society has anything substantive to say to cultures that contain more than one gender. Gilman made it clear that the love on which the Herland dream is grounded is a cultural construction, not a female biological imperative. Thus, just as the many women in Herland who never bear children are dedicated to making the best kind of people, so men can enact this ideal. To be sure, those who share Rousseau's belief that individual traits and qualities are divided up between the sexes, and that the love of children is strictly a female capacity, will disagree. For them, only women can realize the ideal of making the best kind of people. However, according to this ideology, the Herland ideal cannot be realized at all, for the very gender stereotypes that call the love of children a female capacity consider the reason or rationality that is required to fulfill the ideal to be a strictly male capacity. Reject the standard gender stereotypes, however, and there is no reason why all people cannot make the Herland dream their own.

None of this is to say that the theory of education as encounter endorses Herland's philosophy *in toto*. Like Plato in the *Republic*, Gilman in *Herland* abolished the institutions of the private home and family. Our theory, on the other hand, leaves open normative questions regarding the way society should be structured. It also regards education as giving each individual *some* particular shape and form or other, but it takes no stand—as Gilman did—about the partic-ular shape and form that education should give people. Indeed, in conceptualizing education as a series of encounters in which cultural stock and individual capacities become yoked, it does not even say that education should give *one* particular shape and form to all. Maintaining neutrality about which capacities and stock should become yoked together, it recognizes that education turned Victor into a French child, Minik into an all-American boy, and Malcolm Little first into a model schoolboy, next into a pimp and drug dealer, and finally into the world-renowned leader Malcolm X. It is in this minimalist sense that the theory of education as encounter is committed to the thesis that education, be it good or bad, intentional or involuntary, is a maker of individuals.

Still, in this minimalist sense, the Herland dream of making the best kind of individuals has the ring of truth for all lands. Who would want to deny, in the case of one's own culture, that education should make the best kind of people and non-human animals it possibly can? Of course, it stretches credulity to suppose that any culture other than a fictional one could actually achieve the Herland objective of turning every single one of its members into the very best kind of person. It is equally unrealistic to think that pluralistic societies, as opposed to ones such as Herland, could achieve consensus regarding what constitutes the best kind of person or dog or horse, and so on. In addition, there is little reason to suppose, as Gilman's locution "*the* best kind of people" implies, that there is only one best kind of individual. Nor are there good grounds for assuming, as the women of Herland perhaps do, that a culture's definition of "the best" should not change over time. Nevertheless, when the Herland dream is detached from the utopian context in which Gilman set it, and the unrealistic expectations and false assumptions she gave it are rejected, it represents an overarching educational aim or ideal that commands quite general assent.

4. Education as a Culture Maker and Shaper

Subtract the four discredited postulates from Plato's production model of education, dispense with the dehumanizing imagery of the factory version, and take away the intentionality implicit in the sculpture metaphor. What remains is the minimalist conception of education as a maker of individuals that is embedded in the theory of education as encounter. Indeed, this historically anchored model of education follows from our theory by virtue of the fact that, in changing the capacities of individuals, education changes those individuals. If one then removes the assumption that education is a matter of growth pure and simple from the growth model, the Principle of Protection from Harm and the model's child-centered pedagogy can be interpreted as historically grounded advice to those who would wittingly undertake that most difficult and challenging, yet utterly essential, task of making and shaping.

Historically, the idea of education as a maker and shaper referred to the formation of one species of individuals—human beings. The theory of education as encounter extends that insight to all individuals capable of learning and makes it clear that education is also a maker of cultures. To be sure, cultures are sometimes viewed as organisms that have "just grown." Since, however, they are by definition human constructs, it makes no sense to suppose that the changes that take place in them simply follow nature. Besides, it is not only the women of

Herland who shape and form their culture. From time immemorial, people of all lands have tried to do this—or have at least tried to preserve their culture's shape—and some of them have succeeded. For one such example, think of the Amish in the U.S. The bans on electricity, central heating, automobiles; the dress codes; the rejection of formal education beyond the elementary grades and the suspicion of book learning; the liberal use of shunning and excommunication: these are all efforts to keep their culture from losing the form it had acquired.

It is one thing, however, to say that education is a culture maker and shaper—and, in some instances, a culture breaker—and quite another to understand how it goes about its business. Here, Jared Diamond's classic study of cultural collapse is helpful.[17] Diamond did not himself credit education with a role in the successes and failures of cultures, yet his case histories can be read as testimonials to education's contributions to cultural formation.

Diamond isolated five factors that contribute to collapse: (i) the inadvertent damage people inflict on environments, (ii) climate change, (iii) hostile neighbors, (iv) decreased support from friendly neighbors, and (v) a society's responses to its problems. The point at issue is that, whatever may be the beliefs, skills, attitudes, values, worldviews, and the like that enter into these factors, they are not innate; nor, presumably, are they acquired by the wave of a wand or the administration of some drug. In particular, both the damage people inflict on their environments and the ways in which they respond to problems such as climate change or hostile neighbors depend on what items of cultural stock have become yoked over their lifetimes to their capacities. In other words, Diamond's first and fifth factors will be determined, at least in part, by education.

Consider the Viking settlers in Iceland who managed, in the face of great odds, to prevent their culture from collapsing.[18] The Viking colonization began in 870 and, in a matter of decades, the highlands were stripped of vegetation and soil, the grasslands became a desert, and the lowlands started to erode. "When," however, "the settlers finally realized what was happening, they did take corrective action," says Diamond.[19]

Unpack Diamond's statement and one can identify item upon item of cultural stock that must have been part of the Viking settlers' educations: that the Viking culture's educational agents must have yoked to the Viking settlers' capacities at some point in their lives. To be sure, we do not know exactly how or when this education occurred, let alone which educational agents yoked which items of stock to whose capacities. Nonetheless, the theory of education as encounter illuminates the Viking experience.

The realization that a culture's environment cannot support its people's lifestyle is not something that a person is born with or that simply emerges as he or she matures. It is a learned affair and so is taking action upon arriving at such a realization. Moreover, that realization about a culture's environment is not what philosophers call a "basic" belief: one that is not based on, or justified by, any other beliefs. On the contrary, to become aware of what was happening—namely that the herding economy the Vikings had brought with them from Norway and the British Isles was not appropriate to their new surroundings—the settlers had to believe that their wood was almost all gone; that its disappearance was due to their having cleared the trees for pastures (within the first few decades they had cleared about 80 percent of the original woodland); that seedlings were not regenerating as they did back home; that the highlands had been stripped of soil as well as vegetation by their endeavors; and so on. Moreover, there is no reason to think that any of these beliefs were innate or basic either.

Other cultural stock was also necessary if the Vikings were to arrive at the realization that enabled them to turn their culture around. At least some individuals had to have possessed enough curiosity to wonder why the highlands had been stripped of soil and enough imagination to dream up possible explanations, and these too are items of cultural stock. At least some had to have acquired sufficient powers of observation to discover that pigs were rooting out the saplings. And some—perhaps most—of the settlers also had to have been disposed to accept responsibility for the damage they had inflicted on their environment rather than simply blaming their problems on the pigs, the sheep, the weather, or the wrath of God.

In addition to possessing these traits or dispositions, the majority of settlers—or else the most persuasive among them—must have been a relatively optimistic lot: at least optimistic enough to believe that they could improve things by their own actions or that it was, in any event, worth giving it a try. They must also have been willing to cooperate with one another; otherwise neighboring farms would not have begun working together to prevent erosion. Furthermore, they cannot have been so attached to the practices and values they had imported from Europe—as the Norse in Greenland apparently were[20]—that they would not change their behavior. And the fact that they stopped throwing away or burning big pieces of wood, stopped keeping goats and pigs, and more or less abandoned the highlands means that they had to have already had—or else have been able to acquire quickly—the ability to exercise self-denial.

In unpacking these beliefs and character traits, I do not mean to suggest that each and every Viking settler possessed each and every one of them. Given how unlikely it is that the capacities of any two individuals—even identical twins—will become yoked to exactly the same items of cultural stock in exactly the same ways, it is safe to conclude that every Viking's education was, in at least some respects, different. In particular, curiosity, imagination, observational powers, and the like will most likely have been unevenly distributed among the Vikings, just as they are among people today. As would also be the case today, some settlers may have refused to believe that there was a problem to be solved, others may have acknowledged the problem while insisting that it was not of their own creation, and still others may have admitted responsibility only to reject ameliorative courses of action.

Nonetheless, the fact that the Vikings were successful in solving their problem—and that the solution was not imposed from above, as it was in some of Diamond's cases[21]—supports the hypothesis that there was a rather high degree of diffusion of the relevant beliefs and dispositions across the population. To employ the language of our theory, this is to say that there is every reason to suppose that, over a period of time, a goodly portion of the relevant cultural stock—only a few items of which have been identified here—became attached to the capacities of a significant number of Viking settlers.

What does the Viking case tell us about education as a maker and shaper of cultures? Granted, if the Vikings' education had been significantly different—if other beliefs, attitudes, and values had become yoked to their capacities—the culture they had established in Iceland might not have survived. But was it really education that stopped the cultural drift to extinction? Was it not the settlers, individually or collectively, who prevented Iceland's collapse? Did not education, at best, play an indirect role?

When one looks at education from the standpoint of the individual, its role in cultural formation may indeed seem to be indirect. One will see education forming individuals and it may look as if cultural change is a function not so much of education as of the responses those individuals make to problems in their environment. If, however, one looks at education from a cultural perspective, one can see one or more parts of the culture being transmitted. From this perspective, education can be seen as preserving some items of stock and projecting them into the future while relegating other items to the trash bin of history: which is to say that one can see education making and unmaking, shaping and reshaping cultures.

5. Culture Making and Social Engineering

If thoughts of Pygmalion and Galatea spring to mind when education is conceived of as a maker of individuals, forebodings of social engineering arise when it is said to be a maker and shaper of cultures. It seems appropriate, therefore, to take into account the twentieth-century philosopher Karl Popper's strictures against what he called "utopian engineering."[22]

After distinguishing between piecemeal social engineering—the making of small adjustments and readjustments in social institutions—and utopian remodelings of society according to some blueprint, Popper argued that the holistic approach of utopian engineering violates the principles of scientific method and is, in any case, impossible in practice. It is by no means obvious, however, that Popper's distinction holds up under critical examination. Is it really the case, as he said, that large-scale remodelings cannot be pursued with an open mind and that those who seek them cannot learn from their mistakes?[23] Conversely, is there anything to prevent those who seek small social or cultural changes from taking a dogmatic approach and being unwilling to change their minds? Furthermore, since, as Popper himself acknowledged, piecemeal engineers can cherish ideals and have overall goals, and piecemeal methods may result in large-scale changes, may not piecemeal engineering have the same sort of unforeseen effects as the holistic kind?

Even supposing, for the sake of argument, that Popper's distinction is valid, it does not militate against our theory. For the theory of education as encounter is not restricted to, nor does it advocate, one kind of cultural change as opposed to another. It simply assumes that education produces cultural, as well as individual, change and that the effects it has on cultures, like those it has on individuals, can be great or small.

Our theory leaves open the question of the size of the changes cultures undergo and also hesitates to call a culture's educational agents *engineers* of change. In the first place, the minimalist maker model of education encompasses unintended, as well as intended, changes in cultures, whereas engineering is a conscious, goal-directed enterprise. Furthermore, in saying that the piecemeal social engineer is a "technologist" who views institutions as instrumental or functional,[24] has the necessary experimental knowledge,[25] and knows what cannot be achieved,[26] Popper was giving pride of place to means-ends thinking. But there is far more to the process of cultural planning and development than this: among other things, imagination and vision are required if possibilities for action are to be found; courage is needed if strange, new techniques are to be tried out; flexibility is demanded if promising new customs and practices are to be adopted and self-defeating old ones discarded; and commitment to the greater good must take precedence over self-aggrandizement.[27]

Consider two examples from the history of educational thought of what Popper would presumably have called piecemeal social engineering. When, in 1899, John Dewey told a Chicago audience in lectures that were later published as *The School and Society* that the Industrial Revolution had radically changed the American home, he was thinking not of the shopping, cooking, and cleaning that are now known as "housework." He had in mind the production of such things as clothing, furniture, soap, candles, cooking utensils that had been moved into factories. Remarking that it is useless to mourn the good old days as if the past could be brought back by exhortation, he added: "It is radical conditions which have changed, and only an equally radical change in education suffices."[28]

Dewey called for a change in education—or, to be more accurate, for a change in school—because he believed that the changes the Industrial Revolution had wrought in home had put a whole portion of cultural wealth—namely the traits or dispositions of industry, responsibility, imagination, and ingenuity—at risk. This cultural stock had, for centuries, become attached to children's capacities because the nation's young worked alongside adults in the manufacturing occupations done at home; indeed, this cultural wealth was an important component of home's curriculum.

Dewey's great insight was that, if home no longer yoked children's capacities to assets that had, for centuries, been in its keep, school should undertake to do so. Thus, the piecemeal engineering that he proposed was to put the occupations of the earlier home into school, the object being not to preserve the cultural stock represented by the occupations themselves, but to insure that the traits and dispositions they engendered would continue to be passed down as living legacies.

When, in 1907, Maria Montessori gave the speech at the opening of her second school in Rome that was later published as Chapter III of *The Montessori Method*, she also had changes in home on her mind, although not the same ones as Dewey. At the time of Montessori's lecture, new housing had been constructed in the poorest quarter of the city. Upon its completion, the authorities found themselves facing an unexpected problem: the children under school age who were living in the very nice new buildings were running wild. Hoping to solve their dilemma by establishing a school in each building, the Association turned for help to Montessori, then a university lecturer on education, as well as a physician and psychologist. Convinced that these children were neither being cared for properly nor learning what they should at home because both their fathers and their mothers were going out to work each day, she designed the Casa dei Bambini—a new kind of school intended to provide children with the domestic curriculum that was missing from their own homes.

"Casa dei Bambini" has been translated into English as "The Children's House" or "The House of Childhood." Yet, on that opening day, Montessori said, "We Italians have elevated our word 'casa' to the almost sacred significance of the English word 'home,' the enclosed temple of domestic affection, accessible only to dear ones."[29] Even as Dewey perceived the removal of manufacturing occupations to be the all-important change in the U.S. home at the end of the nineteenth century, Montessori took the removal of the adults responsible for the rearing of young children to be the significant change in the homes of the poorest segment of Rome's population. Sharing with Dewey the insight that, when home changes, so must school, she designed a kind of school that would provide a safe and secure, supportive and nurturing environment for children; that would establish an affectionate relationship between the directress and the children and among the children themselves; and that would teach the skills of daily living that home had heretofore been responsible for transmitting.[30]

Because the deep structure of educational thought reduces education to schooling, we tend to forget how much of who we are, how we act, and what we know was learned at home when we were very young. Both Dewey and Montessori understood that home is an educational agent with a curriculum of its own and realized that drastic changes in home can therefore produce serious gaps in children's learning. Instead of proposing that home be restored to its previous condition, they looked to school to fill those gaps and, in so doing, redressed what they perceived to be a potential loss of cultural assets.

In recommending the changes they did for schools, Dewey and Montessori were no doubt viewing school instrumentally and employing means-end thinking. Yet, the engineer as technologist imagery conceals the creative intelligence at work in their respective recommendations.[31] To begin with, each perceived the great changes in home and also realized their relevance to schooling, something other educational theorists apparently did not do. In addition, they were able to imagine school undertaking practices that were then foreign to it.[32] Each also had the courage to make public their convictions, as well as the determination and skill to translate the new ideas into practice.

A minimalist maker model of education does not deny that, on some occasions, cultural planning and development involves relatively simple means-ends thinking. It recognizes, however, that, on other occasions, cultural planning requires far more complex forms of intellectual activity: in particular, a degree of insight and also imaginative powers that may, in fact, enter into the practice of engineering but that do not belong to Popper's conception of the piecemeal variety.

Actually, the engineering as technologist metaphor neglects not only the creative aspects of cultural planning and development and design, but also its moral and political dimensions. Consider the civil rights and the feminist movements in the U.S. in the latter part of the twentieth century and the evangelical movement at the turn of the twenty-first century. Some of the cultural changes that these brought about resulted from the same kind of thinking that underlies the building of bridges and tunnels. Yet, if anything distinguishes these broad-based movements, it is the moral/political visions that they brought to the development of new modes of thinking and living. Similar visions also characterize the changes in school proposed by Dewey and Montessori. Different as the two programs were, they were both motivated by a profound concern for the greater good.

One last problem with engineering imagery is that it tends to conceal the fact that a great deal of the shape and form that education gives cultures is not intentional. Who, in the 1960s, would have dreamed that the principles embraced by leaders of the civil rights movement would eventually under gird judicial decisions sanctioning gay marriage? For that matter, who in the Norse settlement in Greenland from A.D. 984 to somewhere in the 1400s—one of Diamond's clear cases of cultural collapse—could have dreamed that their commitment to European values would ultimately result in the demise of their society?[33] In contrast, the minimalist maker model embedded in the theory of education as encounter has the virtue of encompassing change that is unintended, as well as intended; allowing for imaginative and visionary thought in addition to narrow means-ends reasoning; and countenancing the sad but undeniable fact that education does not necessarily bring about improvement.

6. The Inseparability of Individual and Culture Making

When the individual and the cultural perspectives are joined, it can be seen that the making of cultures and the making of individuals go hand in hand. Cultures are composed of individuals. Thus, when education makes and shapes an individual, it is also making and shaping the culture to which that individual belongs. It stands to reason, then, that one who is designing a culture with characteristics A, B, and C is well-advised to ensure that the members of that culture possess traits that are A-, B-, and C-friendly: in other words, traits that support and maintain A, B, and C—or, at least, are not incompatible with A, B, and C. It is equally the case that those who are attempting to create individuals with traits A, B, and C had better try to ensure that the culture these people will inhabit is A-, B-, and C-friendly; or, at least, that the culture is not actively hostile to A, B, and C. Gilman was doing just this when, in her imagination, she made the women of Herland intent on maintaining a cultural ethos that would foster the kind of people they wanted to make.

Those who want to make and shape individuals tend to forget that the entities they form inhabit cultures. It is common practice for professional educators, politicians, and concerned citizens to draw up lists of attributes to be acquired by, for instance, an educated person, a citizen of a democracy, a patriot, without any acknowledgement that the attributes one thinks an individual should possess are items of cultural stock. Yet, everything an individual learns is an item of cultural stock.

Items of stock will have difficulty flourishing in cultures hostile to them. Thus, as a matter of prudence, a project to make a certain kind of individual must also aim at making the relevant culture or cultures friendly to that being. Just as it is an instance of utopianism to draw up a blueprint for the best kind or kinds of society or culture without thinking about the kinds of individuals who will inhabit it, it is an idle exercise to try to create the best kinds of individuals without attending to the future state or condition of the cultures in which they will live. Indeed, projects to make particular kinds of individuals must take into account the present state of the relevant cultures as well.

Individuals flourish in some environments and not others, and so do items of cultural stock. Take physical health. From time immemorial, this has been considered a praiseworthy individual attribute. That what counts as physical health is an item of cultural stock is evidenced by the fact that different cultures define bodily health differently and that, even within a given culture, the norms of good physical health change over time. That, at this writing, a number of educational agents in the U.S. actively seek to yoke stock that impedes or actually prevents the attainment of good health to the capacities of human individuals can scarcely be denied. The media, in all its guises, as well as the advertising, food, liquor, and cigarette industries deliberately seek to attach the desire and appetite for harmful food, drink, and drugs to people's capacities. Whether intentionally or not, schools, universities, and sports organizations, in their turn, yoke the capacities of young people and their parents to the belief that winning is more important than physical safety and that being a spectator of professional athletes is far more commendable than participating in amateur play.

Literacy, individual autonomy, appreciation of the arts, and any number of other personal attributes can also be cited in support of the point that cultures need to be friendly to the characteristics their members are supposed to possess. Granted, it is possible for a given item of cultural stock to become yoked to the capacities of *some* individuals in a culture that derides, devalues, or positively despises it. But it is, at best, an uphill battle for it to become attached to the capacities of most, let alone all, individuals in a culture hostile to it.

It is not simply the better part of wisdom to recognize that individual and culture making go hand in hand. Every attempt to make or shape individuals involves singling out certain items of cultural stock rather than others and projecting them into the future. In effect, then, every attempt to make and shape individuals is tacitly committed to one rather than another vision of what the cultures those individuals inhabit will be like. To specify, for example, that humans should follow the Golden Rule is to say that this particular item of stock should be yoked to individual capacities in such a way that those individuals consistently act in accordance with the maxim, "Do unto others as you would have them do unto you." And this is to envision a culture in which the Golden Rule prevails.

Just as the making and shaping of cultures is implicated in the project of making and shaping individuals, the making and shaping of individuals is implicated in the project of making and shaping cultures. Every attempt to make or shape a culture also involves singling out certain items of cultural stock rather than others, for the characteristics of cultures are no more given by nature than are the attributes of individuals. And this projection of stock into the future has consequences for individuals.

Some characteristics of cultures are what may be called distributive in that they are, as it were, summations of individual traits. For example, a gun-toting culture is one most of whose members are gun carriers and a smoking culture is one most of whose members smoke. Clearly, to make a culture that possesses distributive characteristic A, one must make individuals who possess A. To be sure, not all the members of a culture possessing a distributive characteristic must themselves possess it, but most members will have to possess it if the attribution of that characteristic to that culture is to be correct. Thus, in the case of distributive characteristics, to make a culture that possesses A entails attaching the capacities of most individuals in that culture—although not necessarily the capacities of any given individual—to A; which is to say it entails making individuals who will fit the culture.

Some characteristics of cultures are not distributive, however. Consider, for example, the trait of being a meritocracy or of having expansionist tendencies. An individual can approve of meritocracies but a meritocracy is not something that a human or non-human animal can be. Similarly, we humans can approve of a nation's occupying other countries but we are not the type of thing that can be expansionist in this sense. In the case of non-distributive characteristics, culture making does not entail yoking that selfsame item of cultural stock to the capacities of individuals. It does, however, entail attaching individual capacities to stock that is friendly to the non-distributive characteristic in question. This is not to say that culture making requires that a given portion of stock be attached to the capacities of every member of the culture. Rather, it entails yoking that portion to the capacities of a large number of members—or at least to a large number of the culture's most powerful members.

It must be stressed that, insofar as the theory of education as encounter is concerned, neither the project of individual making nor that of culture making takes precedence. One can start by specifying the desirable traits of individuals and then try to design cultures that allow these to flourish; or one can begin by listing the desirable traits of cultures and then seek to make individuals who allow them to flourish.

Either way, the process will be interactive. One who begins by specifying desirable individual traits will have to make sure that the culture is friendly to them, but the interaction does not stop here. It may be the case that, in the resultant culture, certain cultural assets will be at risk of disappearing; if so, it will be necessary to build friendliness to those assets at risk into one's design for the culture while, at the same time, amending one's list of the traits that individuals should possess. On the other hand, one can begin by specifying the characteristics that a culture should possess and, on that basis, decide which individual traits to foster. Here, it may turn out that the members of the culture would be much better individuals if they had other traits as well. If so, new individual traits will have to be added to the list and the culture will have to be adjusted accordingly.

Yet, is it not a sign of hubris to call education a maker of both individuals and cultures? In view of how hard it is just to teach children to read and write, should we not be content to assign it a more circumscribed role? On the contrary, to say that education makes and shapes individuals and their cultures is to do no more than acknowledge three basic facts of life: that education takes place not just in schools but in every nook and cranny of society, that it brings about change in both individuals and cultures, and that the change education brings about can be for the better or the worse.

5

CULTURE AS CURRICULUM

In the twentieth century, John Dewey and French sociologist Pierre Bourdieu, among other educational thinkers, told an often-doubting public that culture and curriculum are closely connected. The theory of education as encounter gives this historic insight new meaning. Its illumination of the structure of each and every educational event makes it plain for all to see that the items of cultural stock that become yoked to an individual's capacities represent the content of that individual's learning; similarly, the stock that an educational agent yokes to individual capacities represents the content of the cultural transmission. And this is tantamount to saying that culture—or, more precisely, cultural stock—is curriculum.

1. Scenes from Childhood

Two scenes from childhood, one drawn from Eva Hoffman's memoir *Lost in Translation* and the other from Annie Dillard's *An American Childhood*, lend independent support to the thesis that culture—or, to be more precise, cultural stock—is curriculum.

When Hoffman was seven years old, her mother said to her: "It's time you stopped crossing yourself in front of churches. We're Jewish and Jews don't do that."[1] Thinking back on her childhood in Cracow, Poland, Hoffman reports that it is hard to stop, for Catholicism is "the atmosphere I breathe."[2] She then reports:

> The country of my childhood lives within me with a primacy that is a form of love. It lives within me despite my knowledge of our marginality, and its primitive, unpretty emotions. Is it blind and self-deceptive of me to hold

on to its memory? I think it would be blind and self-deceptive not to. All it has given me is the world, but that is enough. It has fed me language, perceptions, sounds, the human kind. It has given me the colors and the furrows of reality, my first loves.[3]

"Our father taught us the culture into which we were born," writes Dillard:

American culture was Dixieland above all, Dixieland pure and simple, and next to Dixieland, jazz. Our culture was the stock-market crash—the biggest and best crash a country ever had . . . It was the breadlines of the Depression, and the Okies fleeing the Dust Bowl, and the proud men begging on city streets, and families on the move seeking work . . . American culture was the World's Fair in Chicago, baseball, the Erie Canal, fancy nightclubs in Harlem, silent movies, summer-stock theater, the California forty-niners, the Alaska gold rush, Henry Ford and his bright idea of paying workers enough to buy cars, P.T. Barnum and his traveling circus, Buffalo Bill Cody and his Wild West Show. It was the Chrysler Building in New York and the Golden Gate Bridge in San Francisco; the *Concord* and the *Merrimack*, the Alamo, the Little Bighorn, Gettysburg, Shiloh, Bull Run, and 'Strike the tent'.[4]

Culture is the air a young child breathes in; or rather, a particular portion of culture is the air. Had Dillard been born a few years earlier, and in New York City rather than Pittsburgh, she might not have inhaled Dixieland, the Alamo, Little Bighorn, Shiloh, Bull Run and "Strike the tent" when she was young. She might instead have breathed in the New York subway and the Broadway trolley, Joe DiMaggio and Joe Louis, President Roosevelt and Mayor LaGuardia, the Empire State Building and the George Washington Bridge, Charlie McCarthy and Jack Benny, Shirley Temple and Mickey Mouse, *Tom Sawyer* and the game Monopoly, gangster trials and the crash of the Hindenberg. And also Mussolini, Franco, and Hitler.

Although the country of one's childhood gives many adults their first loves, not everyone is so fortunate. The South Africa that Mark Mathabane wrote about in *Kaffir Boy* gave him passbooks, a maximum-security penitentiary that "changed black men into brutes,"[5] and ongoing police squad raids. The air that surrounded him was filled with hatred and fear. My point is not, however, that some cultures turn children's lives into nightmares. Nor is it that every young child breathes in a different portion of culture from every other, although this is also true. Rather, these memories of childhood lend confirmation to the thesis that culture is curriculum.

The history, the geography, the social relations, the images of material phenomena that Hoffman and Dillard recalled are not the first portions of cultural stock to which a human individual's capacities attach. Michael Oakeshott wrote that education as a process of initiation into civilization "begins in the nursery where, for the most part, a child is learning to become at home in the nature-artificial world into which it was born."[6] Certainly, by the time Hoffman was breathing in Catholicism, Dillard Dixieland, and Mathabane Apartheid, all three had already learned to walk, talk, dress, and eat solid food. But the fact that the curriculum of childhood is not an individual's first curriculum does not contradict the thesis that, in childhood and across the life cycle, the curriculum of every individual is a portion of cultural stock.

To be sure, to call what is inhaled with the air "culture" runs counter to definitions that reduce culture to the fine arts and the higher learning, but the theory of education as encounter rejects these. To call what is breathed in "curriculum," in turn, runs counter to three assumptions that follow directly from the deep structure of educational thought: (i) that curriculum is a plan for learning, (ii) that its content is comprised of knowledge alone, and (iii) that school is the sole site of curriculum. Radically narrowing down the concept of curriculum, these corollaries of the deep structure effectively rule out the palpable truth that curriculum is to be found in the cultural air we inhale as well as in the schools we attend.

2. Three Curricular Corollaries

The Restriction of Curriculum Content to Knowledge

In a widely read essay, the nineteenth-century British social theorist Herbert Spencer asked, "What knowledge is of most worth?"[7] In keeping with the deep structure's assumption that the overall aim of education is a cognitive attainment, this has often been called "the" curriculum question. It was Spencer's opinion that science is the knowledge of most worth[8] and others have reached different conclusions. There is no need to decide that issue here, however, for whatever the answer to Spencer's question may be: to make his question decisive in curricular contexts is to beg the question of what should be learned; or, in the language of our theory, of what cultural stock should become yoked to individual capacities.

Philosophers distinguish different kinds of knowledge: for instance, propositional knowledge or "knowledge that," as it is often called; knowledge of how to do something; and knowledge by acquaintance. But, even when the various types of knowledge are taken into account, there is no reason to think that knowledge is the only kind of stock an individual needs or should possess. A human being can know that honesty is a virtue, can have knowledge by acquaintance of honest actions, and can know intuitively in which situations honesty applies, yet consistently act dishonestly because the desire to be honest, or perhaps the strength of character needed to resist temptation, is not yoked to his or her capacities. Similarly, a person can know how to cook healthy meals, yet fail to do so; can know as much as it is humanly possible to know about democracy, yet believe in totalitarian rule; can have encyclopedic knowledge, but lack the capacity to love, empathize with others, and be sensitive to a wide range of social contexts.

The theory of education as encounter rejects the assumption that what is not knowledge has no curricular standing, just as it rejects the narrowly intellectualistic definition of education from which it flows. The assumption that curriculum is a strictly epistemological affair warrants further discussion, however.

Long ago, William Frankena wrote: "Suppose we hold that music is not knowledge. Does it follow that it should not be taught? Not unless we also accept the normative premise that only knowledge should be taught."[9] Frankena was right. If cultural stock consisted of knowledge alone, what may be called "the epistemological fallacy" would not be a fallacy, for there could be nothing other than knowledge in the curriculum.[10] Since, however, the stock of cultures is not limited in this way, it is as much a mistake to believe that curricular content is restricted to knowledge as it is to believe that the meaning of a work of literature can only be determined by reference to its author's intentions; or that the members of a group necessarily possess the characteristics of that group.

Frankena did not identify the different forms the epistemological fallacy can take. Making Spencer's question "the" curriculum question is itself an instance of the epistemological fallacy, but perhaps its most popular incarnation is the claim that only knowledge belonging to one or another intellectual discipline qualifies as curriculum content. The assumption that the structure of knowledge dictates the content of curriculum is also an instance of the fallacy, as is the common belief that only the disciplines of knowledge qualify as school subjects, and that they alone are legitimate sources of subject matter.

The fact is that many widely accepted school subjects—among them, reading, cooking, East Asian Studies, and physical education—are not disciplines of knowledge. Principles that derive from chemistry may be relevant to the subject of cooking and knowledge belonging to physiology may bear on the subject of physical education. But, even supposing it to be true that every school subject is closely related to one or more discipline of knowledge, it is not the case that every curriculum subject is itself a discipline of knowledge.

The Conflation of Curriculum and Curriculum Plans

Give up the deep structure of educational thought's cognitive bias and it becomes apparent that the full range of a culture's stock, and not just one small part of it, provides the content of curriculum. Yet, so long as curriculum is defined narrowly as a plan or design for learning, what Hoffman, Dillard, and Mathabane breathed in with the air will not count as curriculum. For, although some of what they inhaled may have been intended—in Mathabane's case, for instance, fear of the police and, in Dillard's case, a love of jazz—much of it was not.

Mid-twentieth-century curriculum theorists furiously debated whether curriculum is nothing but a plan for learning or if the concept is much broader than this and embraces whatever is learned. When curriculum is defined as an object of intention, it is easy enough to know its content and keep it under control. These benefits would seem to be outweighed, however, by the illusion this narrow definition creates that, in knowing an individual's curriculum, one knows what an individual has actually learned; and that, in knowing what a given educational agent's curriculum is, one knows what that agent has transmitted. Only by repudiating the deep structure's intentional fallacy, and also the reduction of curriculum to a curriculum plan, can a broad understanding of what individuals are learning and educational agents are transmitting be gleaned. That is because only when curriculum is defined broadly can hidden curricula be seen to be curricula.

Logically speaking, the narrow sense of education can be rejected and the narrow intentionalistic sense of curriculum be retained. Yet, as an account that is meant to range over all learning, the theory of education as encounter cannot, in good faith, deny that Hoffman's curriculum included a Catholicism in which she was never formally instructed. It cannot, as a matter of principle, dismiss out of hand the idea that a newborn's curriculum includes gestures and facial expressions that no one is deliberately trying to teach. It cannot deny that Mathabane's curriculum under apartheid included hatred and fear.

Our theory therefore rejects the thesis that education is necessarily a matter of intent and that so is curriculum. It will not do, however, to define curriculum merely as whatever is learned, for that formula views curriculum strictly from the standpoint of the individual, whereas our theory posits an intrinsic connection between culture and curriculum. Thus, to amplify what has already been said here: curriculum is one or another subset of cultural stock that one or more educational agents intend to yoke to or unyoke from—or actually do yoke to or unyoke from—the capacities of one or more individuals.

This definition includes hidden curricula within its scope. It may be helpful to distinguish here between two kinds of hidden.[11] Just as some of the things we describe as hidden—for example, a cure for cancer—are, at a given time, unknown to everyone, there are hidden curricula in which cultural stock attaches to human capacities without anyone's intending or being aware of this. And, just as something can be hidden in the sense in which the penny in the game Hide the Penny is hidden, there are also hidden curricula in which the yoking of particular portions of stock to capacities is known to the educational agent but not to the learner. For example, teachers in the open classrooms of the 1960s and 1970s intended to yoke the three Rs to children's capacities, and usually managed to do so, but the children were not normally aware that the three Rs were part of their curriculum.

No doubt because of the tacit assumption that curriculum is limited to knowledge, it has sometimes been supposed that the difference between a hidden curriculum and what is often called an overt or manifest curriculum, and will here be called a "curriculum proper," is that this latter has to do with academic learning, whereas a hidden curriculum does not. However, the theory of education as encounter leaves open the question of the nature of the content of any given hidden curriculum or curriculum proper. It acknowledges that a curriculum proper can explicitly aim at what is normally thought of as non-academic learning—for instance, the acquisition of moral values, religious attitudes, political preferences, or vocational skills; and that a hidden curriculum can consist of what, normally, would be considered academic learning—for instance, mastery of addition facts, scientific theories, or the principles of democracy. In sum, our theory recognizes that there is no special portion of cultural stock that always and everywhere characterizes a hidden curriculum.

Another common belief is that hidden curricula invariably do harm; in other words, that they necessarily yoke cultural liabilities to individual capacities. That they often do so is indisputable. Thus, the educational reform movement of the 1960s and 1970s uncovered school's hidden curriculum in docility, self-hatred, and learning how to fail. At the close of the twentieth century, a Chinese immigrant to the U.S. remembered that her first-grade classmates called her "Chink eyes" and joked that her hair and skin were pulled too tight: "The children's voices crawled inside me and took residence. I wished I weren't so pathetic. I hated myself almost as much as they did."[12] And a 2003 account of a California public high school strongly suggested that the school was unwittingly teaching that cheating is the best policy and that, in matters intellectual, it is best to play it safe and take no risks.[13]

However, the cultural stock a hidden curriculum yokes to individual capacities can represent assets, as well as liabilities. Consider a family that transmits a love of music or an appreciation of painting and sculpture to its children without ever trying to. Consider also the Yale Sustainable Food Project.[14] To the extent that Yale students were unaware of the project's mission to teach them to eat seasonally, they can be said to have been the beneficiaries of a hidden curriculum of significant worth. In sum, because the cultural stock that an educational agent yokes to an individual's capacities can be a liability or an asset, significant or trivial, of great value or of dubious worth, the stock belonging to a hidden curriculum can have these same attributes.

The Reduction of Curriculum's Site to School

The curricular corollary of the deep structure of educational thought's assumption that school is a culture's one and only educational agent is that school is the sole possessor of a curriculum. Now it is possible in all consistency to reject the false equation between education and schooling, yet hold that school is the sole site of curriculum. But to do so is not only to make it impossible to perceive the curriculum in the air that both children and adults inhale.[15] It also forces school to engage in self-defeating behavior.

Consider a seemingly straightforward instance of curriculum decision-making, namely setting the aim that secondary school students learn the basic structure of evolutionary theory. And now suppose that a young boy has had numerous encounters both at home and in church with the cultural stock that the theory of evolution is the work of the devil. It is likely, in this boy's case, that school's goal will only be achieved if the curricula of his home and church are counteracted: that is, if the stock that they previously yoked to his capacities becomes uncoupled from them.

Imagine now that the desired goal is that schoolchildren acquire an understanding of mathematics. Suppose what again is not unimaginable, namely that a young girl has breathed in with the air the following curriculum of her home and her neighborhood: that she is not smart enough to understand math; and that, in any case, since she will soon be married and bear children, there is no point in her trying to do so. Here, again, school's success in achieving its curricular goal will depend, at least in part, on whether it can counteract this other curriculum; that is to say, on school's ability to unyoke her capacities from previously transmitted stock.

In view of the fact that every group and institution of a society is a custodian of some portion of the culture's stock that could be yoked to individual capacities, our theory holds that every group and institution is the possessor of some curriculum or other. This is not to say that every item of stock in a group or institution's keep will actually become yoked to some individual's capacities. A school may include Latin in its list of subjects but, if no students enroll in the course, the portion of cultural stock known as Latin is not likely to attach to anyone's capacities. Similarly, an archive may preserve on its shelves a historical figure's letters and journals that are never read. Nonetheless, if the stock is in an educational agent's portfolio, there will inevitably be opportunities for the yoking together of capacities and stock—that is to say, for *learning affordances*. And where there are learning affordances, there is curriculum. Thus, an educational agent's curriculum consists in those items of cultural stock that it either attaches to, or has the capability to attach to, individual capacities.

The thesis that every educational agent has a curriculum does not entail that each educational agent's curriculum is absolutely unique. It is seldom, if ever, the case that an educational agent is the sole guardian of any item of stock in its keep. Think, for example, of Beethoven's symphonies. Orchestras, recording companies, music publishers, radio stations, music schools, and conservatories presently have joint custody of this wealth; hence, their curricula overlap. Think of the vast literature on women's history. Here, the curricula of universities, schools, libraries, bookstores, and historical societies overlap, for these educational agents share custody of this portion of stock.

If, perchance, an educational agent does have sole custody of some portion of stock, there is no reason to suppose that this arrangement will persist. Just as our culture's stock changes over time, so do its guardians. As the guardians of a portion of stock change, the custodial arrangements will very likely change, and so will curricula.

In any event, the amount and the type of stock in a given agent's custody will, in all probability, change over time. An art museum may acquire new paintings, a symphony orchestra may commission a new cello concerto, a publisher may add the *Harry Potter* series to its list and remove other books from it, volumes may be stolen from a library, a national park may add a reconstruction of an American Indian village, school may stop offering Greek and Latin. Furthermore, with the passage of time, the value of any given portion of stock can rise or fall. Thus, new data may discredit a scientific theory and the *Harry Potter* series may go out of fashion. To say that a group or institution's stock can change is not, however, to deny that it has a curriculum. It is simply to confirm the well-known but oft forgotten truth that curricula are not writ in stone.

3. School Subjects as Cultural Constructs

Once the curricular corollaries of education's deep structure are identified, it is easy to understand why the insight that culture and curriculum are closely connected has often been met with disbelief and cries of dismay. The intellectual disciplines have traditionally been thought to be so objective and universal as to be culture-free. Thus, when curriculum content is limited to knowledge and the intellectual disciplines are presumed to be the prime sources of curricular content, curriculum, is in effect, "decultured." When curriculum is narrowly defined as a plan for learning and school is considered the only curricular site, the abstraction of curriculum from culture is also fostered, for then the hidden curricula of the full range of a culture's educational agents go unseen.

The deculturing of curriculum is then taken several steps further by a conception of school subjects that, although not entailed by education's deep structure, is basic to thinking about curriculum. According to this widely held dogma, the subjects around which school curricula are usually organized are "givens" that stand outside time, history, and culture. The dogma also holds that there is a shortlist of such subjects to which nothing can be added and from which nothing should be subtracted.

History belies this latter assumption, however. It reveals that what are presumed to be eternal, sacrosanct subjects—for instance, the trivium of grammar, rhetoric, and dialectic; or Greek and Latin; or science, mathematics, history, and literature—have, over time, ceded their places to new and sometimes very different ones. Thus, when the subject social studies was offered as a replacement for history and geography in the school curriculum, there was an outcry in the U.S. "Social studies is not a subject," wrote one critic, "it is a group or federation of subjects."[16] Yet, social studies soon became a staple of the school curriculum. Decades later, there were similar outcries when women's studies was introduced into higher education's curriculum. Yet, before long, it too became an accepted subject.

Even a brief glance at the wide variety of school curricula gives the lie to the idea that there is a short list of school subjects, let alone that the items on the list are all of a piece. School subjects can, of course, be disciplines of knowledge such as physics, chemistry, and biology.[17] However, they can also be languages such as French, Russian, and Japanese; practical activities such as driving and woodworking; and performing arts such as drama and dance. Furthermore, although chairs and hamburgers may not seem, at first glance, to be the kind of things that can be curriculum subjects, chairs would surely qualify as the subject of a curriculum in furniture making, and hamburgers would qualify as the subject of a curriculum for short-order cooks.

The truth is that anything that can function as an object of study can be fashioned into a curriculum subject. The operative word here is "fashioned" for as the theory of education as encounter makes clear, curriculum subjects—whether old or new—are not "givens" that exist outside time, history, and culture. They are constructions made out of the stock of cultures.

Think, for example, of the subject physics. Its point of departure, or *subject-base*,[18] is an item of cultural stock—namely, the science physics—and its subject matter is made up, in part, of the cultural stock belonging to that intellectual discipline. That a good deal of this stock constitutes knowledge is indisputable. But the stock out of which the subject physics is constructed is also composed of attitudes, values, and patterns of behavior; and, although these may involve knowledge, they are not reducible to it. Furthermore, the subject matter of the school subject physics can, and often does, include items of cultural stock drawn from sources other than the science physics—for instance, from the history, philosophy, and sociology of science. This stock is not all reducible to knowledge, either.

What is true of physics is true of all curriculum subjects. They are not given to us from on high and they do not exist outside culture. Something—be it a science, a language, a geographical region, a biological species—attracts interest. Selecting that item of interest as a subject-base and using it as a kind of magnet, we humans pull together diverse items of cultural stock and give them some sort of organization. In other words, school subjects are portions of cultural stock that, over time, people have tied up into neat packages of subject matter and given a seal of approval.

In principle, this means that harvester ants, identity politics, and love can serve as subject-bases for school subjects that supplant traditional ones such as philosophy, mathematics, and physics. That our theory acknowledges the plethora of potential curriculum subjects does not mean, however, that it takes a stand on the value of any given one. The question of what the subjects of any given school curriculum should be is a normative issue that our theory deliberately leaves open. Recognition of the superabundance of potential school subjects does, however, highlight how rich the resources are for those who would engage in curriculum development, and how few of those resources tend to be used.

It may be wondered, however, if there is not at least one group of school subjects—the three Rs, as they used to be called—that defies the present analysis.

Are not they the basics of education and are not the basics immutable givens? Reading, writing, and arithmetic are indeed considered to be education's basic subjects. Like all other subjects, however, they are constructed out of cultural stock. Moreover, they became the basics of education by our decision and serve in that capacity at our pleasure.[19]

It is sometimes said that the three Rs are the basics because they are essential subjects of study, the implication being that we humans have no say in the matter. Even if this were true, what is essential at one time and place might not be at another. As it happens, however, we do not call the three Rs our basics because we consider them essential to study; rather, we consider them to be essential because they seem to us to be so basic.

What is it about the three Rs that justifies our calling them, rather than cooking and driving or science and history, the basics of education? Here, again, the philosophical notion of a basic action is helpful, for, just as basic actions have been said to generate all other acts, the three Rs have been said to be basic because they have generative power.

Of course, from the standpoint of a general theory of human action, reading, writing, and arithmetic are not basic at all: one does not just do them; one does them by doing a variety of other actions. Yet, from the standpoint of education, the decision to call them basic seems to make sense. Every educational encounter involves the kind of change we call learning, and learning is one of those acts one does by doing other things: schools, in particular, assume that learning is done by reading, by writing, and by doing arithmetic. Thus, just as moving one's hand is a building block or generator of the act of opening a door, so reading, writing, and arithmetic are considered building blocks or generators of the act of learning. Actually, and very importantly, the three Rs are assumed to be generators of the acts of living, as well as learning. Indeed, we use them in our roles of parent and caretaker, salesperson and consumer, wage earner and homemaker, citizen and neighbor.

The answer to the question "What makes the three Rs basic?" is, then, that we perform the acts of learning and living by reading, writing, and doing arithmetic. Of course, for some acts of learning and living, the three Rs are all but irrelevant. Furthermore, many acts that can be generated by the three Rs can also be done without their help. Still, we call the three Rs the basics of education because we believe that a great many acts of learning and living must be done by doing them if they are to be done well.

The generative power of the three Rs is neither universal nor eternal, however. In some cultures, fishing and hunting will be far more generative than the three Rs. Then again, even in a culture that considers the three Rs its basics, there are contexts in which they have little, if any, generative power. Within the confines of, for instance, a training program in figure skating, skating on one's inside and outside edges would seem to be far more basic than the three Rs. Furthermore, the activities of learning and living change over time, and substitute ways of performing the same activities can and do become available. Thus, our judgments about the relative generative power of the three Rs may have to change.

Judgments about the three Rs are also subject to change because they are not the only component activities of learning and living. One learns science, for example, by listening and speaking, asking questions and testing assumptions, using one's imagination to conjecture about what might be the case and inventing ways of testing hypotheses, as well as by reading, writing, and doing arithmetic. That we call the three Rs, rather than some other component activities, our basics is a matter, then, of practical decision. Were our perceptions of which activities are most important to change, so might our decision about which ones to single out for special attention.

Lest there be any doubt, rank and privilege attach themselves to those subjects we choose to call the basics of education. No one would ever call one of the basics a "frill;" no one would try to push a basic subject out of the school curriculum in favor of some non-basic subject. On the contrary, the basics are never far from the thoughts of parents, schoolteachers and administrators, and politicians.

Do the three Rs deserve to be called "the" basics? Should other subjects be added to the list? Should anything be subtracted? The dogma that our school subjects are pre-existing, immutable givens lulls us into thinking that the choice of basic subjects is not in human hands. The decision to attach the "basics" label to one portion of cultural stock rather than another is, however, ours to make. Moreover, it is as much a decision about which kind of culture to project into the future as it is one about the individuals who will inhabit that future culture.

Just as our theory leaves open the question of which, if any, subjects should be the basics of education, it leaves open the question of whether the school curriculum should be organized around subjects. In the past, curriculum theorists distinguished between what they called a subject curriculum and a broad-fields curriculum.[20] When, however, it is granted that anything can be a subject-base, the broad-fields curriculum can be seen to be a special case of a subject curriculum: one whose subjects have complex bases—for instance, the conjunction of history, geography, and anthropology; or of reading, spelling, and composition. The subject curriculum also used to be distinguished from the so-called core curriculum. When the concept of a subject is construed broadly, however, this latter also becomes a special type of subject organization: one organized around subjects that are thought to be especially important, or to pull together and make coherent vast amounts of subject matter, and that all students are required to study.

There is at least one type of curriculum organization that cannot always be reduced to a subject curriculum, however, and that is the so-called activity or experience curriculum. To be sure, activities—for instance, reading, carpentry, and film-making—can be the subject-bases of school subjects. When they are, an individual will be expected to learn to do the activity or else simply learn about it. In an activity curriculum, however, an activity serves not as an object of study—not as something for a student to learn about or learn to do—but as a practice or occupation for an individual to engage in.

It is helpful here to distinguish between the points of view of the educator and the educatee. In a subject curriculum, the two standpoints are as one: in the eyes of both parties, the educatee is placed in the role of a student of some aspect of the world. In an activity curriculum, on the other hand, the educator may see the educatee as a student of the world and will certainly be thinking of the activities at issue as vehicles for yoking all kinds of cultural stock to individual capacities, but the educatee will view him or herself, and also the activity, very differently. From the educatee's standpoint, producing a play, publishing a magazine, building a clubhouse, or the like is something to do or an enterprise to be part of—perhaps for its own sake, perhaps because it is an activity the school needs performed, or perhaps simply because it is fun.

Needless to say, the activities in an activity curriculum are themselves items of cultural stock. Moreover, like the items of stock that are our school subjects, their educational value can change over time and space. Thus, an activity that, in one context, engages interest and yokes a large number of cultural assets to capacities may not do so in another.

4. Cultural Liabilities and Curriculum Content

If culture is the stuff out of which curriculum is composed, and it is; then curriculum is the material out of which education fashions individuals and cultures. It might therefore be supposed that the theory of education as encounter must consider "the" curriculum question to be: What cultural stock is of most worth? Yet, once the broad definition of curriculum is accepted, there would seem to be no reason why this or any normative question should take precedence over the empirical question, "What cultural stock is now attaching, or has already attached, to individual capacities?"

Suppose now that one limits one's sights to the normative question of what cultural stock is most valuable. It is a question begging to decide this without determining for whom the stock is most valuable, what makes it valuable, and in what way the most valuable stock should attach to individual capacities. Think of the difference it makes if, for example, loyalty to a political party becomes yoked to a person's capacities as a thoughtful disposition, as opposed to an unreflective habit. Similarly, to ask what stock is most valuable without also asking to whom the stock should be yoked appears to presuppose that everyone's capacities should be yoked to the same cultural stock.

Going on the assumption that the aims of education determine the curriculum, and keeping the cultural component in mind, some might want to insist that "How do we make the best kinds of people and cultures?" is "the" curriculum question. But this question is both too narrow and too broad. On the one hand, it presupposes that we already know which kinds of people and cultures are best.

On the other hand, and assuming that it is agreed that making the best kinds of people and cultures is what education everywhere and always should be doing, it subsumes just about every normative curriculum question one might think of.

Actually, the very idea that there is a single most basic or primary curriculum question is highly problematic. Moreover, it is not clear how one could determine the relative importance of curriculum questions without being arbitrary. And, supposing this latter could be done, one wonders if any single question would come out on top. Might there not be several curriculum questions of equal importance? Or might there be no question that, in all contexts, is most important?

A certain economy would be achieved if the theory of education as encounter could point to one curriculum question and call it "the" question, but the price of such economy is high. Rather than run the risk of cutting off inquiry and short-circuiting decision-making by thinking that there is one, and only one, primary curriculum question when there may either be several, or none at all, the theory of education as encounter resists the temptation to call any question "the" curriculum question. Our theory rests content with allowing new questions to emerge and old ones to be answered that have too often been prejudged. It also seeks to insure that, whatever questions are asked, it is never forgotten that cultural stock includes liabilities, as well as assets; that it is necessary to ask not only what cultural stock should become yoked to the capacities of individuals but also what stock should not become yoked.

In this regard, it is well to remember that the very methods educational agents use in joining stock and capacities together can result in unforeseen and often undesirable yokings of stock and capacities. Thus, in *Experience and Education*, Dewey had this to say about the traditional methods of schooling:

> How many students . . . were rendered callous to ideas, and how many lost the impetus to learn because of the way in which learning was experienced by them? How many acquired special skills by means of automatic drill so that their power of judgment and capacity to act intelligently in new situations was limited? How many came to associate the learning process with ennui and boredom?[21]

When, in the year 2007, hundreds of Protestant churches decided to hold *Halo* nights,[22] the claim that the methods educational agents use really do matter took on new significance. *Halo*, an immensely popular, immersive, and extremely violent video game, was introduced into the churches in order to bring young men and boys into an arena where they would be taught Christian doctrine. Whether the religious lessons that church leaders had in mind did, in fact, attach to the capacities of the game players is not known. *Halo* proved, however, to be an excellent method of gaining the attention of male members of the next generation.

Critics of the *Halo* nights protested that even the most moral ends do not justify the use of immoral means, whereas defenders maintained that killing on a video screen is not really killing. Neither response to the *Halo* case spoke to the central issue, however. As our theory makes clear, the fundamental question the *Halo* case raises is not about the morality of the game itself. It is, rather, what kinds of people and cultures were the church leaders trying to make and shape?

To the extent that the decision to use the game yoked the enjoyment of violence, a delight in cruelty, and insensitivity to the pain of others to the capacities of young American males—or else reinforced previous such yokings—was not the presumed goal of making the best kinds of people placed in jeopardy? To the extent that this decision strengthened these cultural liabilities and projected them into the culture's future, was not the goal of making the best kinds of cultures undermined? Insofar as the decision became incorporated into the hidden curriculum of the churches and other educational agents as a generalized belief that the best way for an educational agent to reach students is through games that equate fun with blowing people up, did it not also subvert the goal of making the best kind of cultures?

Given the undeniable fact that cultural liabilities are as likely to attach to individual capacities as are cultural assets, when the goal is to make the best kinds of people and cultures, an educational agent must do more than simply determine that the content of its curriculum represents cultural assets. "What avail is it," asked Dewey

> to win prescribed amounts of information about geography and history, to win ability to read and write, if in the process the individual loses his own soul: loses his appreciation of things worth while, of the values to which these things are relative, if he loses desire to apply what he has learned and, above all, loses the ability to extract meaning from his future experiences as they occur?[23]

What avail is it, one might add, if, in the process of passing down its most worthwhile assets to the next generation, a culture projects its most problematic liabilities into the future.

An educational agent must try to insure that the methods it uses do not yoke cultural liabilities to individual capacities, and also that the methods are themselves worth passing down to the next generation. Why did the subjects in the obedience studies conducted by Stanley Milgram in the 1960s so willingly accept the idea that someone who delivers electric shocks to people who fail to memorize words on a list is a teacher? The most credible answer is that the belief in the legitimacy of rote learning and punishment as methods of teaching and learning was part of the air that Milgram's subjects had breathed in when they were young. But this is to say that the methods educational agents use to yoke individual capacities to cultural stock are themselves items of cultural stock that are convertible into curricular content.

As medicines have side effects, many of which are undesirable, the methods that produce yokings of stock and capacities can bring about learning that is unwanted. Once more, however, a caveat is needed. In pointing out that the methods or processes that educational agents employ—for instance, drill, rote memorization, and corporal punishment; or, for that matter, lecturing and giving spot quizzes—can convert into curriculum content, I am not suggesting that new educational processes cannot be devised. Of course they can be. Once a new method is created, however, the decision to use it is a decision to project this cultural practice into the future: it is such because repeated use strengthens a method's standing as a cultural practice and thus gives it a kind of legitimacy; and because the belief in its legitimacy easily becomes incorporated into the hidden curricula of school and society.

Whether or not educational methods take on a life of their own as curriculum content, they can, and often do, produce any number of harmful side effects in the form of cultural liabilities that attach to people's capacities. And the same can be said for modes of evaluation, for they too are items of cultural stock that can have unwanted side effects, and they too are convertible into curricular content.

Because hidden curricula are composed of cultural liabilities such as racism, misogyny, dishonesty, and mendacity, as well as assets such as truth telling, honesty, and respect for others; and because such liabilities can attach to individual capacities not just as theoretical knowledge, but also as attitudes, values, and patterns of behavior as well: they can sabotage the best-laid plans for making the best kinds of people and cultures.

5. A Cultural Bookkeeping Project

Yet, can it be known in advance what hidden lessons a given method of instruction or mode of evaluation carries with it? It is difficult enough to be informed about the yokings that school hopes will occur. How can we possibly identify the yokings brought about by school's hidden curriculum, let alone by the curricula proper and the hidden curricula of the culture's other educational agents?

It is no simple matter to track down the unintended yokings of cultural stock and individual capacities. Those in the past who deplored the hidden curriculum of American schooling often left the impression that hidden curricula are all the same; that, if you have found the hidden curriculum of one school, you have found the hidden curriculum of all schools. But the bearers of hidden curricula are educational agents and there is no reason to suppose that different agents will have exactly the same items of cultural stock in their portfolios, let alone attach the same items of cultural stock to the same capacities. Besides, new educational agents with their own hidden curricula are forever emerging and old ones are forever changing. Hence, information gathered yesterday on the hidden curriculum of a given setting may not accurately portray that setting's hidden curriculum today. In addition, what one finds when one investigates hidden curricula is a function of what one looks for and what one looks at. In consequence, the search for hidden curricula must constantly retrace its steps.

Despite the difficulties of gathering the relevant information and finding out the whole story, the existence of numerous empirical studies of the hidden curriculum of schooling, as well as memoirs of life at home, school, the military, and elsewhere, testify that the hidden curricula of a culture's educational agents can be discovered. It is, thus, reckless for the schools, churches, and other educational agents in our midst to proceed as if hidden curricula are not their business. Indeed, the very desire to yoke particular items of cultural stock to individual capacities makes it all the more important to discover what obstacles stand in the way and to determine how to overcome them.

To this end, a *cultural bookkeeping project* is needed—one that seeks to identify the whole wide range of a given culture's educational agents, the full extent of the assets and liabilities in each one's portfolio, and the individuals to whose capacities that stock becomes yoked.[24] Something analogous to this—in effect, a biological bookkeeping system—has recently been developed.

In 2002, E.O. Wilson called for a "full and exact mapping of all biological diversity."[25] Saying, "The biospheric membrane that covers Earth is the miracle we have been given. And our tragedy, because a large part of it is being lost forever before we learn what it is and the best means by which it can be savored and used,"[26] he recommended that each species be identified along with the role it plays in the totality of life. In 2007, Wilson received an award that, along with prize money, grants recipients "One Wish to Change the World." Wilson wished for an encyclopedia of life "as a way to learn about and preserve the earth's biodiversity before it disappears"[27] and, in 2008, The Encyclopedia of Life was launched on the Internet.

How many species are there altogether and where are they? Given that 69,000 species of fungi had been identified by 2002, but approximately 1.6 million species of fungi were thought to exist, the sum total of all species is almost beyond comprehension. The encyclopedia set a goal for its first five years of creating one million species pages on its website, each one verified by a scientific expert.

Similarly, to savor and use well the miracle that is human culture and to minimize the harm that is done, whether by hidden curricula or by curricula proper, every culture needs a bookkeeping system that provides an overview of its stock—its assets and liabilities, the custodians, the methods and processes they use to yoke the stock to human capacities, the designated and the actual beneficiaries of the stock, and so on. A satisfactory cultural bookkeeping project would require a vast amount of research, including: historical studies of the life and times of the various educational agents and portions of cultural stock; philosophical analyses of key concepts such as "educational agent" and the asset/liability distinction; normative work on, for instance, what cultural stock should be preserved and who the various designated beneficiaries should be; and social scientific research on, among other things, the workings of the various educational agents, cultural definitions of cultural wealth, and the actual, as opposed to the designated, beneficiaries of various portions of stock.

Even if a cultural bookkeeping project were restricted to a single locale, it would be an enormous undertaking. Moreover, like The Encyclopedia of Life, this vast research effort would, of necessity, be ongoing, for in a changing world the culture's inventory of educational agents and their assets and liabilities would be in constant flux.[28] Expand the scope of a cultural bookkeeping project to a region, a nation, a continent, the globe, and it will perhaps sound wildly ambitious. But so did the publicly funded human genome project, whose goal was to decipher all 3.2 billion chemical letters of the human genetic blueprint, when it was launched in 1990. And so did Wilson's plan for mapping biological diversity until The Encyclopedia of Life became a reality.

Granted, too much knowledge about a culture's educational agents and the stock in their keep could be a dangerous thing. In the wrong hands, it could be used to gain or tighten control over the populace. However, the domain of cultural bookkeeping includes the culture's assets, liabilities, and educational agents—not the behavior and lives of individuals. Of course, knowledge, like power, can be abused. And it might even be the case that the more knowledge we have, the greater the abuses can be. But the truth is that the kind of knowledge that feeds the appetite of an Orwellian Big Brother to control the private actions of an entire population—or some segment thereof—is increasingly available and is not the result of cultural bookkeeping. Indeed, by tracking the decline of cultural assets such as civic engagement[29] and documenting the increased distribution across the population of such liabilities as political inertia and acquiescence to authority, a system of cultural bookkeeping could serve to thwart Big Brother's totalitarian impulses.

The question remains of what to do with a hidden curriculum when one is found—be it by informal observation, scholarly studies, or a large-scale cultural bookkeeping project. Other things being equal, if a particular hidden curriculum does no harm, it can, with good conscience, be ignored. If, however, a hidden curriculum is known to do—or be likely to do—significant damage, it is, at the very least, counterproductive and may, depending on the nature of the damage, even be positively immoral to leave it intact.

When Dewey found that American schoolchildren were losing their desire to learn because of the endless and meaningless exercises and drills, the strategy he adopted—Progressive Education—was to try to root out the offending practices and substitute better ones in their stead. For some hidden curricula, however, the best policy may be to raise the unintended lessons to consciousness and transfer them into the curriculum proper for all to see and understand. This, for example, is what an Atlanta, Georgia non-profit group did when it held workshops in which teenage girls talked about hip-hop and rewrote the lyrics of songs that degrade women.[30] It is also what a television program did when, in a year of increased sightings of nooses—a symbol associated with past lynchings of African-Americans—it featured a discussion about the history and meaning of lynching in the U.S.[31]

6. Every Individual a Curriculum Worker and a Culture Maker

In 1931, Carl Becker delivered a widely acclaimed presidential address to the American Historical Association entitled "Everyman His Own Historian." "We will suppose," said Becker, "that Mr Everyman is not a professor of history, but just an ordinary citizen without excess knowledge." "In all the immediately practical affairs of life," Becker continued—the example he gave was paying a coal bill—"Mr Everyman is a good historian."[32]

Just as in the immediately practical affairs of life Mr Everyman and Ms Everywoman can be found acting as historians, they can be discovered making one curriculum decision after another. Imagine Ms Everywoman in a toy store. She is looking for a birthday gift for her granddaughter. "Mary has enough dolls," she says to herself. "If I give her this erector set she will learn how to use nuts, bolts, and screws, and all about pulleys and gears. And, if she has fun, she may even decide to be an engineer or an architect." At this point in the soliloquy, Ms Everywoman pauses. "On the other hand, her parents may laugh at her attempts and kill her interest in science. Worse still, their scorn for my gift may teach her to be suspicious of me." "On balance, however," she assures herself as she stands at the checkout counter, "playing with the erector set is likely to make Mary a happier and more capable person. Not to mention the fact that, in defying the gender stereotypes that assign mechanical skills and interests to boys and men, not girls and women, she and I will be making the culture just that much better."[33]

One father plays Dixieland. Another plays Bach and Beethoven. One mother tells her daughters Greek myths. Another shows them how to put on cosmetics. The everyday decisions people make and the mundane things they do have consequences. By virtue of the decisions Mr Everyman and Ms Everywoman do and do not make; by virtue of what they say and do not say; what they do and fail to do; how they walk, talk, and dress: cultural stock becomes yoked to their own capacities and those of others. To be sure, the culture's attitudes and values, perceptions and expectations may, to a greater or lesser extent, determine which items of cultural stock are singled out for yoking. Nonetheless, in addition to being historians, Mr Everyman and Ms Everywoman are educators.

What holds true at home and on a trip to a toy store holds true also for those who work in or patronize supermarkets, hairdressing salons, and automobile agencies; frequent hospital emergency rooms, government offices, and banks; and are members of religious institutions, political parties, unions, community organizations, and neighborhood gangs. When, for example, a beautician recommends color for a customer's graying hair, she is doing curriculum work. So too is a physician who reviews medications but does not talk about exercise and nutrition, a minister who preaches that homosexuality contradicts God's law, a neighborhood youth who tells a new recruit that loyalty to gang members is all that counts.

In revealing that curriculum is in the air we breathe, as well as in the courses of study we follow in school, the theory of education as encounter uncovers the fact that, whether we like it or not, in our daily lives, we full-fledged members of the educational realm are all curriculum workers. In making it clear that every yoking of cultural stock to individual capacities, whether conscious or not, projects that item of stock rather than other items into the future, our theory also makes it clear that we are also culture makers.

Lest it be wondered if animals, as well as humans, are curriculum and culture workers, think about Nim Chimpsky and also Travis, a cross-fostered chimpanzee who, in 2009, attacked a Connecticut woman, causing her serious physical harm. In the 1970s, Nim and other chimpanzees yoked the cultural stock that they were honorary humans to the capacities of any number of people. Here now was Travis unyoking that stock from people's capacities and replacing it with the belief that chimpanzees are, after all, savage beasts. Travis, like Nim before him, was as effective—if unwitting—a curriculum worker as any human could possibly be. As such, he too was also a culture maker and shaper.

The late twentieth-century U.S. was the scene of endless and often bitter disputes—the media called them "culture wars"—about whether works by, for instance, Harriet Beecher Stowe, Virginia Woolf, Langston Hughes, James Baldwin, and Toni Morrison should be brought into the literary canon, and whether subjects such as women's history, African-American literature, gay and lesbian studies, and the like should be included in higher education's curriculum. Although the war imagery may, at the time, have seemed to sensationalize the controversy, it captured the often overlooked fact that curriculum decisions have cultural consequences. To introduce the subject women's history into the college or university curriculum is to give a new lease on life to a portion of cultural stock that might otherwise become extinct. To drop out of that curriculum a Shakespearean play or a John Donne poem in order to make room for a Woolf novel or a Langston Hughes poem is to weaken that item of stock's chances of long-term survival.

The kernel of truth in the culture war imagery is that all curriculum decisions are cultural decisions, and that struggles over curriculum are ultimately struggles about culture. Arguments about the adequacy of the education in the three Rs that children are receiving in school are as much about the importance of preserving certain portions of cultural stock as they are about developing children's capacities. When a university overhauls its undergraduate liberal arts curriculum, its decisions about what courses to offer are as much about the kinds of stock that should be projected into the culture's future as about what an educated person should know. Indeed, the very inclusion of a subject in a school curriculum— even a seemingly uncontroversial subject such as reading or history—strengthens and prolongs the life expectancy of that particular bundle of cultural stock.

It is easy enough to forget that debates about curriculum are ultimately about the kinds of individuals we want ourselves, our children, and the animals in our lives to be. Yet, they are also about the kinds of cultures in which we want ourselves and others to live. It would seem to follow, therefore, that all of us need to practice a kind of double vision throughout our lives and in the various roles we play. Holding the two basic elements of education—individuals and cultures—in focus and attending to the interactions between them, it behooves us to keep our eyes open to both the kinds of individuals we are making when we attach stock to capacities and the kinds of cultures that result.

A caveat is needed here, for to say that all individuals are curriculum workers and culture makers and shapers is not to suggest that they can replace specialists in curriculum planning and development. In calling Mr Everyman his own historian, Becker was not ringing the death knell for his profession. Rather, he was demystifying it by pointing to its continuity with the activities of everyday life. Similarly, the theory of education as encounter points up the continuity between the way all of us behave in our daily lives and what specialists in curriculum planning and development do. The intent here, however, is not so much to demystify a specialized field as it is to heighten awareness that the project of making and shaping individuals and cultures is not solely in the hands of an especially trained few. Every individual is a member of not just one institution but many. Since the institutions to which we all belong are educational agents, this means that all of us are educators many times over; hence that we all participate daily in the making and shaping of people and cultures.

6

EDUCATIVENESS AS A VIRTUE OF INSTITUTIONS AND CULTURES

In view of the fact that a culture's stock includes liabilities as well as assets, a third major implication of the theory of education as encounter is that cultures and their educational agents can be miseducative as well as educative. Of course, differences of opinion will exist as to whether a given culture or a given group or institution within a culture is one or the other. But this does not alter the point at issue. Nor does it mean that the attributes of being educative and miseducative should be regarded as having equal value.

In this regard, being educative and miseducative can usefully be compared to being healthy and unhealthy. Despite the many disagreements about what constitutes good health and the conflicting opinions about which treatments are conducive to it, it is generally admitted that it is better for a person to be healthy than unhealthy. So, too, despite the inevitable arguments over whether specific items of stock are assets or liabilities, it can be agreed that it is a far better thing for a culture and its institutions to be educative than to be miseducative. Indeed, insofar as the dream of making the best kinds of individuals and cultures is adopted as a guiding principle of education, being educative must be considered a virtue of cultures and their institutions, and being miseducative a vice. At best, the yoking of cultural liabilities, rather than assets, to individual capacities places obstacles in the way of realizing the dream. At worst, it transforms the dream into a nightmare.

It may be wondered if it is legitimate to attribute educativeness and miseducativeness to groups and institutions, let alone to whole cultures, given that these are composed of individual human beings. It should be noted that, if this doubt were justified, it would apply equally to the claim made by the twentieth-century philosopher John Rawls that justice is the first or most important virtue of institutions[1] and would also hold good for talk about group actions and institutional responsibilities. As it happens, however, just as it is customary to attribute qualities to a human individual even though he or she is made up of cells, it is standard practice to attribute qualities to a group even though it is composed of human individuals. To be sure, methodological individualism—the thesis that social groups are, in one or another respect, reducible to individuals— has had many defenders over the years.[2] But even if some version of methodological individualism is valid, it does not follow that a general theory of education must abstain from attributing traits or dispositions to groups, institutions, and cultures, or from holding them responsible for their actions.

1. The Virtue of Educativeness

The first thing to be noted about the trait or property of being educative is that it is distinct from that of being educated. One indication that these are independent states is that the relevant contrast to being educated is being uneducated, whereas the relevant contrast to being educative is being miseducative. Another sign is that many people would consider a culture with a high literacy rate to be an educated society, and they would also classify as such a culture most of whose members had attained a higher degree. However, as the case of Nazi Germany clearly demonstrates, a literate culture can be miseducative. So, for that matter, can a culture whose every member has a Ph.D.

A second point to which attention must be drawn is that to call an educational agent "miseducative" is not to say that it is being ineffective or inefficient in transmitting the culture's stock to the capacities of the next generation. To botch this task may well be an indication of ineptitude, but it is not an instance of miseducativeness—unless, of course, the ineptitude betokens negligence. Although miseducation is sometimes due to negligence, the primary reason it is to be avoided is not that it is a job badly done, but that it is the wrong job to do.

Miseducation is a complex phenomenon that includes sins of commission and omission. On the one hand, it involves the yoking of cultural liabilities—for instance rape, murder, racism, dishonesty—to individual capacities. On the other, it constitutes a failure to yoke valuable cultural assets such as honesty, integrity, or kindness to capacities.

Although a miseducational sin of commission is active, in that it succeeds in coupling stock and capacities, this yoking need not be intentional. Suppose, for example, that a television network has no wish to attach individual capacities to unhealthy eating habits but, nevertheless, continually exposes viewers to images of thin, gorgeous, healthy looking people enjoying mountains of luscious looking fattening food and drink. Given the well-publicized knowledge that food of the sort being pictured is conducive to ill-health and the fact, known to this television network, that repeated exposure to such images increases people's appetites for said food and drink, the network can legitimately be said to be miseducative. On the other hand, whereas a miseducational sin of omission is passive, insofar as it consists in the absence of any coupling of stock to capacities, the failure to yoke stock and capacities together can be intentional. As a case in point, consider that nineteenth-century Indian schools in the U.S. deliberately refrained from yoking the capacities of the children in their care to their native languages and cultural practices.

The multiplicity of educational agents and the fact that the same item of cultural stock may be in the keep of more than one agent can make it difficult to pinpoint responsibility for miseducation. Still, that it is not always easy to determine which educational agent has yoked a given cultural liability or failed to yoke a given cultural asset in its portfolio to the capacities of particular individuals does not affect the main point that miseducativeness has two quite distinct aspects.

Similarly, educativeness is a two-sided virtue involving the transmission of cultural assets to individual capacities and the non-transmission of cultural liabilities. The term "non-transmission" is meant to cover two possibilities: that the yoking of liabilities to capacities does not occur; or else, that the unyoking of liabilities from capacities to which they are already attached does occur. After all, some highly educative groups and institutions—for instance, self-help organizations such as Alcoholics Anonymous—devote themselves to this latter task.

Just as being miseducative can, but need not, be a matter of intention, so too being educative may or may not be intended. Good intentions are not enough to establish the educativeness of a culture or one of its educational agents, however. Other things being equal, a culture or an educational agent that consistently attempts to attach the assets in its portfolio to individual capacities but never quite succeeds cannot be said to be educative. This does not mean that a culture or its agent must have 100 percent success in yoking its assets to capacities and preventing liabilities from attaching to them in order to be considered educative. Indeed, the very fact that cultures or institutions can be compared to one another in regard to their educativeness suggests that it is a matter of degree rather than an all-or-nothing affair. Nonetheless, the difference between trying to be educative and actually being educative turns, in part, on the success of the effort.

This said, it must be asked if being educative can legitimately be called a virtue of cultures and their institutions, and being miseducative a vice. To answer this, one has only to reflect upon the property of miseducativeness as exemplified by individuals. Think for a moment of Charles Dickens's *Oliver Twist*. Fagin is an arch villain not simply because he is a thief and kidnapper of boys, although he is both. His most unforgivable sin is that he is a miseducator of boys: he trains the young lads he has kidnapped to be thieves. Think of Dickens's *Great Expectations*. Miss Havisham is the personification of evil not so much because she herself hates men as because she passes down that hatred to her young ward Estella. And now think of Muriel Sparks's *The Prime of Miss Jean Brodie*. If self-absorption is one of Jean Brodie's sins, a far greater one is that she tries so hard, and with notable success, to transmit to "her girls" her own love of fascism.

Literary works are not alone in attesting to the fact that being miseducative is a vice for individuals. When, in everyday life, we say that person X is a bad influence on person Y, what we usually mean is that X, whether intentionally or not, is passing along, as a living legacy to Y, what we take to be a cultural liability; or else that X is encouraging Y to acquire one or another liability as a living legacy by creating a desire—or perhaps inflaming an already existing but latent desire—to do so.

Given that it is wrong for individuals to engage in miseducative behavior, it would seem to be equally wrong for groups and institutions to do so. It makes no sense to blame Miss Havisham for passing down her hatred of men to one young girl or Fagin for turning a score or so of young boys into thieves if, at the same time, we view with equanimity groups and institutions that pass down cultural liabilities to hundreds or thousands or even millions of people. To be sure, disputes over which items of stock are assets and which are liabilities are inevitable in pluralistic cultures. But this is true in the case of individuals as well as institutions, and in neither instance does it militate against our calling educativeness a virtue.

If there were no examples of widespread agreement about the status of particular items of stock, there might be no point in demanding that institutions and cultures be educative. But, even in as diverse a culture as the U.S., there are broad areas of agreement. This is not to say that there is ever unanimity. But unanimity is not required in decisions about a culture's assets and liabilities. Thus, for instance, although people may differ as to whether a murder has occurred, few would consider murder to be a cultural asset; although they may try to justify torture in wartime as a necessary evil, few would consider it an item of cultural wealth; and, although they may say that some poverty is inevitable in contemporary societies, few would deny that it is a cultural liability.

It may be wondered if it is fair to blame institutions or cultures for being miseducative when they are pursuing legitimate ends such as selling automobiles, entertaining audiences, or making money for shareholders and do not engage in this behavior intentionally. Certainly, intention is a relevant consideration, just as it is in the case of individuals. If Miss Havisham had accidentally turned Estella into a hater of men, Dickens would probably not have represented her as the personification of evil. If a school unknowingly fosters cheating in its students, so long as it mends its ways when it finds out, it probably should not be blamed. But groups and institutions sometimes do engage in miseducation intentionally and, when they do, blame may well be an appropriate response. Moreover, if an individual or an institution knows from past experience that certain practices tend to transmit cultural liabilities and yet continues to employ these practices, blame may once again be appropriate.

Blame is not the only relevant issue, however. For, even if a group or institution is not to blame for the miseducation it produces, to the extent that it transmits cultural liabilities it will have failed to exemplify the virtue of educativeness. And that, in itself, is important to know.

In view of the fact that Rawls gave justice pride of place among the virtues of institutions, the question remains if educativeness is distinct from justice or if just institutions are necessarily educative. Will institutions that embody Rawls's principles of justice necessarily pass down cultural assets? Will they prevent cultural liabilities from becoming yoked to human capacities in harmful ways, or at least seek to minimize the likelihood of this eventuality?

Given that Rawls put forward a theory of distributive justice, one should not expect to find in it a mechanism for ensuring that institutions be educative. All that would seem to be required is that his theory take into account the fair distribution of both cultural assets and cultural liabilities. Yet, if justice as fairness does not entail educativeness, was Rawls correct to call it "the" first—as opposed to "one" or "a"—virtue of institutions?

Consider that institutions possessing the virtue of educativeness, but lacking the virtue of justice, could, with impunity, pass down all the culture's liabilities to one individual or to a single class of individuals. This might seem to make justice "the" primary virtue of institutions, for it is an unacceptable situation if there ever was one. However, that claim to special status fades in the face of the fact that institutions embodying the virtue of justice, but not the virtue of educativeness, could, in the name of fairness, pass down to everyone only the culture's liabilities: a situation as malevolent as the other is unfair.

It is not necessary to debate the relative merits of unjust and malevolent institutions here, however. Rather than committing itself to the existence of a single first or most important virtue, the theory of education as encounter simply acknowledges that there are at least two "first" or most important virtues of institutions—educativeness and justice.

2. The Immunization Strategy

Imagine now a culture whose members live forever and into which no new generations are born. Imagine that this culture's stock is entirely composed of cultural assets. And imagine that this culture's educational agents all act in good faith in yoking the wealth in their keep to people's capacities. In such a culture, there would be no such thing as miseducation; hence, there would be no reason to take seriously the virtue of educativeness.

Actual cultures possess very different characteristics, however. In actual cultures, generations die off and new ones take their place, the stock of actual cultures includes both assets and liabilities, and that stock is in the keep of a multiplicity of educational agents who cannot be relied on to yoke as many assets and as few liabilities as possible to people's capacities. In other words, in actual cultures, the virtue of educativeness is something to be achieved, not taken for granted. Furthermore, because individual capacities, a culture's stock, and a culture's educational agents are forever changing, eternal vigilance is required.

In the 1920s, German sociologist Karl Mannheim analyzed the different approaches taken historically to the fact that generations come and go. For Mannheim, who did not take into account the transmission of cultural liabilities from one generation to the next, "the problem of generations" was strictly sociological.[3] When, however, this issue is taken into account and the phenomenon of multiple educational agency is acknowledged, the problem of generations becomes educational.[4] Indeed, it can be seen to be identical with the problem of how the virtue of educativeness is to be achieved; or, conversely, how miseducation's twin sins of omission and commission are to be avoided.

Is it not possible to educate children so that their capacities fail to attach to cultural liabilities and then ignore the virtue of educativeness with impunity? After all, scientists and physicians do not attack an offending virus directly. They seek to prevent people from getting it and trust that, insofar as immunization programs are successful, the disease will be eradicated. Cannot miseducation's sin of commission be avoided by "immunizing" people against cultural liabilities when they are very young, much as they are immunized against smallpox?

The pedagogical experiment that Rousseau carried out in *Emile* is a classic example of an immunization strategy. Believing that society's institutions are miseducative, in his imagination he removed the boy Emile from his home and family at birth and placed him in the hands of an all-seeing, all-powerful tutor named Jean-Jacques, whose job it was to control every detail of the child's daily existence. In other words, Rousseau's strategy was to see that Emile was educated so that only cultural assets would become yoked to his capacities, and then to hope for the best when the boy re-entered society, as in Rousseau's scenario he eventually would.

Like other immunization approaches to miseducation, Rousseau's addresses only the sin of commission. In addition, his plan has a fatal flaw. Having been raised in what amounts to a laboratory situation—a relatively closed system on which the real world only occasionally impinges—and having been given little, if any, knowledge of how to recognize error and vice, let alone how to avoid these when encountered, Emile will not know how to cope with the wide array of educational agents bent on transmitting the culture's liabilities as well as its assets. Cannot Jean-Jacques teach the boy how to cope? Not in Rousseau's experiment. Emile's childhood is to be spent in a veritable Garden of Eden in the company of his tutor, a man intent on keeping from him the knowledge that cultural liabilities even exist.

The Amish in the U.S. employ a different version of the immunization strategy, one that avoids Rousseau's error. A religious sect whose rules cover well nigh every aspect of human behavior and for whom separation from the world is a basic tenet,[5] the Amish are perhaps best known for their piety, pacifism, rejection of modern technology, and distinctive dress. Their relevance to a discussion of the educativeness and miseducativeness of institutions stems, however, from the fact that they represent an experiment in living—if one can call a way of life that originated some 300 years ago an "experiment"—that deals daily with the problem of how to protect children's capacities from becoming attached to the mainstream culture's liabilities.

Just as Rousseau constructed a wall of separation between Emile and the culture's liabilities, the Amish create one between their members and the liabilities of the larger culture. Their wall is more porous than the one Rousseau envisions in that the Amish frequently interact with those on the outside.[6] However, their horses and buggies and their dress create a distance between themselves and others. Furthermore, whereas Emile departs his Garden of Eden forever upon reaching adulthood, the Amish live all their lives behind their wall. In effect, then, theirs is a lifelong immunization process.

The Amish experiment also resembles Rousseau's in that it is premised on the assumption that with the proper upbringing a person will withstand the culture's liabilities. The two ideas of what constitutes a good or moral individual are worlds apart, however. The Amish place a premium on obedience, submission, and humility—all traits or dispositions that Rousseau abhorred. "Let the child do nothing on anybody's word," said Rousseau.[7] "Consider what a head we are putting on his shoulders. In all that he will see, in all that he will do, he will want to know everything; he will want to learn the reason for everything . . . he will accept no assumption."[8] Amish children, on the other hand, are not only taught unquestioning obedience to parents and church. They are brought up to believe that the critical thinking and independent decision-making that Rousseau so admired, and that he wanted Emile's education to foster, are signs of arrogance.

In the humility that the Amish prize, there is no place for thinking and acting on one's own and no place for "book learning" either. Believing that the knowledge to be found in books other than the Bible and those they themselves write comes from pride and disobedience to God and leads to sin and moral corruption,[9] the Amish view it as perhaps the most dangerous cultural liability of them all. "I hate books,"[10] wrote Rousseau, but he did not hate the kind of knowledge and the theoretical understanding they contain. He simply did not want the written word to be a substitute for a child's own first-hand experience. Valuing practical knowledge—especially agricultural skills—but condemning other kinds, the Amish place science, history, literature, philosophy, and the like outside their Garden of Eden. Afraid of what will happen to their children if they are exposed to the various intellectual disciplines, they limit schooling to the elementary grades, disparage both secondary and higher education, and otherwise try to keep the capacities of their members from becoming yoked to the theoretical knowledge that has been amassed by the outside world over the centuries.

Still, although Rousseau and the Amish disagree about what counts as miseducation, both versions of the immunization strategy seek to protect the young from the perceived evils of the world and refrain from educating them to remedy those evils. Emile's education is supposed to keep his capacities from linking up with the culture's liabilities. It is not designed to turn him into a social reformer. Similarly, the Amish strive to protect their own from the perceived wickedness of the outside world while leaving its institutions as they find them.

This is not to say that either Rousseau's or the Amish version of the immunization strategy dispenses with the virtue of educativeness. Although they take the miseducativeness of the culture outside the wall as a given, both Rousseau and the Amish go to extraordinary lengths to ensure that the culture inside the wall of separation is what they consider educative. Rousseau gives Jean-Jacques total control over Emile's education and expects him to know what the boy is doing at every moment of the day and night; which is, in effect, to say that he attributes to the tutor the attributes of omnipotence, omniscience, and omnipresence that are usually reserved for God. The Amish, in their turn, exercise control over almost every aspect of their members' lives, instill in their young the belief that the outside world is evil and corrupt, and employ a system of sanctions and punishments ranging from admonitions by a deacon to excommunication and shunning for life.[11]

3. The Blue-Pencil Strategy

Like Rousseau, Plato wanted to protect children from miseducation, but the approach he took in the *Republic* consisted in removing whatever cultural stock he considered harmful from the culture as a whole, rather than in moving children away from that stock. Thus, re-entry was no problem for Plato. Instead of proposing that the young be reared in a separate purified environment, he wanted to purify the entire culture.

Curiously enough, although justice is the subject of Plato's most famous dialogue, there is but one listing for Plato in the index of Rawls's *A Theory of Justice*, and it refers the reader to a footnote in which Rawls rejects all recourse to devices such as Plato's Noble Lie. In relation to the theory of education as encounter, however, the main point of interest in Plato's account of justice is that it takes the problem of the miseducativeness of institutions seriously.

Whereas the idea of a fair distribution of benefits and burdens lies at the center of Rawls's theory of justice, Plato's theory turns on the idea of a smooth functioning society. In his eyes, the virtue of justice consists in each class of people—the rulers, the warriors, and the artisans—doing their own job and no other. Keenly aware that a culture's stock includes liabilities as well as assets, and convinced that the poets and storytellers of his day were yoking liabilities to the capacities of the young, Plato considered miseducation a formidable obstacle to the achievement of justice.

Think what will happen, said Plato, if children's capacities become yoked to the cultural stock of cowardice and fear of dying. When those children are grown, the people who are supposed to defend the state from its enemies will instead flee from battle and shrink from death. Their miseducation will, in other words, result in their failure to perform the function assigned them; and this, in turn, means that the state will not be just.

In Plato's philosophy, a miseducative society is an unjust society, which is tantamount to saying that, in his eyes, the virtue of justice presupposes the virtue of educativeness. Although he could have addressed the problem of miseducation in the way Rousseau later did, he chose instead to recommend that the offending cultural stock be banished from the state as a whole. Remarking in the *Republic* that the beginning of any process is most important[12] and that the young cannot distinguish what is allegorical from what is not,[13] Socrates called for the expunging of the offending stories.

At first glance, Plato's "blue-pencil strategy" appears to rest on a naive imitation theory of learning: tell children stories of heroes running from battle and, when they grow up, they will run from battle; tell them stories about the gods quarreling and, when those destined to be rulers grow up, they will quarrel among themselves. This reading is inaccurate, however, for the reproduction of depicted behavior is only one of many kinds of learning he had in mind. In the *Republic*, Socrates recognizes that a child who is told a story might well imitate the hero's actions. But he also indicates that a child who does not copy the hero's behavior is apt to acquire the belief that this behavior represents the norm or standard for all people, and he further suggests that a story might affect a child's feelings and emotions.

In the twenty-first century, many are inclined to say that the Socratic Hypothesis that stories can affect children adversely has been confirmed and applies equally to adults. By the year 2000, a review of research on the impact of media violence had reported that the vast majority of studies concurred that media violence has harmful effects.[14] Studies had claimed that a feeling that threats abound in the outside world is common among television viewers of all ages, and that viewers who watch more than three hours of television a day are more likely than others to "feel at high risk of victimization from violence, take their neighborhoods to be unsafe, and regard the world as 'mean and gloomy'."[15] A survey had reported that those under the age of 30 who are "heavy consumers" of violent programming and movies are less bothered by violence on television and less likely than others to feel that violence is harmful to society.[16]

The charge made against the popular early twenty-first-century television program "24" that, in glorifying torture, the first six seasons of the show adversely affected both the attitudes of cadets at West Point, the United States Military Academy, and the behavior of soldiers in Iraq, indicates in its turn that the Socratic Hypothesis cannot be dismissed as a dead relic. "I think people can differentiate between a television show and reality," said "24"'s lead writer[17] but the Dean of West Point and other military officers were not so sure. Apparently, the name of Jack Bauer, the program's heroic U.S. counter-terrorism agent, was frequently mentioned in classes at West Point. After watching Bauer repeatedly administer torture to the suspects in "ticking-time-bomb" plots, cadets protested, "If torture is wrong, what about 24?"[18] And a West Point colonel reportedly said, "Oh, my god! '24' is one of the biggest problems I have in teaching my classes. Everybody wants to be like Jack Bauer. They all think that it may be possible or there are times when you should have to cross the line."[19] An army interrogator in the war in Iraq, in turn, told a reporter, "People watch the shows, and then walk into the interrogation booths and do the same things they've just seen."[20]

Actually, the studies that appear to support the Socratic Hypothesis have all been disputed. No one denies that stories depicting cultural liabilities such as violence are repeatedly being told. The skeptics simply challenge the claim that they do any harm. Indeed, they take to task practically everything about the research: the definitions employed, the reasoning, the statistics, the methodologies, and, above all, the claims to objectivity.[21] As for the cadets' apparent approval of the extreme methods of torture shown on "24," a skeptic would doubtlessly dismiss those reports as "mere" anecdotal evidence and point out that the army interrogator had failed to demonstrate a causal connection between a soldier's watching a television show and committing acts of torture.

Since the validity of research into the harmful effects of stories and images is not easily determined, it is fortunate that this is not a matter that the theory of education as encounter has to decide. Whether or not the Socratic Hypothesis is ultimately confirmed, it tacitly acknowledges what is so often denied, namely that culture is curriculum. In effect, it affirms that the cultural practices, beliefs, skills, and the like that the storytellers yoke to human capacities constitute the content of the curriculum of young and old.

The theory of education as encounter explains why Plato was concerned about the messages that are transmitted by a culture's storytellers and image-makers and why we should be too. Indeed, because of the huge technological developments that make the stories and images transmitted today so much more vivid than they used to be, one would expect us to be far more concerned than Plato or Socrates ever were. However, our theory makes it clear that, in the case of stories and images, miseducation's sin of commission poses two great dangers, not one: the harm that they do and the harm done by expunging them. If critics of the Socratic Hypothesis seem intent on minimizing the damage that stories and images can do, it is because they recognize the perils inherent in the blue-pencil strategy.

It is one thing to praise Plato for recognizing that educativeness is a virtue of institutions and quite another to approve his or any other program of censorship. In the first place, a denizen of the twenty-first century must wonder if, in an age of instant global communication, constant international political and economic interaction, and the continual migration of people, knowledge, and goods across national borders, a policy of purging a culture of its liabilities could possibly succeed. To keep out the offending items of stock, would not the culture in question have to be sealed off from its environs rather as Gilman sealed off Herland and as the Amish seal off themselves?

The practical difficulties facing a blue-pencil strategy like Plato's are the least of the matter, however. A far more basic problem is that his program of censorship is rooted in an untenable epistemology. Attributing infallibility to the knowledge of The Good that rulers of his Just State would presumably acquire through their strenuous philosophical education, he took it for granted that their decisions about which stories to eliminate and which to promote could not be mistaken. However, as John Stuart Mill argued so eloquently in *On Liberty*, no matter how rational and how well educated a human being is, every single one of us is fallible. Thus, regardless of how much research is carried out and how sophisticated it is, we can always be mistaken. To be sure, one or many individuals may experience a psychological state of certainty that a given story or image will harm those who encounter it, but feelings of certainty are not to be confused with the fact of the matter.

It should be noted that, in Plato's eyes, it made no difference if a story was true or false. One of the military's main objections to the torture shown on "24" was that, although Jack Bauer usually manages to extract whatever information his victims have, in real life, torture does not work. For Plato, however, what mattered was not a story's truthfulness but its effect on its audience: the changes in them that would be brought about by their encounters with these items of cultural stock. Moreover, although he had Socrates confine his discussion of censorship to literature and music, we can rest assured that he would have extended his program to include pictures. Thus, a latter-day Plato would not only deny us *War and Peace* because, for example, it depicts Nikolay Rostov, a hero on the battlefield, as confused and full of doubt.[22] He would rule out not just "24" but photographs and films of Allied soldiers weeping when, entering the German concentration camps at the end of World War II, they came face to face with the inmates; Vietnam veterans in the clutches of post traumatic stress syndrome; U.S. military personnel torturing Iraqi War prisoners; and perhaps even the mushroom clouds over Hiroshima and Nagasaki.

In *On Liberty*, Mill did not have pictures on his mind either. But in defining his topic as the "Liberty of Thought" and in discussing the "free expression of opinion," he effectively included them within his compass, for pictures, as well as speech, can express truths and falsehoods. "If all mankind minus one were of one opinion," wrote Mill, "mankind would be no more justified in silencing that one person than he, if he had the power, would be justified in silencing mankind."[23] And, he continued:

> the peculiar evil of silencing the expression of an opinion is that it is robbing the human race, posterity as well as the existing generation—those who dissent from the opinion, still more than those who hold it. If the opinion is right, they are deprived of the opportunity of exchanging error for truth; if wrong, they lose, what is almost as great a benefit, the clearer perception and livelier impression of truth produced by its collision with error.[24]

4. A False Dichotomy: Censorship or Laissez-Faire

For those who value liberty of thought, Mill's defense might seem to rule out the blue-pencil strategy, but two statements in Chapter 1 of *On Liberty* militate against this reading. There, he said: "the only purpose over which power can be rightfully exercised over any member of a civilized community, against his will, is to prevent harm to others."[25] He continued: "Those who are still in a state to require being taken care of by others must be protected against their own actions as well as against external injury."[26]

In light of the acknowledgement by one of history's greatest defenders of freedom of thought that it is acceptable for a government or community to take action to prevent harm to others, it is understandable why opponents of censorship are so quick to challenge research on the harm that stories and images do both children and adults. To be sure, Mill simply said that doing harm justifies intervention; he did not say that it mandates it. Nor did he say that the intervention had to take the form of suppressing the expression of opinion. Still, the skeptics make the tacit assumption that, once it is shown that harm is done, censorship is bound to follow.

Mill did not address the question of how to protect children. Thus, we do not know if he would approve of a blue-pencil strategy for them while condemning it for their parents—assuming it is established that the stories and images passed down by the media and other educational agents do children harm. What is clear, however, is that twenty-first-century children have such easy access to portions of cultural stock judged by their elders to be liabilities that a blue-pencil strategy would require a monitoring of their daily existence, rivaling in intensity that which Rousseau envisioned for Emile.[27] Yet, in cultures where both men and women leave home to go to work and the electronic media have permeated the walls of the presumed sanctuary of the private home, the belief that children can be monitored every waking moment of their lives is unfounded. Few families are apt to have a godlike person at their command whose sole duty is to watch over the children 24 hours a day from birth to adulthood.

Furthermore, to the extent that around-the-clock monitoring of a culture's young is possible, it must be asked how suitable an Orwellian "Big Brother is watching" policy is for children who must one day live in a culture filled with liabilities. Having had no experience of such stock, when they finally encounter it, they will not have learned how to prevent it from attaching to their capacities; on the contrary, they may more easily succumb to its lures. Worse still, with Big Brother dictating how they should act and what they should believe, they will not know how to think, act, or make wise decisions independently.

To be sure, autonomous thought and action are the goals Rousseau had in mind for Emile's education when he instituted his Big Brother policy. But *Emile* is a poor guide for assessing the blue-pencil policy for children. Because Rousseau was conducting an experiment in imagination, he was able to excise what he took to be his culture's liabilities by a stroke of the pen. Emile's tutor does not have to censor the discourse in the boy's environment, keep him away from undesirable companions, and restrict his sphere of action. Rousseau's thought experiment has done all this for him.

In this electronic age, children breathe in cultural liabilities with the air. Is racism the cultural stock to be avoided? Is it misogyny? To keep these from becoming yoked to children's capacities, access to music, radio, television, the Internet would all have to be curtailed, as would interactions with neighbors and strangers alike. Indeed, Big Brother might have to keep children away from playgrounds and even off the streets where they live. Is the cultural liability sexual profligacy? Here, Big Brother's watchfulness would have to know no bounds.

One can well imagine that, in the process of removing cultural liabilities from children's lives, Big Brother would find it necessary to introduce the fear of reprisals into the air they breathe. As for yoking independent thought and action to children's capacities, one suspects that Big Brother would be far more likely to assume that these were cultural liabilities, not assets. Be this as it may, *Emile* is also a poor guide to blue-penciling for children because it fosters the illusion that Emile will grow up to be the very model of an autonomous man. It is not obvious, however, that the adult Emile will be an independent thinker and actor. Never having been exposed to authoritarian political creeds and religious dogmas, he will have been given no defenses against their lures. Having lived under the benign but manipulative rule of his tutor for every moment of every day, he may feel far more comfortable in adulthood functioning as someone else's marionette than as a self-governing person.

Yet, what alternatives are there to a blue-pencil strategy for children if one wishes to protect them from the miseducative tendencies of the educational agents in their midst? Immunization strategies such as those advocated by Rousseau or the Amish do not fit the bill, for they are really special cases of the blue-pencil strategy. Just as the philosopher kings in Plato's Just State are assigned the task of censoring the stories that do harm to children, Jean-Jacques and the ministers and deacons of the Amish must edit them out of their charges' lives. The difference is that, in the latter instances, the censors erect a wall of separation between their charges and the outside world and use their blue pencils only within its confines.[28]

It might seem as if those who give credence to the Socratic Hypothesis but also agree with Mill's defense of liberty of thought are left with two stark options: either allow the vice of miseducation to flourish or impose a thoroughgoing system of censorship. There is, however, no need to choose between a censor's blue pencil and a policy of noninterference where the culture's liabilities are concerned, for there is a middle way between the two extremes.

To be sure, a miseducational sin of commission involves the transmission of cultural liabilities. But cultural stock can attach to an individual's capacities in countless different ways, only some of which do harm. When the stock represents information—for instance, that the Nazis exterminated approximately 6 million Jews—it can become yoked to capacities in the form of a belief; in the form of a feeling or emotion such as abhorrence or fear; in the form of empathy for the victims; in the form of a desire to emulate the Nazis; and so on. Similarly, when the stock is a human practice such as domestic violence, it can attach to capacities as, for example, a more or less automatic habit or a form of intelligent, albeit misguided, behavior.

At the beginning of this chapter, miseducation's sin of commission was characterized as the yoking of cultural liabilities to individual capacities, but this is an oversimplification. To be more precise, miseducation occurs when an educational agent intends to yoke or does yoke one or more cultural liabilities to individual capacities in a form that contributes to the preservation of the liability *as a living legacy*. Conversely, that same educational agent is educative rather than miseducative if it seeks to yoke or does yoke one or more cultural liabilities and individual capacities together so as to transform what is or once was a living legacy into a *dead relic*.

In sum, miseducation's sin of commission is not a simple process of the transmission of cultural stock. It is the more complex one of the linking up of cultural liabilities with individual capacities in ways that do harm: harm to the culture by perpetuating, as living legacies, portions of stock that should either be discarded or else transformed into dead relics; and harm to individuals by equipping them with unpalatable traits and dispositions.

It follows that those who seek to protect children—or adults, for that matter—do not need to expunge the offending stories and images, for there is an alternative to censorship. A middle way can be pursued in which interventions in the educational process either prevent the coupling of cultural liabilities and human capacities or yoke up the two in a manner that does no harm. It goes without saying that this middle way is not always easy to achieve and does not guarantee 100 percent success. But censorship comes with no such assurance either.

5. Middle-Way Strategies

For a good example of a middle-way strategy, one need look no further than at what parents do when they read or tell stories to their children. Acting as interpreters of the text—or, if you will, as mediators between child and text—they explain, clarify, and elaborate upon one or another aspect of a story in order to allay a young child's fears of the villain of the piece, draw out a story's moral, or simply let the child know that "It's just pretend."

Consider the books about the elephant Babar that have been read to and by children across the world since the first one in the series was published in 1931. Critics have called them elitist, colonialist, and racist, and have said that they should be withheld from children.[29] The charges can, of course, be challenged, and the question of whether the proposal to withhold the book amounts to censorship is also open to debate. But supposing, for the sake of argument, that the books do contain potentially damaging messages, a middle-way strategy suggests itself.

Calls for censorship assume that a child's encounter with *Babar* necessarily resembles young Ed Wilson's encounter with the jellyfish—except that racial stereotypes and elitist attitudes, rather than a burgeoning scientific curiosity, will become yoked to the child's capacities. But this scenario is not inevitable. Be it home, school, library, bookstore, television, or the Internet, the educational agent responsible for the encounter with *Babar* can proceed to act as a mediator between the child and the text. And, if it fails to do so, other educational agents can enter the scene and create brand new educational encounters for the child; ones that block or counteract the unwanted yokings of stock. Thus, for example, they can deconstruct the drawings of cannibals and savages for the child, expose the race and gender stereotypes, and critique the colonialism that the books appear to endorse.

What qualifies as good mediation will, of course, depend on the child; or, more precisely, on what cultural stock has already become yoked to the child's capacities and on the form that yoking has taken. For a very young child, it might suffice to point to the drawings in the *Babar* books and say, "See these pictures. Don't the people in them look silly? They are make-believe." For a slightly older child, good mediation might involve explaining that people in Africa do not look like the figures in the illustrations and do not do the things portrayed therein, and showing the child photographs to prove the point. For an even older child, it might be appropriate to raise the presumed hidden curriculum of the *Babar* books to the level of consciousness: to talk about racism and sexism in language the child can understand; and to try, with the child's help, to figure out what in the book might lead people to call it racist or sexist.

As the case of "24" indicates, mediation can be undertaken for adults as well as children. In 2006, the Dean at West Point, together with several experienced military interrogators, met with the creators of the show. Presumably, their hope was that "24" would modify the way torture was represented. Whether or not it did so to their satisfaction is not really the concern here. For us, the point of interest is that they requested help in what was, in effect, an attempt to mediate the show for the cadets. In particular, they wanted to convince them: that "24" was fiction, that actual occasions for torture seldom arise in "ticking-time-bomb" situations, and that, in fact, torture rarely, if ever, works. As a result of the meeting, the star of "24" agreed to visit West Point to discuss with the cadets why torture is wrong[30] and the lead writer agreed to be filmed for a video being produced by a human rights organization for showing at West Point and elsewhere.[31]

Mediation resembles the immunization strategy in that its object is to prevent people's capacities from attaching to cultural liabilities in the form of living legacies. But, instead of banning stories and images that portray a given liability, this middle-way approach seeks to neutralize the power of the stories to do harm. Furthermore, young and old alike can learn to be their own mediators; that is, to be self-educators when encountering potentially harmful stories. The educational agents in their lives can yoke cultural stock to their capacities that enables them to detect for themselves and to neutralize the cultural liabilities that a given image or story might otherwise transmit. Indeed, insofar as they acquire the tendency to engage in mediation, this strategy would seem to offer more protection than censorship against the onslaught of the cultural liabilities that fill the air around them.

Mediation is but one middle-way strategy. Another is the proliferation of stories and images designed either to prevent some cultural liability from yoking to children's capacities or to weaken an already existing coupling. Aesop's *Fables* and Heinrich Hoffmann's *Der Stuwwelpeter* are classic examples of this approach, and it is also the strategy that pressure groups embrace when they lobby for non-violent "child-friendly" television programming. Parents and teachers, in their turn, adopt it when, for example, they teach the children in their care to convert their superhero play so that the characters they assume are flying around helping people instead of killing monsters and terrorizing the community.

In general, if the culture breathed in with the air is filled with stories and images that portray a cultural asset such as honesty as the norm and present it in a favorable light, the existence of a few isolated yokings to individual capacities of that asset's opposite, namely the cultural liability of dishonesty, will be of no great concern. Granted, it is always possible for a single encounter with a story to bring about the yoking of a cultural liability to a child's capacities as a living legacy. Then again, censorship does not provide absolute protection against potentially damaging stories and images either. When, however, stories and images that portray some cultural liability as exciting and attractive or as the norm saturate the air people breathe in, the problem of generations can become acute. This is when censorship exerts its pull. But it is also when the middle-way strategy of proliferating stories and images having the potential to counteract the ones that do harm would seem to be a promising option.

One precondition for the success of strategies that turn occasions for imposing censorship into opportunities to launch genuinely educative practices is acceptance by all and sundry of the existence of multiple educational agents. It is thus worth noting that neither the critics of "24" nor commentators in the press appeared to consider the possibility that television is an educational agent and that what was happening to the cadets, the soldiers in the field, and who knows how many members of the program's multimillion audience was miseducation. Yet, the fact that television was functioning as an educational agent was precisely the issue that motivated the meeting.

The problem "24" posed West Point was that the show was attaching beliefs, attitudes, and value to the cadets' capacities that were undermining the military academy's educational goal of persuading cadets that torture is illegal, immoral, and ineffective. In the case of soldiers in Iraq, the problem "24" posed was slightly different, but no less one of education—albeit of the miseducative variety. According to a military interrogator, he and his cohort had been trained to follow the Geneva Conventions but, upon their arrival in Iraq, the U.S. administration had led them to believe that the rules did not apply to their situation. Into the breach—or, if you prefer, into the educational vacuum—stepped "24." In the interrogator's words, "we had no training, basically on what we were supposed to do, what our limits were . . . And so we turned to television."[32]

Our theory makes it clear that miseducation can be perpetrated by any educational agent, and can occur anywhere and at any time. The challenge for those who would eradicate it by following the middle way is to ensure that educational agents of all stripes make the virtue of educativeness their own. Of course, it would be a mistake to rely purely on the good intentions of institutions whose primary objectives are to entertain the public or sell cars or maximize profits, and so on. Thus, the challenge is also to convince the culture as a whole that, whatever else a publishing company, a television network, a museum, a bank, an Internet company, a website, a supermarket, a governmental department, may be: it is also an educational agent that should be held accountable for what it does.

Is it unfair to hold one educational agent such as a television show responsible for yoking cultural liabilities to individual capacities when other educational agents do the same thing? If the claim were that this particular agent was the *only* one doing harm, the argument would be valid. But shared responsibility is still responsibility. To hold one educational agent accountable for the miseducation it brings about is not to deny that other educational agents might also be held accountable. Moreover, although it is unrealistic to rely exclusively on the good intentions of groups and institutions, just as some corporations have begun to take seriously the pollution of the atmosphere and to change their technologies accordingly,[33] so some educational agents can be expected to take seriously the virtue of educativeness and their own complicity in the problem of miseducation.

Interestingly enough, reports of the discussion between the military and the creators of "24" suggest that, in the course of the meeting, the TV people began to take into account the unintended consequences of their show. To be sure, one man reported that the "24" people "were a bit prickly. They have this money-making machine, and we were telling them it's immoral."[34] Yet, calling the meeting "an eye-opener," a representative of "24" said, "We hadn't really thought a lot about torture as anything more than a dramatic device."

6. Addressing the Sin of Omission

Miseducation is, however, a compound vice. Hence, charting a middle way between a do-nothing stance and censorship does not address the second aspect of the problem of generations, namely how to maximize the yoking to the next generation's capacities of the culture's assets. When, for example, farmers stop yoking the old agricultural knowledge, skills, attitudes, and perspectives to the capacities of their sons and daughters; when home stops yoking the three Cs of care, concern, and connection to its young; when local communities stop yoking the virtues of kindness to the elderly and neighborliness to the disadvantaged: what is to be done?

If an educational agent shows signs of no longer being able to yoke the cultural assets in its keep to the capacities of its designated beneficiaries, one obvious course of action is to try to persuade or force it to mend its ways. This, indeed, is what the American colonies attempted. Thus, Bernard Bailyn reports:

> Within a remarkably short time after the beginnings of settlement it was realized that the family was failing in its more obvious educational functions. In the early 1640's both Virginia and Massachusetts officially stated their dissatisfactions in the passage of what have since become known as the first American laws concerning education.[35]

These and similar laws reminded families of their educational duties and threatened punishment for irresponsibility.

Large-scale social, economic, and technical forces often make it impossible to stem the tide, however. In such cases, a more effective strategy may be to find or invent a substitute educational agent—a functional equivalent, as it were—to shoulder those aspects of the role that the original agent is no longer able to carry out. The Puritans did just this when, in the 1640s, they "quite deliberately transferred the maimed functions of the family to formal instructional institutions."[36] It is also what Dewey did when he proposed that work be placed at the center of the school curriculum and what Montessori did when she established her Casa dei Bambini in Rome.[37]

For the "functional-equivalency" strategy to bear fruit, one or more individuals must perceive that a given group or institution has undergone radical change; and must realize that, in consequence, it is no longer able to carry out its educational responsibilities. The strategy also calls upon the ability to envision a group or institution in an unaccustomed role, and a willingness to create new agents if such are necessary. This latter is, for example, what Jane Addams and Ellen Starr Gates did in Chicago when, in 1889, they established Hull House, a settlement that was to serve as a replacement for the close-knit, social, supportive, educative environment that the local community no longer was.

The case of the United States Department of Agriculture's Extension Service demonstrates, however, that it is not always possible to find a functional equivalent for an existing educational agent. In 1862, U.S. President Abraham Lincoln signed the Morrill Act, establishing at least one college in each state whose mission was to teach agriculture and "mechanic arts," along with the liberal arts and sciences, to "the people."[38] Twenty-five years later, Congress supplemented the Morrill Act with the Hatch Act, authorizing the establishment of experiment stations that were to be connected to the Land Grant schools. As the mission of the Land Grant colleges and universities was to teach agriculture and mechanic arts, theirs was to carry out research in those areas. And then, in 1914, the Congress passed the Smith-Lever Act, establishing the Extension Service that was supposed to diffuse "among the people of the United States useful and practical information on subjects relating to agriculture and home economics, and to encourage the application of the same."

The extension work authorized by the Smith-Lever Act was to be carried out in connection with the Land Grant schools and was to consist of instruction and practical demonstrations. At first thought, one might wonder why a new educational agent was needed. Perhaps the experiment stations were not designed to transmit the knowledge they were producing directly to farmers, but did not the Morrill Act take care of this problem? On the contrary, although the stated mission of the Land Grant schools was to teach agriculture, the designated beneficiaries of the cultural stock in their keep were not for the most part farmers who were then at work in the fields. As the Smith-Lever Act, in effect, acknowledged when it said that the extension work was for "persons not attending or resident in said colleges," the creation of a new educational agent was essential for this population.[39]

Like Hull House, the Extension Service was established to satisfy a perceived cultural need. What were considered to be important cultural assets were not becoming yoked to the capacities of the nation's farm population; in consequence, the designated beneficiaries were deprived of valuable knowledge, skills, and technology, and the stock itself was at increasing risk of extinction. In contrast to Hull House, a new institution that was meant to play a role that a pre-existing educational agent—namely the local community—had been playing, the Extension Service was meant to fill a new niche; that is to say, to carry out a function that no agent had previously performed.

But now consider the Norse Settlement in Greenland where, from AD 984 to some time in the 1400s, Scandinavians built a thriving community that then vanished. Why, asked Jared Diamond, did they ultimately fail to master Greenland's problem whereas the Inuits, who inhabited the same land from about 1200, succeeded?[40]

The Norse case stands in stark contrast to that of the Extension Service. In the latter instance, the cultural assets—namely the knowledge and skills having to do with agriculture and mechanical arts—existed and the beneficiaries of this cultural wealth had been named. All that was missing was an educational agent that would link the two together. In the Norse case, the culture's educational agents—its families, churches, and so on—did not possess the assets that were desperately needed if the culture was to survive. Practices such as using blubber for heating and lighting, using sealskins to build kayaks, and constructing housing out of snow that had long been yoked to the capacities of the Inuit were not included in the portfolios of any of its educational agents.

Does a culture's failure to yoke assets to individual capacities qualify as miseducation when those assets do not even belong to that culture? Just how far must a culture go to acquire the cultural stock that needs to be yoked to its members' capacities if its educational agents are to escape the charge of being miseducative? These questions do not have to be decided here, but in light of the fact that the needed items of stock did indeed belong to the neighboring Inuit culture, it must be asked why the Norse did not beg, borrow, steal, or reinvent them. Were their capacities yoked to cultural stock that prevented them from appropriating for themselves the stock belonging to another culture?

A willingness to change one's ways, the belief that a culture other than one's own can possess stock of value, and an appreciation of the possible value of another culture's stock for one's own culture would seem to be prerequisites for the begging, borrowing, stealing, and reinventing that the Norse were apparently loath to do. But whatever steps one thinks an educational agent should take in order to acquire the items of cultural stock it needs, to the extent that the Norse believed that the practices they had imported from Europe comprised the one right way, and to the extent that they denigrated Inuit practices that might have solved their problems, one can judge their various educational agents to have been miseducative.

Writing to his brother William in 1867, novelist Henry James said that Americans "have exquisite qualities" in that "we can deal freely with forms of civilization not our own, can pick and choose and assimilate and in short (aesthetically, etc.) claim our property wherever we find it."[41] James might have been referring to the Peabody sisters. Perceiving the need for early childhood education just a few years before James wrote that letter and, seeking in vain for stock in the portfolios of the educational agents of their own U.S. culture that addressed the problem, Mary Peabody Mann and Elizabeth Peabody had no compunctions about borrowing the necessary cultural assets.

In 1860, after becoming acquainted with the great German educational thinker Friedrich Froebel's philosophy of education, and more particularly with his idea of kindergarten, Elizabeth Peabody established the first English-speaking kindergarten in the U.S., where she adapted this portion of Germany's cultural stock to the American situation.[42] In 1863, she and her sister published a widely read book in which they explained their Froebelian approach,[43] and, in the very year that James wrote that letter to his brother, Elizabeth Peabody traveled to Germany to study Froebel's methods. Then, in 1872, she invited Maria Kraus-Boelte, a German who had trained under Froebel's widow, to New York to establish a kindergarten. Accepting Peabody's invitation, Kraus-Boelte soon become a pioneer of Froebelian education in the U.S.

It need hardly be said that the need for new cultural stock was not as dire in the kindergarten case as in the Norse Case. Nonetheless, the kindergarten example demonstrates how valuable one culture's receptivity to the practices of another culture can be. In general, to be educative, a culture would seem to require that a sufficient number of its members possess a certain kind and degree of flexibility and open-mindedness. More important still, it would seem to require that as many of its institutions as possible take seriously the virtue of educativeness. How else can those institutions be brought to acknowledge their status as educational agents? How else can their miseducativeness be curbed?

PART III
Applications

7

MAKING DEMOCRATIC CITIZENS

A very general theory of education cannot be expected to tell school teachers what they should do in class next Monday or parents how much television their children should be watching on Saturday mornings. It should, however, be capable of illuminating pressing practical problems. In this chapter and the next two, the theory of education as encounter will be put to this test.

The education of a democratic citizenry—that is to say, the making and shaping of democratic citizens—is arguably the most important task a democratic society has. It thus represents a good proving ground for our theory's applicability. Affirming democracy's dependence on education, Thomas Jefferson wrote in his *Notes on Virginia*:

> Every government degenerates when trusted to the rulers of the people alone. The people themselves therefore are its only safe depositories. And to render even them safe their minds must be improved to a certain degree. This indeed is not all that is necessary though it be essentially necessary. An amendment of our constitution must here come in aid of the public education.[1]

Seconding Jefferson's argument, John Dewey said, "the devotion of democracy to education is a familiar fact."[2] And more recent theorists of democracy have said, "democracy can not thrive without a well-educated citizenry;"[3] "a commitment to the democratic system of government implies a concern for the education of every citizen;"[4] "a basic knowledge of the nation's constitution and legal system, of its political history and institutions, and of its culture and political practice is obviously indispensable to democracy in any form."[5]

One need only read Plato's *Republic* or think of Hitler's Germany and Stalin's Soviet Union to know, however, that, although an educated citizenry may indeed be a requisite of democracy, there is no similar guarantee of education's allegiance to democracy. Whatever devotion education has to democracy does not inhere in it. On the contrary, a citizenry's determination to make and shape a democracy is a quality difficult to achieve and easy to forfeit.

The theory of education as encounter makes education's neutrality vis-à-vis democracy explicit: whether or not the individuals and the cultures that education forms are democratic will depend on the nature of the stock that the myriad educational agents transmit, and on whether the relevant items of stock become yoked to individual capacities as living legacies or dead relics. Bringing to light the kinds of questions that proposals for the education of democratic citizens must answer, and exposing the false presuppositions of standard approaches to the education of democratic citizens, our theory offers fresh insight into what must be done to cultivate education's devotion to democracy—and, once cultivated, to sustain it.

1. Gaps in the Standard Approach

Deliberative, aggregative, procedural, majoritarian, participatory, representative, equilibrium: this list does not begin to exhaust the varieties of democracy that political theorists have distinguished.[6] Yet, as important as it is for some purposes to identify the various kinds of democracy and determine the relationships of one to another, it is not necessary to undertake that task here. Just as the women of *Herland* want to make the best kind of people, political and educational thinkers describe what they believe are the best kind of democratic citizens and formulate proposals for their education accordingly. Although the proposals vary according to the type of democracy being espoused, they share a large enough set of characteristics to justify the abstraction from them of a common or standard approach to the problem.

First and foremost of these common features is a reliance on the standpoint of the individual. To be sure, the various proposals take democracy as their starting point and that is an attribute of groups, organizations, cultures, and other large-scale entities, not individuals. But having acknowledged that, if you want a nation or culture with democratic characteristics A, B, and C, you had better make sure that the members of that nation or culture possess traits that are A-, B-, and C-friendly, the proposals ignore this proposition's converse. They uniformly disregard the fact that, if you want people who possess traits A, B, and C, you had better make sure that the culture is friendly to A, B, and C; that it encourages their flourishing or at least allows them to flourish.

Taking the perspective of the individual for granted, discussions of the education of democratic citizens start from the valid belief that being a democratic citizen is an acquired characteristic. To be sure, a child born in a democratic country, or one whose parents are citizens thereof, will in some instances automatically be a citizen of a democracy. But a de facto citizen of a democracy is not necessarily a democratic citizen. Quite simply, newborns have not yet encountered, and their capacities have not yet become yoked to, the relevant items of cultural stock. Moreover, these yokings do not just occur as children mature; rather, they are the results of education.

From the fundamental truth that being democracy's best kind of person is a learned affair, the proposals leap to three false conclusions, the first of which is that only children are and should be the "recipients" of citizenship education. Forgetting how porous national borders have become, the proposals fail to take into account the fact that some adult newcomers to democratic nations are likely to resemble newborns in having encountered little or no democratic cultural stock thus far in their lives. They also assume, without justification, that whatever stock pertaining to democratic citizenship that does attach to the capacities of a child will remain yoked over a lifetime.

The second false conclusion is that school is democracy's one and only educational agent, and the third is that education is a purely intentional affair. Putting all of education's eggs in one basket, namely school; assuming that a democratic society has no other educational agents, or else that the ones it has do not engage in political education; and committing the intentional fallacy: the standard approach to the education of democratic citizens thus ignores the democratic miseducation in school's cultural surround.[7]

To assess the poverty of an approach to citizenship education that does not take seriously the existence of multiple educational agency and that commits the intentional fallacy, consider the case of Elaine Mar, whose family emigrated to the U.S. from Hong Kong when she was a young child. In her memoir, Mar described being taught authoritarian values by her mother, "a traditional Chinese." Mar's mother "saw herself in relation to family. She was a daughter, sister, and aunt. She spent her life waiting to become a mother."[8] Mar recalled her mother once looking "down in shame" and saying, "How dare I question you?" after challenging something that Elaine's grandmother said.[9] Mar wrote, "From birth I was expected to abide by the adults' rules."[10] Her mother told her, "This is what it means to be an adult—you learn to be cautious and follow your elder's lead."[11] On the subject of punishment, Mar said, "I didn't think I had anything to worry about. Didn't everyone always say how clever I was? And didn't 'clever' mean the same as 'obedient'?"[12] Before long, however, Mar's mother was beating her whenever she spoke up or disobeyed.

The attitude a citizen of a democracy is supposed to have to the law is a trait so basic that most discussions of citizenship education forget to mention it. In an authoritarian system, the individual is expected to obey laws enacted by others, and that is that. In a democracy, the individual is both the subject and the author of the law. In other words, democratic citizens are their own governors: the laws they obey are ones that they or their chosen representatives have written.

Furthermore, in a democracy, as opposed to a dictatorship, everyone is equal before the law and is also subject to the law. No individual or group is above it. People who are their own legislators are not unthinkingly and unquestioningly supposed to obey laws made by others; on the contrary, they are expected to speak out when they do not approve of what their representatives are doing.

Mar's case is a poignant reminder that home does not necessarily instill in its young the fundamental principles of democracy, and another such reminder is to be found in this vignette from the 2005 memoir of a New York City schoolteacher:

> Augie was a nuisance in class, talking back, bothering the girls. I called his mother. Next day the door is thrown open and a man in a black T-shirt with the muscles of a weightlifter yells, Hey, Augie, come 'ere.
>
> You can hear Augie gasp.
>
> Talkin' a yeh, Augie. I haveta go in there you wish you was dead. Come 'ere.
>
> Augie yelps, I didn't do nothin'.
>
> The man lumbers into the room, down the aisle to Augie's seat, lifts Augie into the air, carries him over to the wall, bangs him repeatedly, against the wall.
>
> I told you—*bang*—never—*bang*—never give your teacher—*bang*—no trouble—*bang*. I hear you give your teacher trouble—*bang*—I'm gonna tear your goddam head off—*bang*—an'stick it up your ass—*bang*. You heard me—bang?
>
> . . . the man drags Augie back to his seat and turns to me. He gives you trouble again, mister, I kick his ass here to New Jersey. He was brought up to give respect.[13]

According to a newsletter of the Child Rights Information network, "As part of their daily lives, children all over Europe are spanked, slapped, hit, smacked, shaken, kicked, pinched, punched, caned, flogged, belted, beaten and battered by adults—mainly by those whom they trust the most."[14] It is possible that other parts of the world at the turn of the twenty-first century differed from Europe in this regard. Yet, one must wonder in what percentage of homes one of the basic tenets of democracy is put into practice.

Home is not the only educational agent that yokes unquestioning obedience to children's capacities. Thus, for example, scouts in the U.S. take an oath to follow Akela, their pack leader, and the boys and girls enrolled in Chicago's Middle School Cadet Corps after-school programs who "learn how to stand, turn, and salute in synchronization" must do 10 push-ups when they disobey an order.[15] Moreover, children are not the only individuals whose capacities are apt to attach to the cultural stock of unquestioning obedience. Banks and nursing homes post warnings to their employees that read, "Yours is not to reason why!" and the punishment of whistle blowers in companies and corporations large and small is an established fact of life.

As for the United States Marine Corps, here is a recollection of boot camp, taken from a 2003 memoir of a lance corporal in a scout/sniper platoon during the Gulf War:

> Burke punched the recruit square on his forehead. He swayed but his knees did not give. The recruit had made the mistake of using personal pronouns, which the recruit is not allowed to use when referring to the drill instructor or himself. The recruit is the recruit. The drill instructor is the drill instructor or sir.
>
> Burke surveyed the platoon, hands clasped behind his back.
>
> He yelled, addressing us all, "I am your mommy and your daddy! I am your nightmare and your wet dream! I am your morning and your night! I will tell you when to piss and when to shit and how much food to eat and when! I will teach you how to kill and how to stay alive! I will forge you into part of the iron fist with which our great United States fights oppression and injustice! Do you understand me, recruits?"[16]

Unquestioning obedience is but one of the items of undemocratic cultural stock that some very powerful educational agents daily yoke to the capacities of adults. Consider self-esteem, a virtue often included on lists of traits that every citizen of a democracy must possess, and think of the companies in the U.S. who laid off thousands and thousands of workers in the last decades of the twentieth century and the first years of the twenty-first century. "Everything you think is important and do for your life's work, isn't. To have someone senior in the company say that so bluntly in public is terrible," an executive told an interviewer.[17] As a prominent political theorist noted, "In political debate in the public arena people have to have a certain economic security, otherwise they are likely to feel adrift, anxious and victims of circumstances beyond their control."[18]

Think of Enron. Here was an energy giant whose stated values were respect, integrity, communication, and excellence, but whose culture increasingly fostered and rewarded greed, selfishness, arrogance, hypocrisy, deception, self-indulgence, ruthlessness, and disdain for the greater good.[19] To be sure, no single item in Enron's hidden curriculum, except possibly disdain for the greater good, can be considered undemocratic in and of itself. Still, the hidden curriculum of the Enron culture as a whole appears to have been inconsistent with the requirements of democracy.[20]

Think too about trust and honesty, personal traits that also appear on lists of democratic virtues. "Washington has become the home of the permanent campaign, a game of endless politicking based on the manipulation of shades of truth, partial truths, twisting the truth, and spin," a former press secretary of the then President of the United States wrote in 2008.[21]

When the subject is the education of democratic citizens, it is sheer folly to overlook the hidden curriculum of the culture's dominant educational agents.[22] A sustained cultural bookkeeping project is required if all the sources and the full content of a single nation's democratic miseducation of young and old are to be documented. Here, it suffices to note that, with young children being exposed to political miseducation at home and in their communities, and with mature men and women encountering cultural stock that conflicts with democracy at work and in the world, education for democratic citizenship is best thought of as a lifelong process.

Lifelong does not necessarily mean linear. An individual's self-esteem can go up and down, the skills of critical thinking can be turned on and off, democratic virtues can atrophy over time, and undemocratic attitudes and values can take root. Furthermore, the democratic miseducation of one group can rub off on another. Remarking that lay-offs are a trauma to the entire family, a psychiatrist who treated a number of patients for "laid-off related ailments" said:

> All of a sudden the parent sits at home and can't find a job and is depressed. And suddenly the child's role model sort of crumbles. Instead of feeling admiration for the parent, the child eventually begins to feel disrespect. Because the children identify with the parents, they begin to doubt that they can accomplish anything. They feel they won't be successful in life and their self-esteem plummets.[23]

2. A Truncated Conception of Democracy

In treating school as the only educator of citizens—or else, as the only educator worthy of attention—and committing the intentional fallacy, the standard approach to the making of democratic citizens reflects the deep structure's truncated conception of education. Interestingly enough, the standard approach's conception of democracy is also truncated. Interpreting democracy as a political phenomenon and defining politics as narrowly as the deep structure of educational thought defines education, it equates the political realm with one of its many sites, namely formal government. Yet, government is no more the one and only locus of democracy and its antitheses than school is the single locus of education and miseducation.

Think of Elaine Mar's and Augie's homes. Indeed, think of the fact that home is, by nature, an undemocratic institution in that children do not choose their parents and are not, in general, the authors of the commands or rules they are supposed to follow. Think also of the military. Ordinary service men and women do not originate the commands they follow, nor do they choose the officers who issue the commands. Now consider hierarchical religions such as the Roman Catholic Church. Catholic laypeople do not choose the Cardinals who elect the Pope. Recall those college and university presidents in the U.S. who, in response to the student protests of the 1960s, proudly proclaimed that institutions of higher education were not democracies. Remember, too, the many businesses that could be but are not organized according to democratic principles. And, for that matter, consider the rigid hierarchical structure of untold numbers of schools and classrooms, as well as the fact that students rarely choose their teachers and school administrators and are seldom the authors of the rules they are told to follow.

The theory of education as encounter leaves open the question of whether the economic, social, religious, and other institutions in a political democracy should be organized around democratic principles; indeed, it leaves open the question of whether democracy is the best form of government. It makes it clear, however, that, when the subject is the making and shaping of democratic citizens, it is self-defeating to think only about the political realm—and, more particularly, only about government.

Just as the full range of a culture's groups and institutions are sites of education, so schools, homes, religious organizations, corporations, charitable foundations, and all the rest are arenas of democracy, authoritarianism, or something in between. Thus, insofar as those potential sites of democracy are authoritarian in their structures or ideologies, they may be yoking undemocratic and perhaps even anti-democratic cultural stock to the capacities of individuals. To the extent that they do this, they place obstacles even in the path of those who would simply educate citizens for political democracy.

In light of the deep structure of educational thought, it is not surprising that resistance to acknowledging the contributions of non-school agents to the education of democratic citizens is strong, and is especially unyielding in the case of home and family. Throughout history, most political theorists and philosophers in the Western tradition have embraced the public/private split. Moreover, contemporary thinkers concerned with the education of democratic citizens appear to have accepted its educational corollary that home and family fall outside the educational realm. In consequence, even those who say that home influences children's learning tend to treat schoolchildren as blank slates on which home and community have never written.

The theory of education as encounter takes no position on what the nature and structure of homes and families should be. It does, however, consider the disregard of home's role in citizen making as one more reason for rejecting the deep structure of educational thought. "A popular Government without popular information or the means of acquiring it, is but a Prologue to a Farce or a Tragedy or perhaps both," said James Madison after the U.S. Constitution was adopted. One might venture the same opinion about a democracy that denies itself information about democratic miseducation. "People who mean to be their own Governors, must arm themselves with the power knowledge gives," Madison added.[24] So, too, people who mean to turn children into their own governors had better arm themselves with the power that knowledge can give. For when the contributions of home—and also, of course, of religion, the media, government, and so on—to the education of a nation's young are hidden, there is no way of knowing if a child needs remedial work in democracy when he or she enters school.

It goes without saying that democratic citizen making should not proceed in a totalitarian fashion or violate people's rights. There is no need, however, to make a forced choice between two evils: either act in a totalitarian manner or ignore the reality of multiple educational agency. There is nothing undemocratic about acknowledging that children experience one or another degree of democratic miseducation before they ever arrive at school and continue to do so throughout their years of schooling and beyond. There is nothing sinister about admitting that, if school is to teach democratic citizenship successfully, whatever democratic miseducation children are receiving elsewhere will have to be counteracted. There is no risk of totalitarianism in recognizing that the whole range of a culture's groups and institutions are educational agents and that the education for democracy they provide can be for the better or the worse.

Just as the theory of education as encounter is neutral on the hotly contested issues of whether economic, social, religious, and other non-political institutions should or should not be organized according to democratic principles, it leaves open the question of how homes and families should be structured. I hasten to add, however, that this neutrality does not preclude it from issuing the advice that the yokings of individual capacities to undemocratic stock in the portfolios of undemocratic economic, social, and religious institutions warrant the attention of those who care about the future of democracy. Whatever stance is taken regarding economic and other forms of democracy, the problem of what to do about democratic miseducation is possibly the most pressing one of all for those who would educate a democratic citizenry.

In sum, a narrow political conception of democracy makes it difficult to achieve the very goal that the standard approach to citizenship education posits, namely creating citizens of a nation with a democratic form of government. To conceptualize democratic citizenship narrowly also loses sight of all those aspects of democracy that go beyond voting and decision-making; for instance, respect for others, concern for the greater good, the belief that no one is above the law, and a devotion to freedom of thought and action.

In *Democracy and Education*, Dewey wrote, "A democracy is more than a form of government; it is primarily a mode of associated living."[25] Others have said, "The open air of a democracy invites individuality and variety . . . Conflicting ideas and attitudes produce a vitality that enriches the experience of all"[26] and "Democracy, first and foremost, is a shared way of life."[27] A mode of living, a way of life: this is how anthropologists and sociologists define culture and it is well known that one becomes a member of a culture by being immersed in it. Two-day-old Henri does not learn to be a Frenchman by studying the history, geography, and governmental structure of France. He becomes French by breathing in the culture of France with the air.

The narrow definitions of democracy and education adopted by the standard approach to citizenship education do not allow one to ask if democracy is being breathed in with the air: its sole concern is school's curriculum proper. Yet, if it is not known what undemocratic and anti-democratic messages the members of a culture are receiving daily—that is to say, what undemocratic and anti-democratic items of cultural stock are being yoked to their capacities—how possibly can they be counteracted?

Here are some examples of the hatred that was transmitted to the American public in the first decade of the twenty-first century by some very powerful educational agents. The author of one best seller called liberals "'the enemy within our country;' 'an enemy more dangerous than Hitler;' 'traitors' who are 'dangerous to your survival' and who 'should be placed in a straightjacket'." A talk radio host whose listeners numbered in the millions told a gay man, "You should only get AIDS and die, you pig. How's that? Why don't you see if you can sue me, you pig. You got nothing better than to put me down, you piece of garbage. You have got nothing to do today, go eat a sausage and choke on it. Get trichinosis." An equally important radio personality reported that Muslims "don't eat during the day during Ramadan. They fast during the day and eat at night. Sort of like cockroaches." Yet another repeatedly called the National Organization of Women "the National Organization of Whores."[28]

The commentator who reported on this scene said plaintively, "God knows the price we pay when we turn political opponents to be debated, into mortal enemies to be eliminated." It does not require omniscience to know that the price of yoking the capacities of millions of people to a belief system that equates Muslims with insects, gay men with garbage, women who seek equality with whores, and turns those with whom you disagree into traitors is the democratic miseducation of a significant portion of a citizenry. The theory of education as encounter makes this perfectly clear. And it also makes it clear that a democracy that ignores the democratic miseducation being transmitted by the culture's educational agents can place at risk its central project of making and shaping a democratic citizenry.

3. Liberal Education and Democratic Citizenship

The standard approach to the education of democratic citizens makes no attempt to determine what democratic miseducation schoolchildren may have received in the past. Nor does it seek to ensure that school children breathe democracy in with the air. Rather, it draws up a list of traits or dispositions that every citizen must possess and treats these as the aims of school's curriculum proper.

The lists differ considerably in their content. Thus, two theorists of deliberative democracy say:

> To prepare their students for citizenship in a deliberative democracy, schools should aim to develop the capacities of students to understand different perspectives, communicate the understandings to other people, and engage in the give-and-take of moral argument with a view toward making mutually justifiable decisions.[29]

Hope and confidence, courage, self-respect, friendship, trust, honesty, and decency, along with "the bedrock democratic dispositions of justice, tolerance, and personal autonomy" appear on the list of a British philosopher of education.[30] And a philosopher who conceptualizes a democratic citizen as a world citizen identifies three capacities "essential to the cultivation of humanity in today's world:"[31] the capacity for critical examination of oneself and one's traditions; the ability to see oneself as a human being bound to all other human beings by ties of recognition and concern; and the capacity of narrative imagination.[32]

Nevertheless, there is wide agreement that the attributes of a democratic citizen are to be acquired through study of the three Rs and the disciplines of knowledge—in particular, the natural sciences, mathematics, the social and behavioral sciences, and the humanities. In sum, apart from the three Rs, the subjects prescribed for the making of citizens are the very ones that belong to the twentieth century's idea of a liberal education.

Whether democracy is defined narrowly as a form of political organization or broadly as a way of life, the deep structure's divorce of mind from body and liberal education's devotion to the project of developing mind cast doubt on its adequacy for the task of making democratic citizens. You can teach Augie the three Rs; all the history, literature, science, economics, political philosophy you wish; and also the skills of critical thinking and political deliberation. But, if the cultural stock that represents democracy's "middle way" between unquestioning submission to authority and rampant disobedience of the law does not attach to his capacities as living legacy; if he does not learn to respect both majority rule and minority rights; if he does not come to believe and act as if no one—not Augie and not Augie's father—is above the law; and if he does not also become disposed to protect his own rights and those of others, and to speak out when he sees democracy being subverted: he will not have learned to be a democratic citizen.[33]

What kind of people does liberal education aim at making and are these the best kind from the standpoint of democracy? Liberal education, as it has traditionally been understood, tends to form observers or spectators of democracy rather than active participants in it. If successful, a liberal education will yoke the capacities of its recipients to cultural stock that enables them to understand and interpret experience. But appropriate democratic action does not follow from these cognitive achievements. Even if this stock encompasses knowledge about democracy and the rule of law, there is little reason to think that it will include a disposition to care if people's freedoms are denied them; little reason to think that it will become yoked to individual capacities in such a way that people will feel society's injustices, be moved to action by concern for its future, or be able to translate the knowledge acquired into practice.

I do not mean to say that items of cultural stock that promote active democratic participation cannot become yoked to the capacities of the recipients of a liberal education. The source of such yokings will not necessarily, however, be the liberal education that the standard approach prescribes.

Advocates of deliberative democracy may protest that a liberal education is indeed designed to shape participants for at least their kind of democracy. To make their case, they will remind us that deliberative democracy is:

> a form of government in which free and equal citizens (and their representatives), justify decisions in a process in which they give one another reasons that are mutually acceptable and generally accessible, with the aim of reaching conclusions that are binding in the present on all citizens but open to challenge in the future.[34]

And they will ask what kind of education could possibly be better suited to the task of turning out rational decision-makers than one that aims at the development of mind.

For the moment, let us assume that a liberal education is, in fact, the best possible vehicle for creating rational decision-makers. One has only to think of Augie to know that the skills of rational decision-making are not the only items of cultural stock that need to attach to the capacities of the citizens of a democracy. To be sure, the definition of deliberative democracy cited here gives the impression that its essence is decision-making. But that definition is unduly narrow, even when democracy is itself construed as merely a governmental form.

Just as the deep structure of educational thought turns education into a purely cognitive enterprise whose sole object is the acquisition of knowledge and understanding, the above definition and portrayals of deliberative democracy more generally turn democracy into a decision-making process whose most important characteristic is reason giving. It is undeniable that decision-making by citizens or their representatives is an important element of democracy.[35] But, just as there is far more to education than the acquisition of knowledge and understanding, there is far more to democracy—even to political democracy—than rational deliberation about the significant political issues of the day. Thus, for example, democracy is distinguishable from totalitarianism—and also from anarchy, the form of government with which Plato equated it—by virtue of its fundamental belief in the capacity of people to govern themselves, its acceptance of some form of majority rule, and its willingness to protect the rights of the minority.

R.S. Peters replied to critics who pointed out that his analysis of education was unduly narrow by admitting that a broad sense of the term "education" existed while insisting that it was not of philosophical interest. Political theorists might, in their turn, grant the existence of a broad sense of "democracy" but say that it is of no interest to them. The knowledge, skills, attitudes, and values that narrow construals of democracy leave out must, however, be of interest to those whose concern is the making of democratic citizens.

The definition of deliberative democracy under discussion here resembles the dictionary definition of "armchair." An armchair, so the dictionary says, is a chair with arms. Using that formula, a carpenter who knows what a chair is can fashion an armchair, but someone who has no idea of the basic attributes of chairs cannot. Similarly, political theorists tell us that a deliberative democracy is a democracy in which the deliberation of free and equal citizens and their representatives is paramount. As the definition of armchair presupposes knowledge on the part of its makers of what a chair is, the definition of deliberative democracy presupposes knowledge of the ABCs of democracy.

When the subject is education, it is tempting to try to "peel off" curriculum recommendations from the leading theories and narratives of the various intellectual disciplines. Considering how reductive the definitions of democracy provided by cutting edge political theories can be, however, it would seem to be self-defeating to let them dictate curriculum. Try to imagine a populace whose every member is a rational decision-maker. Would these be the best kind of democratic citizens? Would they not lack the other attributes of democratic citizenship? Would they know anything about how to build or sustain democratic institutions?

It is far from clear, however, that, when the cultural stock singled out by advocates of deliberative democracy is yoked to individual capacities, the resultant people will be the desired kind of decision-makers. Here is a small sampling of the problems that arise in contemporary democracies: global warming, the violence and the increasing number of displaced people in the Congo, the increased opium trafficking in Afghanistan, North Korea, health care, steroid use among professional baseball players, the elk population of Rocky Mountain National Park, the former Laotians who were hired by the U.S. during the Vietnam War and are still in the jungle, the militant Islamic organization Hamas, trade with Cuba, the Gulf of Mexico oil spill, the recession.

Just as liberal education has historically been contrasted with vocational education, it has been differentiated from specialized and technical education. Yet, a fund of specialized and often very technical information is required to decide the kinds of problems listed above. Thus, it is an open question if a liberal education could provide the knowledge and skills people need to deliberate intelligently enough to reach justified conclusions about all of these.

It must also be noted that the problems or issues that the citizens of a deliberative democracy are supposed to decide do not necessarily belong to any of the disciplines of knowledge that make up the liberal curriculum. Which discipline enables a person to decide whether the elk population of Rocky Mountain National Park is out of control and, if so, what to do about it? Which one supplies the knowledge needed to decide what to do about the trafficking of opium in Afghanistan or the situation in the Congo? To be sure, the study of history, literature, science, and the rest may shed light on the displaced people in the Congo and on these other issues but that light will often be indirect. Thus, even if a liberal education did supply the requisite specialized and technical information, it would be inadequate to the task of turning out people whose decisions about the issues of the day are rational and justified.

The question remains of whether a liberal education is necessary, even if not sufficient, for the citizens of a democracy. The theory of education as encounter strongly suggests that it is not. Let us grant that there are indeed specific items of stock that must become yoked to an individual's capacities if that person is to be a democratic citizen. Even if some of these items are part of the content or subject matter of subjects that have traditionally been belonged to a liberal education, they are detachable from those subjects. For example, although the school subject politics lays claim to the belief that, in a democracy, no one is above the law, other subjects can also lay claim to this item of stock. Moreover, items of stock can attach to individual capacities independently of their role as the subject matter of some school subject: for instance, a person can encounter the belief that, in a democracy, no individual is supposed to be above the law, by reading a book or watching television. Thus, even if the yokings of certain items of stock to capacities are required for democratic citizenship, a liberal education as traditionally conceived is not.

Here, an important caveat is in order: to say that having a liberal education is neither a necessary nor a sufficient condition for being a democratic citizen is not to deny its value. In an impassioned defense of a liberal education that is at once Socratic and pluralistic, the American philosopher and classicist Martha Nussbaum wrote in the last days of the twentieth century:

> If we cannot teach our students everything they need to know to be good citizens, we may at least teach them what they do not know and how they may inquire. We can acquaint them with some rudiments about the major non-Western cultures and minority groups within our own. We can show them how to inquire into the history and variety of gender and sexuality. Above all, we can teach them how to argue, rigorously and critically, so that they can call their minds their own.[36]

Nevertheless, the theory of education as encounter challenges the widespread assumption that a liberal education, as it has traditionally been understood, is essential for the citizens of a democracy, if not actually sufficient. Indeed, insofar as the goal of liberal education is considered to be the development of mind alone, our theory challenges the assumption that, even if it is not absolutely essential for democratic citizenship, it is the most appropriate kind of education there can be.

4. School's Role

Let us perform another experiment in imagination. Picture a state or nation whose various educational agents are engaged in a joint venture in citizen making that is so effective that all children breathe democracy in with the air from Day 1: their homes induct them into a democratic mode of living and so do all the other educational agents in their lives. How easy the making of a democratic citizenry would then be! The full range of a culture's educational agents would do the bulk of the work and school would at most have to add the finishing touches.

In contrast, real democratic states contain groups and institutions that wittingly or not engage in democratic miseducation on a daily basis: that is to say, they yoke undemocratic cultural stock to individual capacities and they also fail to transmit the stock associated with democracy as a way of life. In real democratic states, therefore, an adequate approach to citizen making must combat miseducation's twin sins of omission and commission. It must seek ways to counteract the cultural liabilities that fill the air and either find or construct a site where children can experience democracy as a way of life.

The fact that citizen making begins before children go to school, continues after they leave school, and occurs outside school's walls does not release school from its culturally assigned task of educating a democratic citizenry. Given that school is the one place where vast numbers of children meet each day for a considerable amount of time, what educational agent is better suited to serve the function of initiating or inducting children into democracy by providing an atmosphere in which they breathe democracy in with the air?[37]

It is important here to distinguish between school actually being a democracy and simply being a site for learning democracy as a way of life. In light of the fundamental inequality at the heart of schooling, it is far from obvious that a school—at least a school for children—can or should be a democracy. Granted, the members of a democracy do not have to be equal in all respects in order to be treated equally: they can, for instance, differ with respect to height, weight, eye color, class, race, gender, ethnicity, and so on. But these inequalities are not relevant to democracy's purpose or function, as it were. In contrast, the inequality between teachers and students is directly connected to school's *raison d'être*. Whatever the particular missions of any given school for children may be, to achieve these it must transmit the cultural stock in its portfolio to its students. Hence, its teachers are, presumably, individuals who possess what its students do not, namely the knowledge and skill that enables them to do so.

The fact that school is not itself a democracy does not mean that it cannot be a site for learning to live in and maintain democracy as a way of life. Actually, it is necessary to speak of school *becoming* such a place, for in many instances it is not. One does not have to agree with the sentiment that schools "conduct themselves as the least democratic institutions"[38] to believe that the great majority of schools would have to undergo significant change for them to make the grade:

governing structures are often hierarchical; rules are not always applied equally to children of different races, classes, genders, and so on; and many classroom practices deny children such fundamental democratic rights as freedom of speech and association. Still, although it may not, in all cases, be easy for schools to become sites where children experience democracy on a daily basis, it is certainly possible. Indeed, numerous schools that describe themselves as democratic and are deemed by others to be so have existed in the past and exist today.[39]

Even the most cursory survey reveals a surprising degree of variation in such schools. One lesson to be learned from the differing accounts is that there is no one right form that school must take in order to induct children into democracy. Another lesson is that several characteristics that have often been singled out as necessary ingredients of democratic schooling are not actually essential.[40]

One such feature is that the students choose to study whatever they want. Although some democratic schools claim to enact a free choice principle of this sort, one wonders if they would, in fact, be prepared to follow it to its logical conclusion and allow a child to study how, for example, to be a murderer or a rapist. Be this as it may, many schools that can legitimately be described as inducting children into democracy as a way of life do not endorse this principle.[41]

"We want to make democracy a living force in the lives of our children; we want to translate its tenets into the practical terms of everyday thinking and acting. It is a process which begins in the nursery group and which continues straight through to the highest grades in the School" wrote Agnes De Lima in *The Little Red School House*, a book with an introduction by John Dewey about a school with that name founded in New York City in 1932.[42] Yet, despite the school's commitment to being a site in which lessons in democracy are breathed in with the air, it roundly rejected the idea that children should choose their own subject matter.

Grounding their belief in a planned curriculum in their many years of teaching experience, the Director and faculty of The Little Red School House insisted that the teacher is "better able to weigh the possibilities of a proposed program and to relate it to the general plan of the school."[43] In a democratic class, they explained, the teacher "must always remain the leader and the guide. The children must be given as much choice as is consistent with healthy growth, and those realms of choice must be defined. Children will respect a teacher who frankly says, 'In this you may choose for yourself, but in that you may not'."[44] Lest they be thought dictatorial, they added that sufficient flexibility remained "for the children not to feel regimented"[45] and then said:

> we do not consider our present choice of subject matter anything final or inviolable. In fact, we do make changes from time to time; but this is done after careful consideration by the whole staff and always in relation to the total program of the eight elementary school years and their relation to the secondary school.[46]

Another characteristic that is often thought to be a mark of democratic schooling is that each student be in charge of his or her own learning. Once again, some democratic schools embrace this practice: their students set their own goals, choose their own projects, make their own schedules, and manage their own time accordingly. The principle that learning should be brought under the control of the student or anyone else does not, however, fit comfortably with the approaches to learning taken by many democratic schools. The theory of education as encounter teaches that, even when a school employs standard learning activities such as reading textbooks, listening to the teacher, memorizing facts, and taking tests, the chances are great that any number of unexpected items of cultural stock will become yoked to individual capacities. In schools that have a broad conception of what counts as a valid learning activity, the difficulties of managing what and how and when an individual learns are magnified.

In the 1930s, the subjects of study at The Little Red School House included Manhattan, American Indians, city housekeeping, the ancient Hebrews and Egyptians, America from 1600–1850, and American life from the Civil War to the present.[47] In studying these unconventional subjects, the children engaged in equally unconventional learning activities: they took trips around New York City to museums, markets, garbage dumps, courthouses, fire departments, and police stations; wrote stories and poems and painted murals about what they saw and heard on the trips; created, produced, and acted in plays about Shays' Rebellion and the Hebrew slaves in Egypt; participated in daily class discussions about the trip just taken, the play under rehearsal, or an incident in the playground. In addition, the children at The Little Red School House performed school services such as making repairs around the building, serving as school librarians, decorating the walls with their murals, and planting bulbs. In view of the countless learning affordances built into these activities, the very idea that the children *should* manage or be in control of their own learning makes little sense because it is far from evident that they *could* do so.

Finally, some proponents of democratic schooling hold that, without student participation in the school's governance, democracy cannot be achieved. Here, too, however, what is put forward as a necessary condition is not, in fact, one. Although some democratic schools enact a principle of participation in governance, others do not.[48] "The democratic way of life, like every other way of life in which we believe, is not won through shouting pious slogans, through oratory in high places, or even through daily affirmation of its virtues," wrote De Lima:

> Rather it is a slow and almost insensible process built into the consciousness and subconsciousness of our people through a multitude of small and apparently insignificant acts. When we at The Little Red School House say we have a democratic setup, we don't mean the outer trappings which pass for democratic. We have no multiplication of student committees; we

have no elaborate machinery of self-government. We do not ask children to make decisions which they are too young to make.[49]

The question naturally arises of what makes a school an induction center for democracy if not its devotion to the principles of free student choice in what is studied, student control over learning, and student participation in governance. In the case of The Little Red School House in the 1930s, the answer was an overall curriculum in democracy—much of it hidden in the hide-a-penny sense of the term—that actively sought to combat the democratic miseducation in the cultural surround.

It will be apparent that the school was not itself a democracy: the director and teachers did the hiring, developed the curriculum proper, chose many of the children's learning activities, and made other important decisions. Yet, occasions for yoking the cultural stock of democracy to the children's capacities and for uncoupling undemocratic stock from them were everywhere.

"The lessons to be learned on the playground are of incalculable value," wrote De Lima. "Here, in terms which children of this age readily understand, we can discuss the meaning of democracy, of majority versus minority, of the claims of the weaker on the stronger." In addition to the lessons of the playground, folk dancing brought "the girls and boys into pleasant, easy relations."[50] Shop classes offered "special opportunity for the development of both self-assurance and social responsibility:"[51] the children made shelves for the library, counters for the school store, tables for classrooms, storage space for music equipment and they endlessly repaired chairs. Trips around the city brought the children into contact with people old and young, rich and poor, black and white, immigrant and Native American; and with railroad men and sanitation department workers, city councilors, and a Texas cowboy who they ended up inviting to sing to them in a school assembly.

Furthermore, long before the invention of women's studies and African-American studies, The Little Red School House had its children read about, write plays about, give reports about, and otherwise learn about Frederick Douglass, Booker T. Washington, Nat Turner, Harriet Tubman, Sojourner Truth, Phyllis Weatley, Lucretia Mott, and Susan B. Anthony. Before the Civil Rights Movement in the U.S. drew attention to the nation's history of racism, the school was yoking to its children's capacities a particular kind of understanding of all groups, races, and religions. Wrote De Lima:

> We wish to go beyond tolerance of another race; we want to learn to understand and appreciate the contribution which this race is making to our American life. We want to rid ourselves of the tawdry stereotype to be found in the ordinary work of fiction, movie or radio script, where the Negro is portrayed as a clown, a lackadaisical, shiftless good-for-nothing, or the abjectly devoted menial.[52]

Thus, before media studies came into existence, the school was teaching its children that "you cannot believe a thing just because a book says it is so"[53] and encouraging them to take a critical attitude toward the media of the day: the radio, the movie, and the newspaper. "Needless to say," De Lima added, "critical thinking involves freedom of speech in the classroom. The child is not told what to think but . . . is continually being challenged for his facts."[54]

The wealth of detail, the insightfulness of its commentary, and its tacit honoring of the distinction between a school being a democracy and being a site where democracy is learned make De Lima's account an invaluable resource for those who would rethink the education of democratic citizens. I do not for a moment mean to suggest, however, that The Little Red School House's solution to the problem of how to induct children into democracy was "the one right way" for its time and place, let alone that it should be treated as a model that can be lifted out of its historical, sociological, and geographical context and automatically transplanted elsewhere. On the contrary, it is merely one clear instance of democratic schooling to which the stereotypes of children doing ludicrous things, learning nothing of any significance, and running wild simply do not apply.

On the other hand, it would be a mistake to think that, because The Little Red School House solution was developed in the 1930s, when democracy was under threat from fascism and Nazism, or because it was located in a major city, its practices have no relevance for other contexts. The school's belief that education is everywhere—at the playground, on the radio, and in the city streets, as well as in classes of formal instruction—has broad applicability. So do its tacit assumptions that no encounter between a child and some item of undemocratic or anti-democratic cultural stock is too trivial to be taken seriously; that a school's hidden curriculum is at least as important as its curriculum proper; and that race, class, religious, and ethnic hatred are as much the enemies of democracy as is totalitarianism.

5. Joint Ventures

Some educational thinkers have held that schools should not be in the business of teaching values. In their eyes, it is the job of home and religion to teach what is good and bad, right and wrong; school's one and only task is to teach the three Rs—or perhaps the three Rs and disciplines of knowledge such as history and science.[55] But this reductive conception of schooling clearly contradicts the Jeffersonian belief that the formation of citizens is a fundamental task—some have gone so far as to say *the* fundamental task—of schooling in a democratic society. It flies in the face of historical studies showing that, in the nineteenth and twentieth centuries, the public school system in the U.S. served as a mechanism for assimilating immigrants into the dominant culture.[56] And it overlooks the fact that school inevitably yokes values to children's capacities, whether through its hidden curriculum or its curriculum proper. The question for those who care about the fate of democracy is not, *Should* school be in the business of transmitting values to the next generation? It is, *Which* values should school be transmitting?

The claim that school should not be in the business of teaching values does, however, point up a contradiction between assigning school the task of turning young children into democratic citizens and the deep structure's assumption that the object of education is the acquisition of knowledge and understanding. Even on a narrow construal of democracy, democratic citizens—as opposed to mere de facto citizens of a democracy—must learn to *believe in* the principles of democracy; or at least they must come to *be committed to* democratic practices— and this is something quite different from simply acquiring *knowledge about* democracy. In other words, the very kind of education that democracy requires is precluded by the deep structure's split between mind and body and the consequent divorce of thought from action.

The inconsistency can be avoided if one holds that the citizens of a democracy do not need to acquire positive attitudes toward and values regarding democracy, but this is patently false. The claim that belief in democracy is so fundamental that it is misleading to call it a value or attitude does not get around the inconsistency either. Call it what you will, a belief in or commitment to democracy is an acquired characteristic that goes well beyond mere knowledge or understanding.

The thesis that belief in democracy is so basic that it must be learned before a child enters school does not dispose of our problem either. By locating a vital portion of education for democracy in the sphere that the deep structure excludes from the educational realm, it simply shifts responsibility for the contradiction from one part of that belief system to another. Furthermore, in tacitly affirming what is true—namely, that the private home and family do engage in education— it presupposes what is patently false: that the dominant educational agents in a child's early life can be counted on to instill the basic attitudes and values of democracy.

As a last resort, it might be argued that belief in democracy is the exception that proves the validity of education's deep structure. But, on the contrary, the contradiction between the deep structure and the educational requirements of democracy represents one more nail in the deep structure's coffin.

Still, to affirm that, in a democracy, one of school's tasks is the making and shaping of citizens is not to say that school must do this job by itself. Citizen making in a democracy requires the cooperation of the many significant educational agents in the lives of both children and adults—school, home, neighborhood, religion, the media, the government, and all the rest.[57] Moreover, to the extent that any significant non-school educational agent undermines school's designated task of educating for democratic citizenship, democracy's health or well being is to that degree in jeopardy.

The cooperation of a culture's educational agents in the joint venture of educating a democratic citizenry is not to be confused with conformity of belief or the suppression of dissent. In music, dissonance is one form of harmony. Similarly, in a democracy, a culture's educational agents can work together to foster democratic citizenship while disagreeing about matters large and small. Which is worse: genocide or widespread disease and poverty? Should pensions be the responsibility of individual corporations or of the state? Is there such a thing as a just war? Since freedom of thought is a basic tenet of democracy, it would seem imperative to encourage rather than stifle differences of opinion, whether they be about individual morality, public policy, or the nature of democracy itself.

Making the education of a democratic citizenry a joint venture does mean, however, that a wide range of groups and institutions must acknowledge their status as educators; and this, in turn, means acknowledging that they have an obligation to be educative vis-à-vis democracy rather than miseducative. In a pluralistic culture, there will no doubt be educational agents whose cooperation in the joint venture is precluded by their explicitly anti-democratic missions, as well as agents whose missions may be compatible with democracy but whose structures and practices tend to yoke undemocratic cultural stock to individual capacities.

Fortunately, however, 100 percent cooperation in a joint venture for the education of a democratic citizenry is not required; indeed, the success of the joint venture is best conceptualized as a matter of degree and not an all-or-nothing affair. Thus, provided that the anti-democratic groups and institutions in a culture—for instance, neo-Nazi organizations—are neither too many nor too powerful, the fact that their cooperation cannot be enlisted is not of prime importance. It does, however, seem essential that the cooperation of institutions with undemocratic, as opposed to anti-democratic, structures be enlisted in the joint venture.

Can home be prevailed upon to instill democratic values and attitudes? It does not follow from the fact that homes with young children are, by their very nature, undemocratic institutions that home must inevitably be miseducative where democracy is concerned. Cultural stock can attach to individual capacities in a variety of ways that fall along a continuum from dead relic to living legacy. Furthermore, the unquestioning obedience that a small child learns at home can attach to his or her capacities as a living legacy that will last forever, but it does not have to. It can instead attach as a temporary disposition that will one day be shed. This latter form of yoking is quite consistent with a joint venture in the education of a democratic citizenry. Granted, it takes effort on home's part to yoke the kind of obedience that is required of very young children to their capacities so that it does not become a living legacy. Granted, this is not the only problem home must solve if it is to cooperate with our joint venture. But untold numbers of homes bear witness to the fact that home can be an active partner in and not a subverter of the education of a democratic citizenry.

Can the military be a participant in our joint venture? Although obedience to command is one of the core items of cultural stock in the military's portfolio, there is no requirement that it be yoked to a given individual's capacities forever. In fact, it is a disposition that an individual is expected to shed when his or her military service is over. Moreover, obedience in the military is normally meant to be a highly context-specific disposition in that a service man or woman is expected to obey not just anyone who issues an order, but a commanding officer. Indeed, the problem the military in a democracy faces in its capacity of educational agent is that of how to attach obedience to people's capacities without its spilling over into non-military contexts, be it momentarily or for a lifetime. Given that service men and women have, at times, been held responsible for following immoral or unjustified orders issued by commanding officers, it would seem that this question is—or at least should already be—on the military's docket.

The case of authoritarian religions differs from that of the military in that the disposition of unquestioning obedience is supposed to become yoked to individual capacities as a lifelong legacy. This disposition is, however, context specific: an individual is expected to obey the commands of God, priest, church, or some other religious entity, and not the orders of just anyone. It seems, then, that whether a religion can cooperate in our joint venture will depend on the content of the commands issued. If the religion orders its advocates to vote for one candidate for office rather than another, or to support one governmental policy rather than another, its ability to cooperate is to that extent diminished. And so it also is if it forbids advocates to read certain political and philosophical works, believe certain ideas, or enter into certain intellectual fields of study.

Religious institutions change over time, however. Thus, for example, the Roman Catholic Church's Index Librorum Prohibitorum forbidding the reading of most of the greatest philosophical works in the Western canon is no longer enforced. Educational agents who can plausibly be charged with subverting our joint venture at one moment in history might, at another historical moment, therefore, be prepared to cooperate with it. Still, religion's cooperation is something to be courted by those whose concern is the education of a democratic citizenry and not taken for granted—as, to be sure, is the cooperation of home, the military, and all other educational agents.

Yet, is it not unduly optimistic to think that the vast majority of "for profit" groups and organizations would cooperate in a venture that did not make, and might in fact lose, them money? Once again, their cooperation cannot be assumed. However, the profit motive does not function as an absolute. "Shoddy electrical work by private contractors on United States military bases in Iraq is widespread and dangerous, causing more deaths and injuries from fires and shocks than the Pentagon has acknowledged, according to internal Army documents" the *New York Times* reported in 2008. One company spokesperson denied the allegation, but accuracy is not the issue here. In affirming the company's unwavering commitment "to the safety of all employees and those the company serves," the spokesperson acknowledged that, even in capitalist regimes, the profit motive is supposed to be moderated by concern for the general welfare.[58]

If a group, organization, or institution can take into account the population's physical well-being, even if to do so reduces profits, why cannot it also be expected to take the population's political well-being into account? Granted, for-profit organizations frequently try to evade responsibility for the harm they do the public while proclaiming their commitment to its well-being and they might act in similar fashion when confronted with evidence of the harm they were doing democracy. But this is merely to say that a group or institution's acknowledgement of its status as an educational agent is but a first step—although, admittedly, not necessarily an easy one—if the smog of democratic miseducation is to be cleared away.

Political theorists tell us that there is no single right path to democracy: it can be the result of, for instance, evolution, revolution, imitation, or imposition.[59] The theory of education as encounter strongly suggests, in turn, that there is no single best way to become a democratic citizen. The called for changes in an individual can be undergone by young or old; they can be the result of evolution, revolt, imposition, imitation, all of the above, or something else entirely; and they can be brought about by a progressive pedagogy or in a very different manner.

Yet, even as our theory holds that there are many different ways to create democratic citizens, it seconds Rousseau's insight that democratic miseducation requires attention. Indeed, it maintains that, whether the source of the miseducation is home, church, neighborhood, the media, or some other institution, it is folly to assume that it will take care of itself. And, finally, because the theory of education as encounter emphasizes the fact that education involves changes in cultures, as well as in individuals, it opens up the possibility of a rapprochement between democracy and the array of educational agents whose cultures conflict with that of democracy. If the education of a democratic citizenry is to be the joint venture it needs to be, many of the cooperating partners will themselves have to undergo change. Just as a democratic culture or society must have citizens who are democracy-friendly, so too democratic citizens must have institutions whose cultures are democracy-friendly.

8

THE "WOMAN QUESTION" IN HIGHER EDUCATION

The "woman question" is as old as the hills and as shifting as the sands. Are women rational enough to be full-fledged citizens of the state? Should the rights of men be extended to women? Should women be given the vote? Should they be given the same education as men? Should they be admitted to medical schools? Law schools? Business schools? Engineering schools? This chapter will bring the theory of education as encounter to bear on the "woman question" in higher education.

In 1944, the Swedish economist Gunnar Myrdal published *An American Dilemma*, a 1,500-page work documenting the huge gap between the principle engraved in the Declaration of Independence that all men are created equal and the reality of African-American lives. Today, there is a another dilemma and this one is worldwide: the huge gap between the principle inscribed in the United Nations' Universal Declaration of Human Rights of the equal and inalienable rights of all members of the human family and the reality of women's lives. The woman question in higher education is one part of this global dilemma.

One who looks at higher education through the lens of the theory of education as encounter will see an educational agent with a unique threefold culturally desig-nated mission. Higher education is expected to preserve that portion of cultural stock known as "the higher learning," transmit it to the next generation, and produce brand new stock. One will also see—and this is what gives the woman question in higher education its special significance—that at least some of the cultural stock in higher education's ever expanding portfolio has the capacity to improve the lives of those in the furthest corners of the earth, and the potential to contribute to the solutions of the pressing problems that now confront the world.

The theory of education as encounter allows us to break down higher education's woman question into a number of interrelated queries. Among them is the distribution question: Does higher education yoke the cultural assets in its keep equally to the capacities of men and women? The production question is equally pressing: Are women equal creators or generators of the wealth higher education produces? There is also the relevance question: Does the cultural stock that higher education preserves, transmits, and generates apply equally to the lives, experiences, work, and deeds of women? And, of course, there is the cultural liabilities question: Is higher education—either wittingly or unwittingly—yoking cultural stock to the capacities of men and women that contributes to and perhaps aggravates its own woman question?

Although some academicians have claimed that to talk about women as a group is essentialist, racist, and classist, let me assure readers that, in focusing on higher education's woman question, I do not attribute some sort of essential nature to women. On the contrary, I leave open both the definition of "woman" and the issue of whether or not women and men have essential natures. Nor should it be thought that higher education's woman question concerns only white, middle class, heterosexual women. In fact, it has to do with all women, which is not to say that women of all classes, races, sexual orientations, and so on experience higher education in the same way or are treated exactly alike.

1. The Missing Students and the New Gender Tracking

Although the doors that once barred women from higher education are now open, untold numbers of the women students who walk through them go missing from the fields of science, technology, engineering, and mathematics.[1] In the last decades of the twentieth century, reports began to circulate of an unexpected gender tracking in higher education across the globe. Even in countries in which women made up at least half of all students, fields of study were proving to be sharply divided according to sex, with women tending to predominate in the so-called "soft" areas of the arts, languages, and literature, as well as pre-professional fields such as nursing, education, and social work: that is, in fields having low academic standing and reduced job opportunities.[2]

The same year in which the new gender tracking began to be noticed at the undergraduate level, the U.S. National Research Council reported that, whereas the majority of doctoral recipients in English and American Languages and Literatures and in Foreign Languages and Literatures were women, men represented about seven-eighths of new Ph.D.s in the so-called "hard" areas of engineering and the mathematical and physical sciences.[3] According to more recent figures, women in the U.S. received 60 percent of the doctor's degrees granted in English and 59 percent in foreign languages, but only 21 percent of the ones granted in engineering and in computer and information sciences, 30 percent of the ones granted in mathematics and statistics, and 32 percent in the physical sciences.[4]

From a historical standpoint, this gender tracking system is noteworthy because the relative absence of women from the "hard" subject areas defeats the aim of the centuries long co-educational movement to extend men's education to women. The prevailing wisdom is that the movement succeeded and women are now equal beneficiaries of what used to be men's education. However, the facts suggest otherwise. Let us assume that women have officially been granted equal entry to what once was considered men's higher education. The data show that this *de jure* success is effectively cancelled out by women's de facto move away from some of the fields that once belonged to men's curriculum.

In the name of equality, there is no more reason to demand that everyone study or learn identical subject matter than that everyone be given the same medical treatment no matter what their ailment. Thus, the new gender tracking does not warrant attention merely because it results in different curricula for different people. Rather, it is problematic in relation to the ideal of gender equality because it routes men and women into subject areas having unequal status in the eyes of both the academy and the world, and from these into occupational areas of unequal pay and prestige.[5]

Now, all this is readily comprehended without the help of the theory of education as encounter. The new dimension our theory introduces is that the gender tracking distributes the culture's wealth unequally to men and women. Seen through its lens, a tracking system is a mechanism for distributing the stock in an educational agent's portfolio. In particular, the new gender tracking constitutes a mechanism by which higher education yokes the knowledge, skills, attitudes, values, methodologies, and worldviews belonging to the fields of science, technology, engineering, and mathematics to the capacities of far fewer women than men. Because the culture places a lower value on the stock belonging to the "soft" areas, the new gender tracking is, therefore, a mechanism for the unequal distribution of higher education's cultural assets.

There is another reason, too, why the new gender tracking deserves attention. Global warming, peak oil, tuberculosis, AIDS, a flu pandemic, the protection of the food supply, water shortages, the collapse of bridges, the world economy: the list of pressing real-life problems whose solutions depend on the yoking to individual capacities of the cultural stock of the sciences, technology, engineering, and mathematics is well nigh endless. In failing to attach these assets to the capacities of large numbers of women, the new gender tracking creates a gap in their knowledge and understanding of the world around them. Unless the deficiency is overcome, this, in turn, means that it is harder for women than for men with the same number of years of schooling to contribute to the solution of many of the world's most serious problems. To put the matter starkly: in failing to yoke the cultural assets of science, technology, engineering, and mathematics to the capacities of countless women, the new gender tracking deprives women of the opportunity to do some of the world's most important work and deprives the world of the opportunity to benefit from the missing women's "brain power."

It must be stressed that the theory of education as encounter does not attribute the gap in women's understanding to their "native" intelligence; rather, it takes it to be a function of their unequal higher education. Still, one can readily imagine someone protesting at this point that so long as women have the opportunity to study the same subjects as men, gender equality is achieved. After all, if a woman does not choose to avail herself of the curricular opportunities offered her, is that not her prerogative?

It is indeed customary to use the language of "choice" when discussing the new gender tracking, and for good reason.[6] There are no rules forbidding women from studying science and mathematics or requiring them to study languages and literature. No official gender quotas are imposed on the "hard" areas of higher education's curriculum. Rather, the fact that a high percentage of women students go missing from the "hard" subject areas is an unforeseen consequence of higher education's elective system: a large-scale by-product, if you will, of many small individual choices. The terminology can, however, be deeply deceptive for a person's choices are not always free from outside influences and pressures and they are not always fully informed.[7]

As it happens, choice is a surprisingly minimal concept. All that is needed for someone, X, to make a choice is that: (a) alternatives exist; (b) X perceives them *as* alternatives; (c) even if X does not like any of the alternatives, X prefers one to the others; and (d) X picks said alternative. Thus, a woman who majors in French, art history, or education probably has chosen to do so. But a choice such as this is not necessarily made freely, is not necessarily rational or autonomous, is not necessarily fully informed, and is not necessarily in the chooser's best interest. To put it bluntly, choosing is compatible with compulsion, conformity, self-delusion, and just plain ignorance.

Oedipus chose to marry Jocasta but he did not choose to marry his mother, even though marry her he did. Less dramatically, a woman who chooses to major in education is not necessarily choosing a low-paying occupation, although this is where she will very likely land. And one who chooses to study French or art history is not consciously denying herself access to the cultural stock she needs to contribute to the solution of, for instance, global warming.

Two lessons emerge from this sketchy conceptual analysis. The first is that, when the subject is women, choice rhetoric is a double-edged sword. Because choice is conceptually related to freedom, autonomy, and self-government, use of the term serves as a reminder of the historic battle to extend the "rights of man" to women—and with these rights the duties of citizenship. It signals that women are indeed moral agents fully capable of making their own decisions. However, the reverse side of moral agency is responsibility. And so the language of choice can constitute a way of saying that the new gender tracking and the paucity of women in the higher ranks of the professoriate are perfectly just: that the reason women are missing is to be found not in men, the socio-economic systems, or the culture, but in women themselves.[8] The second lesson is that it is important to look behind the rhetoric of choice to see what, if anything, is being concealed.[9]

When the subject is the missing women students, the language of choice renders invisible the fact that history is repeating itself. Instead of the old official gender tracking system of separate schools with different curricula for males and females, there is now a de facto gender tracking system *within* co-education. Thus, co-educational environments have come to perform a sorting function analogous to the one that the formal mechanism of separate sex institutions once did. Although today's co-educational system sends both men and women into the world of work, politics, and the professions, by failing to make an equal distribution to women of the cultural assets belonging to science, technology, engineering, and mathematics, it delivers men and women once again into differentially valued occupational areas.

The language of choice also masks an irony. When education had two distinct and clearly labeled gender tracks, few women could elect to study the "hard" areas. Today, most women can, at least in principle, choose to do so. Yet, large numbers of women instead opt for the "soft" areas, many of which lead to public world versions of the very "female" occupations that used to be located in the world of the private home—for example, teaching, nursing, social work.

Choice rhetoric does not merely hide history. It also screens out the chilly co-educational climate for women students. Studies at all levels of schooling have shown that co-educational environments are often less hospitable to girls and women than to boys and men.[10] In higher education, the different treatment of male and female students in co-educational settings produces a chilly climate for women that takes myriad forms, extends beyond classrooms to halls, cafeterias, gymnasiums, athletic fields, residential settings, and extracurricular sites, and ranges over college and university experiences both great and small. If, as seems likely, the climate is chillier for women in the "hard" areas of study than in the "soft" areas, this would go far toward explaining the new gender tracking.

In higher education, the "micro-inequities" of the chilly co-educational classroom climate for students include teachers calling directly on men but not women, calling men by name more often than women, addressing their classes as if no women were present, coaching men but not women for correct answers, waiting longer for men's answer than women's, asking women lower-order questions, and giving longer responses to men's questions. The chilly climate's not-so-micro-inequities include teachers counseling women students to lower their expectations or switch to a "softer" specialty, nominating men and not women for awards and prizes, and inviting men but not women to share the authorship of articles. Interestingly enough, the research indicates that, in co-educational settings, both men and women teachers engage in these often unwitting practices.

The chilly classroom climate's gross inequities include the use of demeaning language and sexist "humor." Thus, for example, law school students call women in their classes "man-hating lesbians" and "feminazi dykes."[11] An instructor shows a slide in an accounting class of a bikini-clad woman "guaranteed to provide accurate measurements." A physics lecturer demonstrates the effects of a vacuum by changing the size of crudely drawn women's "boobs." A surgery professor pinches the breast prothesis of a mastectomy patient and then the breast of a woman radiologist saying, "I'd like to bump into either one of you in an elevator any time."[12] A physics professor includes on a test, "Starting with the lungs and using Bernoulli's equation, describe in full physical detail the production of the sound 'Ohhh' by our lone sophomore female physics major. An anatomical sketch would be helpful."[13]

Comparative research on the climate of different subject areas within higher education is needed. If, however, one conceptualizes co-education as a matter of degree, it seems reasonable to suppose that the climate will be more hospitable for women in fields that are populated mainly by women. And, if this hypothesis is correct, then the mystery appears to be solved of why women students choose to major in the arts, the humanities, and pre-professional fields such as education, nursing, and social work even though it would seem to be against their self-interest to do so.

In many women's eyes, being in a friendlier climate or culture here and now may well outweigh whatever loss of prestige they suffer and whatever economic consequences they anticipate. Needless to say, higher education's chilly classroom climate does not lower the self-esteem or shake the self-confidence of *every* female student. Thus, research is also needed to determine why some women do not seem to experience the climate as chilly, some experience it as such but do not care, and some find it intolerable. Another reasonable hypothesis, however, is that, among those who flock to the "soft" areas, are women who might have stayed the course in the "hard" ones had the climate there been more hospitable; had it supported rather than undermined their confidence in their own capacity to "master" the "hard" subjects.

2. The Missing Faculty and the Attrition in the Professoriate

Even as women students go missing from higher education's fields of study with the greatest prestige, women faculty go missing from the highest ranks of the professoriate. Across the world, women's progress through the ranks has been slow and has been marked by attrition. Although in the U.S. in the year 2007 females accounted for 57 percent of enrollments, in four-year post-secondary institutions 48 percent of all assistant professors, 40 percent of all associate professors, and 36 percent of all full professors were women.[14] In 2006–2007, 44 percent of bachelor degrees in mathematics and statistics, but only 30 percent of doctor's degrees, were awarded to women; similarly, 41 percent of bachelor degrees in the physical sciences, but only 32 percent of doctor's degrees, were awarded to women. Interestingly, the attrition holds true even for the "soft" areas. The 70 percent of bachelor degrees in English awarded to women turned into

60 percent of doctor's degrees in 2006–2007, and the 70 percent of bachelor degrees in foreign languages turned into 59 percent of doctor's degrees.[15]

At the highest ranks of the professoriate everywhere, and in the most prestigious institutions, there are many more men than women. Thus, in 2004, women represented only 18 percent of the faculty at the renowned Massachusetts Institute of Technology[16] and, in 2006, women represented less than 25 percent of the tenured professoriate in 10 of 13 Harvard University faculties.[17] Moreover, as one goes down the ranks, the percentage of women increases. In addition, women cluster in non-tenured positions as adjuncts, part-timers, instructors, or lecturers and are also concentrated in two-year institutions, are more likely to be teachers than researchers, and tend to be heavily represented in low status fields.[18]

Like the gender tracking of women undergraduates into the "soft" devalued subject areas of higher education, the attrition of women in the graduate student and faculty ranks can be represented graphically by a pyramid. In the subject areas pyramid, there are relatively few women in the most highly rewarded subjects at the top, but huge numbers in the less prestigious subjects at the bottom. In the professoriate pyramid, there are few women in the full professor category at the top, and huge numbers at the bottom in positions of lower pay, higher teaching loads, and less prestige.

The attrition differs from the gender tracking, however, in that it is not a matter of the unequal distribution of cultural stock. Rather, it denies women whose capacities have already become yoked to the cultural assets of their fields of choice access to the material resources—the money, the time, the colleagues, the research assistants, the laboratory space—that would allow them to use those cultural assets to generate new cultural wealth.

Authoring or generating new knowledge is one of the things that many, if not most, of those who have earned doctorates have learned to do, and it is what tenured professors at many colleges and universities are able to do. It is difficult, however, for people at or near the bottom of the pyramid or who leave the academy altogether to undertake research projects, publish articles, or write books. In consequence, these individuals—a large proportion of whom are women—do not have an equal opportunity to create, invent, and author new cultural wealth; hence, the larger culture is once again denied the potential benefits of women's "brain power."

The rhetoric of choice is used in reference to the attrition of women in the professoriate just as it is in discussions of the new gender tracking, and, once again, it hides the way history repeats itself. Women used to be excluded from the professoriate as from other male professions by fiat. In the twenty-first century, they are welcomed into it, yet once in the pool—or, as some prefer to say, the pipeline—of candidates for tenure, promotion, and the other rewards of academia, many women go missing.[19]

As in the case of the missing students, the language of choice diverts attention from the unfriendly atmosphere in which women faculty find themselves.[20]

The co-educational classroom climate can be as chilly for women faculty as it is for women students. Indeed, in one study, 48 percent of female faculty reported experiencing at least one form of sexual harassment by students, these ranging from sexist comments to sexual assaults.[21] The academic work environment outside the classroom can also be woman-unfriendly. In the 1980s, for example, a Canadian professor told an interviewer, "I don't think a day goes by that some kind of comment isn't made about my being a woman."[22] In the next decade, $20,000 worth of feminist journals devoted to the study of women were stolen or destroyed at the University of New Mexico, five shelves of journals were replaced with Nazi books, and feminist journals were left on the shelves with swastikas and "bitch propaganda" written across the pages. In 2008, an Internet search turned up scores of reports on the ongoing sexual harassment of women by both students and colleagues on faculties ranging from the arts and sciences to engineering and medicine.[23]

At the time of writing, the percentage of qualified women who leave higher education's workplace for the express purpose of staying home with their children—or who, for that reason, do not enter it in the first place—is a matter of dispute. Regardless of the numbers, however, it seems unproductive to resort to the rhetoric of choice. At the very least, it masks a climate so unfriendly for women who are mothers that these women feel it necessary to "cover": a law student hides her husband and child until she gets a clerkship; a professor of medicine talks to students about obstetrics without alluding to her own visible pregnancy.[24] It also conceals the fact that, whether or not women leave the professoriate with the express intent of becoming full-time mothers, those who have or hope to have young children are being pulled apart by two polar opposite cultures.[25]

3. The Missing Subject Matter and the Stock Imbalance

The attrition in the ranks of the professoriate notwithstanding, in the U.S. today, almost every subject area within higher education includes one or more women on its faculty. Furthermore, in many fields, at least one of these women is a feminist scholar. From the standpoint of gender equality, this is surely a welcome departure from the past. A philosophy or history or economics or art department's courses used to have next to nothing to say about women or gender or feminism. In the early twenty-first century, the resident feminist scholar might well offer a whole course on one of these topics. Nonetheless, the "mainstreaming" of feminist scholars represents another ironic twist of history.

Most early advocates of co-education assumed that the curriculum of higher education already contained a full and accurate account of human civilization. In the name of equality, they simply wanted this presumably objective, unchanging, and universal knowledge to be transmitted to both sexes. It was only in the last decades of the twentieth century, when the new scholarship on women revealed that women's lives, experiences, works, deeds, and ideas were missing from, or else misrepresented in, the theories, narratives, and analyses of the various fields of knowledge, that this judgment was widely questioned. Because higher education draws its subject matter from the cultural stock that these disciplines generate, the discovery of women's "epistemological inequality" in the disciplines of knowledge meant that there also was "epistemological inequality" in the curriculum.

The immediate response to the newly perceived gender gap in higher education's curriculum was to create a brand new curriculum subject called women's studies. From the beginning, however, a number of those who agreed that women were not adequately represented in higher education's curriculum expressed the fear that the creation of a separate subject devoted to women would "ghettoize" the new research. They argued, instead, for the "mainstreaming" of the new scholarship across the disciplines: the integration of the material on women into every subject of the liberal curriculum and, if possible, every course. There is no need to take sides in this debate here.[26] The point of interest for us is that, despite the proliferation of women's studies programs in the U.S. since the 1970s, the generous funding of some mainstreaming projects, and the mainstreaming of women faculty, a genuine "co-curriculum"—one in which women and men are equally represented—does not appear to have been established.

A cultural bookkeeping project that keeps track of women's studies programs and the mainstreaming of scholarship on women is required if we are to know for sure what proportion of the cultural stock in higher education's curriculum proper is devoted to women. It appears to be the case, however, that, with the mainstreaming of women scholars, the very condition that those early feminist critics of women's studies wanted to avoid has come to pass: the segregation of scholarship on women. To be sure, the original concern was that a single enclave for this scholarship would be created within the liberal curriculum as a whole. In the event, separate enclaves have developed within the various areas or departments of higher education. Thus, a history department will offer one or two courses on the history of women, a philosophy department will offer a course on philosophy and feminism, a psychology department will offer one course on women's psychology or development and another perhaps on gender, a political science department will offer a course on women in politics, and so on. Supposing, for the sake of argument, that the lives, experiences, and deeds of women are well represented in those few courses, it is far from clear that the vast majority of courses in each department have added, let alone integrated, women into their subject matter.

Periodic surveys of higher education make statistics available regarding the number and percentage of women in the various subject areas and the several ranks of the professoriate. A culture-wide bookkeeping project could, in its turn, provide relevant data about: (a) the number of higher education institutions that have women's studies programs, departments, concentrations, majors, or the like;

(b) the number of women's studies courses there are in these institutions and their percentage of the total number of offerings; (c) the number and percentage of students enrolled in women's studies courses; (d) the number and percentage of departmentally based courses that take women as their point of departure or include a significant portion of cultural stock about women in their subject matter; and (e) the number and percentage of students taking these courses.

If, as appears to be the case, there is still a gender imbalance in higher education's curriculum proper, it does not follow that there is one in the cultural stock higher education produces. Logically speaking, it is possible that research across the disciplines is generating theories, narratives, analyses and the like about women's lives, deeds, and experiences, and that these items of stock are not then being incorporated into higher education's curriculum. A bookkeeping effort that tracked both the production and transmission of stock about women could determine whether this is, in fact, the case.

Does the epistemological inequality of women in the cultural stock that higher education produces and distributes to its students matter enough to undertake one or more bookkeeping projects devoted to the subject? If one agrees with the statement of the former president of Harvard University that a part of higher education's mission is to pass down as "straight, honest, accurate, and comprehensive" a record of human civilization as possible, then the lack of a gender-balanced stock portfolio and the absence of a genuine co-curriculum matters enormously.[27] Moreover, interviews with women students suggest that the lack of a co-curriculum contributes to both the new gender tracking and the attrition in the ranks.[28]

A woman who does not see herself in the subject matter of her courses will not necessarily switch fields or leave school. Multitudes who never once encountered a healthy, happy, productive woman in her official curriculum are living testimony to this. Nonetheless, the impact on one who finally sees herself and her concerns represented in the literature of her field can be enormous.

Like the gender inequality of the professoriate, the imbalance in the curriculum deprives women students of positive mentors and role models. It reinforces, in the minds of both sexes, the prevailing view that women are not capable of doing meaningful work outside their private homes, let alone of doing significant scholarly research. Above all, by depriving women of contact with the very people, situations, topics, and problems they most readily identify with, it denies them emotionally charged studies. One can only speculate as to how many women might have been inspired to undertake academic pursuits of their own—thus significantly increasing the number of women in the pool from which the professoriate is drawn—had they been able to see themselves in their course materials.

It is also worth noting that most of the authors or generators of cultural stock that represents women's lives, experiences, and so on faithfully are women. If this or any stock is to be projected into the future as living legacy, rather than dead relic, it is well nigh essential that it be included in the curriculum of the next generation. Thus, to the extent that stock about women dies "on the vine" more rapidly or in greater quantities than stock about men, both the women who produce it and the stock itself can be viewed as having received unequal treatment.

4. The New Two-Sphere Ideology

The tendency is to view the new gender tracking, the attrition of women in the professoriate, and the lack of a genuine co-curriculum as separate, unrelated issues. Keep the deep structure of educational thought in mind, however, and these superficially disparate phenomena can be seen to have a single source. When women's place is assumed to be the world of the private home and family, and the function of education is assumed to be the preparation of people for life in the public world of work, politics and the professions, it stands to reason that the cultural stock higher education produces, preserves, and transmits will be mainly about the public world and the men who are believed to inhabit it. It also is to be expected that its assets will, for the most part, be produced by, transmitted by, and distributed to men.

To be sure, one might have thought that the several entrances of women into higher education would have brought about the demise of that old two-sphere ideology. Yet, the labels "hard" and "soft," the new gender tracking, a climate in which women can still be reduced to body parts and portrayed as freaks of nature, and the eerie historical parallels testify to the ideology's continued existence. A skeptic might want to insist that the demeaning language and sexist humor are signs of nothing more than "free-floating" misogyny, that the terms "hard" and "soft" are meaningless vestiges of the past, and that the historical parallels are mere coincidences. However, these ad hoc responses conceal the connections between and among the various phenomena.

The terms "hard" and "soft" not only have gendered connotations, with "hard" being associated with males and masculinity and "soft" with females and femininity. The items of cultural stock that the "hard" areas claim as their own— for instance, objectivity, logical analysis, mathematical expertise, and an aggressively intellectual stance—are the very ones that have historically and culturally been associated with the world of work, politics, and the professions, and have been thought to belong to the men whose place that was believed to be. Similarly, the items of cultural stock that the portfolios of the "soft" areas of study are said to contain—for instance, empathy, connectedness to others, and a concern for human relationships—are ones that have historically and culturally been associated with the world of the private home and family, and have been thought to belong to the women who dwell there.[29]

In other words, the cultural stock in the portfolios of the areas of study into which the new gender tracking tends to place men and women is gendered.

Not surprisingly, the labels "hard" and "soft" also carry with them the value hierarchy that was presupposed by the old public/private split. Just as the world of work, politics, and the professions was considered to be of much greater importance than the world of the private home and family, the "hard" areas of study are considered more important than the "soft" areas. Indeed, the distinction within higher education between the "hard" and "soft" areas of study is drawn in such a way that it can be considered a version of the public/private split. To be sure, the "hard" and "soft" areas are fields of study, not spheres of society. But, with the cultural stock of the "hard" areas genderized in favor of males, and the stock of the "soft" areas of study genderized in favor of females, the two sets of fields represent, as it were, higher education's equivalent of the public and private worlds.

Why are co-educational classrooms and the academic workplace so often unfriendly to women? One reason is that there is a mismatch between the gender assignment of the items of stock in higher education's portfolio and that of the women to whose capacities that stock is supposed to attach. Immanuel Kant was reading from a cultural script when he said, "Laborious learning or painful pondering, even if a woman should greatly succeed in it, destroys the merits that are proper to her sex" and "A woman who has a head full of Greek . . . or carries on fundamental controversies about mechanics . . . might as well even have a beard."[30] When masculinity and femininity are culturally constructed as polar opposites and intellectual activities are considered to be male or masculine items of cultural stock, the more items of "male" or "masculine" cultural stock that become yoked to the capacities of a female individual, the more likely it is that she will be perceived as lacking the femininity that culturally defines a female human being.

In *The Subjection of Women*, John Stuart Mill wrote: "Women who read, much more women who write, are, in the existing constitution of things, a contradiction and a disturbing element."[31] Think now about a woman student in one of the "hard" areas of higher education's curriculum. If she is to succeed in her chosen field, her capacities must become yoked to mathematical knowledge and analytic skills: in other words, to stock that the culture considers to be the property of biological males. This means that, unless she goes out of her way to ward off perceptions of masculinity, she is at risk of being seen as a freak of nature.[32]

Both the outright hostility to women in co-educational classrooms and the more subtle behaviors that can make them feel like second-class citizens are explained when the climate is understood to be a surface manifestation of the two-sphere ideology; or, rather, of an updated version of that ideology. The idea of two separate spheres, one the domain of men and the other the domain of woman, is often portrayed as a historically interesting item of cultural stock that, in the twentieth century, became a dead relic. It is true that twentieth-century women gave the lie to the ideology by gaining access to higher education, winning the vote, and making their way into what had, historically, been men's jobs and professions. Yet, fundamentalist religions continue to yoke the two-sphere ideology to the capacities of millions of men and women as a living legacy.[33] There is ample evidence, moreover, that, for many men and women, the old two-sphere split has been replaced by a "post-feminist" version of that ideology.

Recognizing that the world has changed, the updated public/private split acknowledges women's suffrage and their right to men's education. In addition, it takes it for granted that women will work outside the home; indeed, that they will be not only teachers and nurses, but also doctors, lawyers, factory workers, bankers, and perhaps even miners, engineers, physicists, and computer scientists. It clings, however, to the old gender stereotypes, the vision of the two spheres as polar opposites, and the belief that, if a woman becomes a mother, her proper place is, once again, the world of the private home.

Commentators on higher education tend to assume that participation in academic life is time consuming. When ruminating publicly in 2005 about the missing women in science and engineering "in the highest ranking places," the then president of Harvard University said that these fields, like almost all the "high-powered" professions, "expect a large number of hours in the office, they expect a flexibility of schedules to respond to contingency, they expect a continuity of effort through the life cycle, and they expect . . . that the mind is always working on the problems that are in the job, even when the job is not taking place."[34]

According to the old two-sphere ideology the world of the private home and family is equally demanding for women, and so it is in the updated version. To be sure, a good mother is allowed to buy take-out and perhaps let the dust accumulate. But she should never let her baby cry, she has to be on call to nurse all day and night, she must continually devise new ways to stimulate her child's intellect, she must oversee the homework of her older offspring and chauffeur them to their myriad after-school activities, and she should probably consider no babysitter good enough for him or her.

"I was haunted by the stereotype of the mother whose love is 'unconditional'; and by the visual and literary images of motherhood as a single minded identity," wrote American poet and feminist theorist Adrienne Rich about the period when her children were very young.[35] The generations come and go, but the stereotype survives and so does maternal guilt—and paternal guilt as well. In the 1940s, a teenager was informed that her father felt embarrassed and humiliated because her mother, a schoolteacher, worked outside her home. In the 1960s, a pregnant woman was told by a man interviewing her for an academic position that, when her child was born, she, being a normal woman, would want to stay home with him or her. In the first years of the twenty-first century, a pregnant woman was pressured by her women friends to give up her tenure-track position once her baby was born and an exhausted instructor at a community college felt guilty for not being a stay-at-home mother.

Insisting that mothers are better suited than any other women to make and shape their own children, what has been called "the new momism"[36] makes no allowance for the fact that a woman who becomes a mother may want to keep working outside the home; that she may have to do so for economic reasons; or that it may be prudent for her to do so in case her husband loses his job, becomes incapacitated, dies, or leaves her. In its eyes, if a woman does not devote herself to full-time mothering, her children will suffer irreparable harm.[37]

In the course of discussing civilizations and religions, Nobel Prize-winning economist Amartya Sen described a " 'solitarist' approach to human identity, which sees human beings as members of exactly one group."[38] The "solitarist approach" also characterizes the culture of home as defined by the new momism. In 2004, the researchers who coined that term wrote that it "redefines all women, first and foremost through their relationships with children. Thus, being a citizen, a worker, a governor, an actress, a First Lady, all are supposed to take a backseat to motherhood."[39]

Expecting its members to devote practically all their time and energies to its designated tasks, duties, and responsibilities, higher education also takes a solitarist approach to human identity. Just as in home's culture being a teacher and scholar or researcher is supposed to take a backseat to being a mother, in higher education's culture being a mother is supposed to take a backseat to being a teacher and scholar or researcher. Historically tailored for men who either had no family obligations, or else had a wife who stayed home and took care of the children, its ideal worker was an individual with minimal domestic responsibilities. One might have thought that the fact that those stay-at-home wives may now be colleagues would have brought about significant change in the workplace, but it has not.

Think about the time demands. Think about the assumption that the mind must always be on the job. Think about the fact that higher education's tenure policies impose "a rigid tenure clock that requires a period of intense effort at precisely the period when most families have young children."[40] Think about such seemingly trivial academic mores as the practice of holding departmental and committee meetings in the late afternoon, the very time of day when children are tired, restless, and hungry. There is no sinister plot here. No one consciously designed higher education's way of life so that women who entered the professoriate would go missing. Forgetting that women have no wives, the academy has simply clung to practices that presuppose the outsourcing of the professoriate's childrearing and other domestic responsibilities to wives.

When there were two formally distinct educations—one for males and the other for females—the relatively few women students who walked through higher education's doors crossed the gender tracks with round-trip tickets in their hands. Whereas the men's destination upon graduation was the world of work, politics, and the professions, the women were expected to return to the world of the private home from whence they had come. And, for the most part, they did. By the late twentieth century, however, women students in higher education were being issued one-way tickets: their destination, like the men's, was the public world. The problem that continues to face that subset of women who choose to enter the professoriate is that, after officially welcoming them into its faculty ranks, higher education has done little to accommodate its new workers. Regardless of whether a woman is a faculty member in a "hard" or a "soft" area, she has either to eschew that heaviest of domestic responsibilities—childrearing—or risk being torn apart.[41]

The yoking to the capacities of both men and women of an updated two-sphere ideology goes far toward explaining the disappearance of women in the "hard" areas of study and in the professoriate, and is also the key to understanding the gender imbalance in the cultural stock that higher education preserves, generates, and transmits. One might have expected that, with the entrance of women into the professoriate, the gender imbalance in the stock would disappear. To the extent that it has not, it is tempting once again to resort to choice rhetoric and say that women scholars, like men scholars, tend to choose "gender-neutral" topics. However, the language of choice masks faculty women's reality.

There is, in the first place, the simple fact that many of the women at the bottom of the pyramid are not in a position to engage in research. When, moreover, the two-sphere ideology is taken into account, it also becomes apparent that women who study women have two strikes against them. The first stems from the fact that a researcher will inevitably possess a number of items of stock that, at present, are genderized in favor of males. Thus, women who do research are, from the start, at risk of being perceived as freaks of nature. In addition, higher education subscribes to a version of the principle of guilt by association by which an individual has only as much status as his or her objects of study have in the culture at large.[42] The two-sphere ideology leaves little doubt as to the status in the culture at large of cultural stock associated with women. It would thus seem to be far more prudent for an academic woman to choose to do research on topics that are presumed to be gender-neutral, rather than on women or ones that are women-related.

5. The "Man Question" in Higher Education

The theory of education as encounter takes no stand as to whether higher education ought to attempt to solve the problem of its missing women; indeed, it takes no stand as to whether higher education should have opened its doors to women in the first place or, for that matter, on the very ideal of gender equality. It notes, however, that, should higher education want to solve its "woman question," it will have to address its "man question."

Even as the new gender tracking distributes one part of the wealth in higher education's portfolio to too few women, it distributes another part of the wealth to too few men. Why does one seldom hear of official inquiries whose mission it is to discover why there are not more men in the areas of language, literature, and the arts? Why are few, if any, commissions set up to find out why there are not as many men as women in the nursing, social work, and school teaching pipelines? The failure to care that men go missing from the "soft" areas of study signals the belief that the stock in the portfolios of those fields has little value. This assessment of the stock's value is one more bit of evidence that the two-sphere ideology continues to inform educational thought. The assumption that it does not matter that higher education is failing to yoke the cultural stock in the portfolios of the "soft" areas of study to the capacities of a great many men does not withstand scrutiny, however.

Consider Martha Nussbaum's impassioned defense of the thesis that the literary imagination is a part of public rationality. "The person brought up solely on economic texts has not been encouraged to think of workers (or, indeed, anyone else) as fully human beings, with stories of their own to tell" wrote Nussbaum.[43] The very form of mainstream realistic novels, she went on to say,

> constructs compassion in readers, positioning them as people who care intensely about the suffering and bad luck of others, and who identify with them in ways that show possibilities for themselves. Like the spectators of tragic drama in ancient Greece, novel-readers have both empathy with the plight of characters, experiencing what happens to them as if from their point of view, and also pity, which goes beyond empathy in that it involves a spectatorial judgment that the characters' misfortunes are indeed serious and have indeed arisen not through their fault.[44]

The question of whether reading realistic novels or any other form of literary study is the only route or the best route to the goal of yoking a concern "for the good of other people whose lives are distant from our own"[45] need not concern us. Perhaps historical study can bring about the same result. Perhaps the goal can be achieved equally well through the study of social work cases. The point at issue, and that Nussbaum's extended analysis of public rationality brings out so beautifully, is that at least some of the items of cultural stock in the keep of higher education's "soft" subject areas have immense value.

Consider, too, that, among the traits and dispositions that contemporary theorists of democracy claim a democratic citizen must possess are mutual respect, understanding different perspectives, empathy, listening, and the imaginative reconstruction of self as other[46]—all of which items of cultural stock are to be found in the portfolios of the "soft" areas of study. The receptiveness to art and literature from other places that is said to be an attribute of world citizenship or cosmopolitanism[47] can also be found there. And, for one last example of the importance of stock belonging to the "soft" areas, think about Le Chambon, a village in Southern France, whose inhabitants saved the lives of thousands of Jewish children and adults during World War II. The traits and dispositions they drew upon included responding directly to the plight of others, giving oneself as opposed to merely giving things to those in need, and living in intimacy with others.[48]

At the start of this chapter, the new gender tracking was shown to cause higher education to fall short of the ideal of gender equality because it fails to yoke the assets in the keep of the "hard" subject areas to many women. Higher education now can be seen to fall short of the ideal on two counts, for it also fails to yoke the assets in the keep of the "soft" areas to the capacities of many men. Indeed, the new gender tracking provides us with a reenactment, as it were, of Rousseau's story about Sophie and Emile.

If Rousseau came back today as a ghost, he would doubtless be dismayed to learn that, in the centuries since the publication of *Emile*, higher education gradually opened its doors to women. He would presumably be delighted, however, to discover that many women go missing because higher education has put an updated version of that ideology in its place. Rousseau would feel compelled to remind us, however, of the conclusion he drew when he divided up traits and dispositions according to gender and assigned "masculine" ones such as rationality, objectivity, and logical acumen to the boy Emile and "feminine" ones such as the three Cs of care, concern, and connection to Sophie. Recognizing that some of Emile's and also some of Sophie's traits were essential to morality, he pointed out that neither Sophie nor Emile was capable of being a fully moral individual; that, on the contrary, only the two of them together—or, to generalize his point, only a heterosexual couple—could be a fully moral person.

Rousseau did not believe that women could or should be citizens of a democracy, and so he did not have to consider the inherent conflict between the two-sphere ideology and democratic theory. Two-hundred-and-fifty years later, the clash cannot be ignored. Granted, higher education's new gender tracking does not make it absolutely impossible for a man or woman to be a genuinely democratic citizen. In spite of the tracking, the supposedly masculine and feminine items of cultural stock that theorists of democracy say a citizen should possess can and often do become yoked to the capacities of single individuals. But the new gender tracking means that, for the most part, a man who is tracked into the "hard" areas will have to pair up with a woman tracked into the "soft" areas in order to qualify as such; and vice versa.

In sum, higher education has a heterosexual bias. It also has a "democracy question" that, like both its "woman question" and its "man question," turns on the two-sphere ideology. To be sure, theorists of democracy tend to assign the task of citizen making to lower rather than higher education. Still, insofar as higher education withholds the cultural stock out of which democratic citizens are made from either men or women, it can be said to undermine that project. Furthermore, and quite aside from the issue of democracy, to the extent that higher education keeps the cultural assets housed in the "soft" areas from attaching to the capacities of men, it makes it that much more difficult to solve its "woman question."

6. At the Clashing Point

Modest measures, ranging from the establishment of better childcare facilities and "opt-out" policies for tenure-track faculty who become new parents to the creation of study centers for students in undergraduate science courses, have been proposed in response to higher education's "woman question." Yet, helpful as these may be, more far-reaching changes are also required.[49]

Writing about the fundamental novelties in science that he called anomalies, Thomas Kuhn said that the scientific assimilation of an anomalous fact "demands a more than additive adjustment of theory."[50] Pointing out that anomalies are "produced inadvertently by a game played under one set of rules," he argued that their assimilation "requires the elaboration of another set."[51] Because the presence of significant numbers of women is a genuinely anomalous fact for higher education, "piecemeal tinkering" to solve its woman question is akin to science's additive adjustments to existing scientific theory. Just as science requires a new paradigm if an anomaly is to be assimilated, higher education requires a transformed culture if the women who go through its doors are to be fully integrated. It needs to change not only its practices but also its beliefs, attitudes, values, and worldviews. Given that the larger culture shares the pertinent aspects of higher education's culture, this is no simple task. Yet, who ever said that the ideal of gender equality could be easily achieved?

Higher education is not the only institution that must undergo a sea change if the problem of its missing women is to be solved. Even as it relinquishes its definition of the ideal faculty member as someone with either no domestic responsibilities or else a wife at home, home and family must abandon definitions of a good mother that envision childrearing as a full-time, all-encompassing occupation for which only women are qualified. Otherwise, the women who use higher education's childcare facilities will continue to feel that they are not good enough mothers, while those who seek new kinds of work schedules will be made to feel that they are not good enough scholars.[52] And otherwise many of the men who try to do their fair share of childrearing will be treated as unqualified, and those who might want to be stay-at-home fathers will feel they are not suited for the job.[53]

In "The Two Cultures," a lecture delivered in Cambridge, England in 1959 that drew international attention, British novelist and scientist C.P. Snow examined the intellectual life of Western society and found that it was split into two separate, polar opposite cultures. "At the one pole we have the literary intellectuals," said Snow, and "at the other scientists."[54] Between these two cultures he discerned "a gulf of mutual incomprehension." "Their attitudes are so different," he added, that even on the level of emotion, "they can't find much common ground."[55]

Snow's lecture would seem to be far removed from our subject: the literary culture he described was mainly located outside the academy, and the population of both it and his scientific culture was almost 100 percent male. However, the areas of study that constitute the "hard" areas of the new gender tracking are, in effect, Snow's scientific culture in contemporary guise. The arts and humanities can, in turn, be considered his literary culture in modern dress and they map nicely onto the "soft" areas; or, rather, an updated literary culture along with the professionally oriented areas of education, nursing, and social work represent the "soft" category.

Do the "hard" and "soft" areas of the academy qualify as cultures? Defining "culture" in roughly the same way it has been in this volume, Snow assured his audience that the sciences really do constitute a culture for "there are common attitudes, common standards and patterns of behaviour, common approaches and assumptions."[56] And, in an exegesis of his lecture, he made explicit what earlier he had simply assumed, namely that the literary culture is also really a culture.[57] So, too, higher education really is a culture, and its "hard" and "soft" areas are also cultures.

More germane to this discussion, however, is Snow's finding that the literary and scientific cultures could not talk to one another. Whether or not this holds true for higher education's "hard" and "soft" areas, his discovery is more than matched by the lack of communication between the two cultures at issue here—home's and higher education's. The deep structure of educational thought makes it difficult for higher education to talk *about* the world of the private home and family, let alone talk *to* it. Placing home outside the boundaries of the educational realm and defining education as preparation for life in the world of work, politics, and the professions, it renders inquiry into and discussion about life at home irrelevant, if not actually dysfunctional. From the standpoint of the deep structure, for higher education to think seriously about home's relationship to the workplace is to devote its energies to an unworthy subject, thereby deflecting attention from what counts—namely, preparation for life in the public sphere of work, politics, and the professions.[58]

Because higher education's distinctive mission as an institution dedicated to the generation of new cultural stock and the transmission of both new and old stock makes it uniquely qualified to solve its woman problem, Snow's opinion of what, in the best of all possible worlds, can occur at the clashing point of two polar opposite cultures bears repeating:

> At the heart of thought and creation we are letting some of our best chances go by default. The clashing point of two subjects, two disciplines, two cultures—of two galaxies, so far as that goes—ought to produce creative chances. In the history of mental activity that has been where some of the break-throughs came. The chances are there now. But they are there, as it were, in a vacuum because those in the two cultures can't talk to each other.[59]

In the past, the peaceful coexistence of the public and private spheres was taken for granted. That supposedly happy yin-yang state depended on women and men knowing their "places," and on both sexes agreeing that women's place was in the home. The world has changed, however, and women now stand at the clashing point of the cultures of two polar opposite realms. What Snow perceived to be creative chances are there. The question is: Will the phenomenon of the missing women become the occasion for breakthroughs that bring the cultures of higher education and the private home and family into a new improved relationship?

Snow looked to schooling to bring his two cultures together.[60] Recognizing that school is but one of many educational agents, and not necessarily the most effective one, our theory counsels a healthy skepticism regarding the power of formal educational institutions. Nevertheless, the theory of education as encounter makes it clear that, if the problem of the missing women is to be solved, higher education must do its part. The unequal distribution to women of the cultural assets belonging to the "hard" areas of study, and to men of cultural assets belonging to the "soft" areas, is higher education's doing. So is the withholding from large numbers of qualified women the material resources needed to create new cultural assets. In addition, higher education is guilty of what, from the standpoint of the ideal of gender equality, constitutes a sin of commission.

It is easy to shrug off old, accepted practices on the grounds that they are so trivial as to be innocuous. How, for example, can it possibly matter that universities talk about "training" teachers and "educating" doctors, lawyers, and engineers? What difference can it make that the buildings in which teachers are "trained" are often located at the geographical fringes of university campuses? What difference that few, if any, courses offered by philosophy departments take as their points of departure cultural stock associated with the world of the private home and family? Or that, in the field of psychology, the area of cognitive psychology has far more prestige than child development?

One major lesson our theory teaches is that even seemingly trivial practices can yoke items of cultural stock to people's capacities. When the several practices listed here are added to the many other apparently trivial ones of higher education that slight areas of study and topics culturally associated with the private home and family, the sum total can be seen to be a hidden curriculum that helps perpetuate the two-sphere ideology.

There is no doubt that the deep structure of educational thought places higher education in a bind: to solve its woman problem, it has to talk about what its own deeply held beliefs say is taboo. Were it to break its silence, however, it could martial the considerable intellectual resources of both the "hard" and the "soft" areas in the hope of improving the lives of those who walk through its doors. In addition to launching an inquiry into the nature, structure, and function of work and home, this broad-based interdisciplinary study could survey alternative designs for living and encourage the search for new options.

Were higher education to defy the deep structure's taboo on talk about the private world of home and family, it could also undertake a self-study—a kind of internal bookkeeping project—to determine which of its practices perpetuate the two-sphere ideology. By no stretch of the imagination can higher education be considered the first or the only educational agent to yoke one or another aspect of the two-sphere ideology to the capacities of those who walk through its doors. Home, family, religious institutions, community organizations, school, the mass media, and more will have performed this job beforehand for untold numbers of those individuals and will be continuing to do it. It should not be supposed, either, that every individual inside higher education's gates embraces the ideology. Nevertheless, if higher education is to do its share in resolving its "woman question," it will, at some point in the process, need to acknowledge its own miseducative sins of omission and commission, as well as those of others; which is to say that it will need to identify the aspects of its culture that perpetuate the very problem of the missing women it is trying to solve.

Supposing that higher education does start talking, there is no guarantee that a breakthrough that transforms the two polar opposite cultures of higher education and home will in fact occur. Taking the path of least resistance, higher education could convert the problem of the missing women into an abstract theoretical conundrum and stop there.[61] On the other hand, just as there have in the past been experimental colleges that sought to integrate the two supposedly polar opposites of work experience and academic learning,[62] some institutions of higher learning could become "laboratory colleges," as it were, whose object was to integrate the polar opposite cultures of home and academia in the hope of thereby resolving higher education's "woman question."

To be sure, commentators on higher education who argue that it has one and only one goal, namely "the mastery of intellectual and scholarly skills"[63] will reject any suggestion that it take on a "non-academic" mission of this sort. But the plausibility of this narrow conception of higher education's business rests on the deep structure of educational thought's narrow conception of education. Once that is rejected and it is seen that education is everywhere, and is not necessarily intentional or beneficial, a more expansive conception of higher education is required.

If, in order to solve the problem of the missing women, one or more institutions of higher learning were to join theory and practice, how exactly would they be designed? Would the cultures of home and higher education continue to be polar opposites or would they become sufficiently similar to qualify as a single culture? Would gender still be a relevant category? Would women continue to have primary responsibility for childrearing or would men become equal partners in all aspects of the process? Would men need compensatory education in the three Cs of care, concern, and connection in order to do the job well? If women flocked into the "hard" areas of study, would those fields change? Would men really move into the "soft" areas or would those fields start to wither away?

A theory of education, no matter how broad, cannot possibly predict what changes a breakthrough would bring about. It is safe to say, however, that profound questions will arise should the two-sphere ideology become a pressing item on higher education's agenda because the lesson to be learned from the phenomenon of the missing women is that both cultural and individual transformation are likely to become the order of the day.

9

WHAT SCHOOL CAN AND CANNOT DO

In the last days of the twentieth century, Amartya Sen exhorted his colleagues to look at particular institutions together in order to see what they can and cannot do in combination with one another.[1] For the better part of that century, anthropologists and sociologists had tended to take an integrated approach to institutions, but he was concerned about the tendency of economists to focus almost exclusively on the market and to treat it as an entirely separate entity. This same propensity prevails with respect to school.

Assuming falsely that school is a culture's one and only educational agent, the deep structure of educational thought has cast the large constellation of educational agents in shadow. In consequence, school has been expected to perform such miracles as single handedly putting an end to a nation's social ills or making it a leader in the global economy. Viewing school together with its sister and brother educational agents, and going on the assumption that ought implies can, the theory of education as encounter provides insight into what school can and cannot do, and thereby illuminates what it should and should not set out to do.

1. The Division of Educational Labor

If an institution has a monopoly over X, it does not have to worry about the role of other institutions in relation to X. Should that institution lose its monopoly, the actions of those others may become pressing matters. So it is for a company with a monopoly over the production of oil and so it is with school's presumed monopoly over education. When education is reduced to schooling, it makes no sense to ask what the other educational agents in the culture are doing, let alone if they are working in harmony or at cross-purposes with school, for there is thought to be only one such agent. Acknowledge the brute fact of multiple educational agencies and the tasks of the whole range of educational agents become a matter of concern.

In an illuminating discussion of his discipline's methods, a mid-twentieth-century anthropologist wrote that he first saw a community as an intuited whole and then moved from what was immediately visible to an understanding of the character of its life.[2] School is immediately visible to anyone interested in education. Someone who keeps looking may then discern home and ask how the educational labor is divided between the two.[3] Perhaps churches, mosques, and synagogues will next come into view, or perhaps the media, the military, and governmental agencies will suddenly appear. Regardless of the order of the sightings, as the landscape becomes crowded with educational agents, the questions multiply. That the numerous questions about the way a culture divides up its educational labor are infrequently, if ever, given voice is a measure of the deep structure of educational thought's neglect of the standpoint of the culture and mute testimony to its acceptance of the false equation between education and schooling. Happily, the theory of education as encounter provides a framework within which these questions can be articulated.

How many educational agents are there, what items of cultural stock are in their respective portfolios, and to which individuals do they distribute the stock? A cultural bookkeeping project can provide answers to these basic queries but our theory invites questions that go beyond mere bookkeeping, for instance: Are the various educational agents mutually supportive or do they undermine one another's efforts? Do their responsibilities overlap or are they separate and distinct? Has one or another educational agent stopped fulfilling one or more of its educational functions? If so, should another agent step into the breach? Does the culture have educational needs that no educational agent is presently meeting? If so, should a new agent be created?

Discussions of how best to divide up the labor go back at least to Plato's *Republic*. As Socrates launched the thought experiment that yielded his Just State, he asked if people should specialize or be as self-sufficient as possible. His answer was that each person should perform the task that he or she was born to do—whether it be providing food, building ships, making shoes, or governing the state.

A culture's educational agents do not have innate natures in Plato's sense. Some of them—for instance, kindergartens, military academies, and schools of law and medicine—will have been designed to serve specific educational purposes. But Plato considered a person's inborn nature to be fixed and immutable, and he also assumed that each individual is suited, by nature, to do only one task well. History reveals, however, that educational agents can change over time and that, when they do, their educational functions may change. Thus, for example, home and family underwent such great changes in early colonial America that they could no longer fulfill the educational duty of "imparting civilization to the young" that had long been theirs.[4] In that same period, the institution of apprenticeship changed sufficiently that, although it continued to transmit skills, it stopped providing the instruction in literacy that had been another of its educational functions.[5] Moreover, by the nineteenth century, apprenticeship was no longer providing the manual training it once did.

There are, in sum, no good grounds for believing that an educational agent has an immutable or essential nature. Nor is the Platonic assumption warranted that an educational agent can perform only one task well. Nonetheless, Plato's solution to the problem of how best to divide up the labor required by his Just State is instructive. Whereas financial profit or some other form of self-interest has tended to be the motive behind division of labor thinking, Socrates' objective was to achieve the greater good.[6] Although he clearly valued efficiency, his ultimate concern was the well-being of the state as a whole. It was for this reason that he insisted that each individual do only the job that he or she is best suited by nature to do. Otherwise, he said, the result would be a malfunctioning, unhealthy city-state. The theory of education as encounter, in its turn, heightens our awareness that, if a culture's educational agents work at cross-purposes, rather than in harmony, the culture as a whole is likely to be miseducative.[7]

In his classic study of the subject, French sociologist Emile Durkheim wrote that the division of labor in society "cannot be effected according to any preconceived plan . . . The division must come about of itself, and progressively."[8] Whether this rule holds for the division of educational labor is a question for future investigation. It should be noted, however, that our theory does not specify the particular form that a culture's division of educational labor should take. Rejecting the notion that institutions have essential natures, it maintains a strict neutrality regarding the question of which educational agents are directly responsible for which educational tasks. Nor does the theory of education as encounter say if all the partners in the educational enterprise are equal or if some are more senior than others; which educational agent should prevail when one of them is subverting the work of another; or when, if ever, new educational agents should be created. Rather, it assumes that every culture will answer these in light of its own circumstances.

The theory of education as encounter does recognize, however, that new educational agents are continually emerging to share the work, and that the educational labor to be done in a given culture also changes. Who, 100 years ago, would have dreamed that the electronic media would be one of the most powerful educational agents in young people's lives or that the yoking of computer skills to individual capacities would become a crying educational need? Who would have thought that English speakers would do well to learn Chinese and Arabic and that nations whose inhabitants had been leaving in droves for foreign lands would be playing host to immigrants of their own? Who, even 50 years ago, suspected that climate change and the global economy would be topics that people needed to know about? For that matter, who could have known that, because of the invention of Velcro, young children would no longer need to learn how to tie their shoelaces?

Furthermore, our theory alerts us to the fact that there is no guarantee—no invisible hand of the sort posited by Adam Smith—to ensure that a culture's educational labor will be divided in a manner that benefits all. For an example of a culture's educational agents working together for the general welfare, consider Denmark's early twenty-first-century effort to fill its roads with electric cars. To the uninitiated, this might appear to be a technological feat pure and simple. In fact, however, education was one of its main ingredients. Briefly, the extraordinarily high taxes that the government imposed both on gasoline and on gas-operated vehicles served to yoke to individual capacities positive attitudes toward the new technology, as well as the requisite patterns of behavior. Industry, then, did its part in creating a new mindset in the populace, and so did home and family.[9]

For an instance of a culture's educational agents failing to work together for the greater good, consider the case of SEED, a publicly funded public boarding school in Washington D.C. founded in 1998 for the express purpose of preparing inner-city students for college.[10] SEED's success in accomplishing this goal has been celebrated. However, the very fact that it was deemed necessary to take Rousseau's advice and remove teenagers from their homes, neighborhoods, and local schools strongly suggests that the existing division of labor was not satisfactory. For reasons that may well have been beyond their control, one or more of the major educational agents in those young lives had presumably found it difficult to yoke the relevant cultural assets and to refrain from yoking damaging cultural liabilities to the young people's capacities. This is not to say that any one of those educational agents was to blame for the miseducation that was occurring. They may not have been able to act otherwise. Nonetheless, the positive outcomes for which SEED is justly praised highlight a spectacular failure of the existing division of educational labor.

2. No School Is an Island

Throughout its history, school's educational mission has been contested. In recent memory there have been "back-to-basics" minimalists who reduce school's responsibility to the teaching of the three Rs of reading, writing, and arithmetic; so-called "romantics" who see school as the place where children's natural talents can flourish; and "essentialists" who take school's job to be the passing down of the cultural heritage, by which they mean the West's literary canon and its so-called "higher" or academic learning. As well, there have been those who hold that school's main purpose is to prepare the next generation for college and careers, and those who have wanted school to transform society.[11] The theory of education as encounter takes no stand as to which, if any, of these positions is to be preferred. When questions arise about school's functions, it does, however, advise one and all to remember that, to paraphrase the English poet John Donne: no school is an island entire to itself; it is a piece of the continent, a part of the main.

Newborns do not move directly from the womb to school. Home, family, and any number of other educational agents write on those supposedly blank slates long before school does. Indeed, school is neither the first educational agent to yoke cultural stock to a given individual's capacities nor the only one to do so when a child is in attendance there. On the contrary, schoolchildren have "extra-school" educational encounters when the bell tolls each afternoon, some of which may support and sustain school's efforts, some of which will perhaps have no effect on these, and some of which may hinder or actually undermine the yokings of cultural stock to individual capacities that school is trying to bring about. Thus, whatever one believes school's responsibilities are or should be: to carry these out well, school needs some idea of what cultural stock the other educational agents in its students' lives are yoking to their capacities.

Think of SEED. Although it was successful in sending its graduates to college, a number of students dropped out before graduation. SEED's student body was composed mainly of African-Americans from the inner city. When they went home on weekends and summer vacations, they re-entered a culture in which the beliefs prevailed that it is not okay to be intelligent, that academic learning is for whites only, and that SEED itself is a "D Block," one definition of which is "The worse block in the worst hood of the city" and another is "Death Row."[12]

A common theme in the first-hand reports of those who have moved from one socio-economic class to another is guilt for having betrayed those who are left behind.[13] Guilt is not a feeling or emotion that just happens to develop. It is an item of cultural stock that is yoked to people's capacities by family, friends, local community, the media, or some other educational agents. It would not be surprising, then, if the very educational agents that transmitted a disdain of academic learning to SEED students also yoked the capacities of at least some of them to the belief that, in attending a college preparatory boarding school, they were betraying their friends and families, and even their race.

Distrust of school, disdain for academic learning, guilt, and self-hatred: insofar as educational agents in school's cultural surround are yoking items of cultural stock such as these to the capacities of schoolchildren, it is well-nigh self-defeating to treat school as an island entire to itself. Besides, in deciding what school's responsibilities should be, it is important to know if the culture has any vital educational needs that are not being met.

Here is one last thought experiment. Subtract school from the large con-figuration of educational agents and determine what cultural assets the remainder transmits to the next generation. Then, ask yourself what especially valuable cultural assets, if any, are not being yoked to individual capacities. If you can identify such assets, ask yourself if the educational agent whose responsibility it has been to do this part of the culture's educational labor is no longer able to do it; or, if, perhaps, these items of stock are so new—or else, so newly thought to be valuable—that no existing educational agent has taken on the task of transmitting them.

Needless to say, the deep structure of educational thought denies the premise upon which this experiment rests, namely that a culture divides up its educational labor among numerous educational agents. Yet, even as that belief system views school as a self-contained entity, it assigns functions to school that presuppose the prior yokings to children's capacities by other educational agents of a goodly amount of cultural stock. In particular, without the walking, talking, eating cooked food, dressing, and linguistic skills that home and family have long been expected to yoke to young children's capacities before they arrive in school, school could scarcely proceed to prepare them for life in the world of work, politics, and the professions.

Given that school relies on the work of other educational agents, the pressing question is not whether it should be aware of whatever educational gaps there may be in its cultural surround. Of course it should. The question is what, if anything, school should do about it.

In the second half of the nineteenth century, American educator and pedagogical theorist William Torrey Harris gave what amounted to an answer to this question. Taking it for granted that school was not his culture's only educational agent, he declared that school should teach what students do not pick up from the others.[14] Harris may have been too strict in rejecting all overlap between school's teachings and those of other educational agents. Might it not, in some instances, be beneficial for school and other agents to reinforce one another's yokings of stock to capacities? Nevertheless, his basic premise that school belongs to a constellation of educational agents whose actions and inactions school cannot safely ignore was correct, and so was his assumption that the remainder of educational agents in the constellation do not necessarily meet all of a culture's educational needs.

In fairness to Harris, it should be noted that he held that school should do *only* what the other educational agents in the constellation do not do; he did not claim that school should do *everything* they do not do. But, even so, it may be wondered if an "into the breach" conception of school's role is viable. Would not school undergo so many changes if it consistently played a stepping into the breach role that it would lose its identity and no longer be school? On the contrary, history demonstrates that school resembles other institutions in having no fixed, unchanging nature. In the U.S. colonial period, for instance, the teaching of literacy was not a primary function of schooling. Today, it is. Nor in that time and place was it school's job to teach occupational skills, yet, by the twentieth century, school had taken on that task. Just as a radical change in technology can convince a corporation to develop a new product, one that results in what amounts to a new identity for the corporation:[15] a radical change in home or some other educational agent can cause school to take on a new educational function, one that brings about a new identity for school.[16]

Another likely objection to an into the breach conception of school is that it turns that institution into a kind of utility infielder: an educational agent not quite good enough to play a regular position on the team, yet with sufficient ability to fill in on a temporary basis where needed. There is, indeed, no doubt that, in rejecting the false equation between education and schooling, the theory of education as encounter reduces the power or influence over individuals and cultures that is now attributed to school. Under the aegis of the deep structure of educational thought, school is "the one and only," whereas, in our theory, it becomes "one among many." But an into the breach conception of school does not have to be demeaning. Indeed, individuals who step into the breach are often viewed as heroes who save the day.

A very different concern is that an into the breach conception of school turns it into a predator institution that robs other educational agents of their functions and seeks, ultimately, to reinstate its monopoly over educational agency. Consider what historian Lawrence Cremin had to say on this subject. Like other early-twentieth-century progressives, wrote Cremin, John Dewey realized that homes, shops, neighborhoods, and churches were no longer performing their educational functions. And so, ergo, he made "the *grand jeté* of twentieth-century educational theory:"[17] he leaped to the conclusion that school must take them on. In consequence, Dewey "effectively removed the agencies of informal education from the purview of public educators."[18]

Whether it is fair to hold Dewey responsible for the deep structure of educational thought's embrace of the false equation need not be decided here. It suffices to say that the very idea that school could gain a "de facto" monopoly over educational agency in place of the official "de jure" monopoly that the deep structure awards is illusory. So long as groups and institutions other than school exist in a culture, the educational labor will be divided among them. Furthermore, although it is true that school can take on so many functions that it has too much to do, the theory of education as encounter neither requires school to step into every breach nor bars it from so doing.

Assuming that school's standing vis-à-vis the other educational agents in the constellation may change over time, and will differ from culture to culture, our theory simply makes it clear that school can shed old educational tasks and responsibilities, as well as take on new ones. Just as it can step into the breach when an educational agent stops yoking the cultural assets in its portfolio to individual capacities, some other agent can do so when school stops transmitting cultural assets in its keep to the next generation. In addition, and as history confirms, when it is perceived that an educational need is not being met, a new educational agent can be created for the purpose.

Which tasks or functions might school share with other educational agents?[19] Vocational training? Science teaching? Computer literacy? If school had the sort of essential nature that Plato believed individuals possess, one could follow his advice and simply specify that it perform only those jobs for which it is well suited by nature. Our theory does not offer this option. With the help of cultural bookkeeping, it is possible, however, to discover what tasks school is expected to do at any given place and time, and which, if any, of these school is finding it difficult or impossible to carry out. If it is decided that school's failures or near failures represent miseducative sins of omission, other educational agents can be encouraged to share those responsibilities with school, or else relieve school of them entirely.

In sum, because school is not an island entire to itself, it cannot, in good conscience, ignore the miseducation in its cultural surround, be this due to a sin of commission or one of omission. Whether school should actually step into the breach in any given situation will depend on whether the miseducation is serious enough to warrant school's intervention, and also whether some other educational agent in the large configuration is better suited than school to come to the rescue. In addition, and very important, one or more of those other agents can step into the breach when school commits—or appears to be on the verge of committing—a miseducative sin of its own.

3. Revisiting The Schoolhome

Recall now Dewey's edict that, when home changes radically, so must school. In the terms of our theory, he understood that: (i) home is an educational agent, (ii) when it is transformed, its educative role is likely to change, and (iii) insofar as this results in a miseducative sin of omission, some other agent should take over the educative functions that home is no longer able to perform. Because Dewey knew that home and school are not a culture's only educational agents, he would have been the first to say that Cremin's *grand jeté* was not entailed by his premises. Nonetheless, Dewey concluded that school should step into the breach. When Montessori established her first Casa dei Bambini in Rome, her reasoning was similar. So too was the reasoning of the Puritans when, in the formation of American society, they "deliberately transferred the maimed functions of the family to formal instructional institutions."[20]

Following this same train of thought, and alarmed by the increasing violence in children's lives in the late-twentieth-century U.S., I argued in *The Schoolhome* that home was the educational agent whose traditional responsibility it was to yoke the cultural stock belonging to the so-called private or domestic sphere to the capacities of the nation's young; however, because of the social transformations in the last decades of the twentieth century, home could no longer be counted on to do so. The cultural stock I had in mind was the three Cs of care, concern, and connectedness to others, and the basic activities of living in human civilization that Victor did not acquire in the woods. In consequence, I said, a significant portion of the culture's wealth was at risk. Finding no evidence that other educational agents were prepared to step into the breach, I recommended that school take on the task. I did not suggest that school appropriate for itself all of home's educational functions. Rather, I proposed that school share with home the labor of transmitting the culture's domestic curriculum to the next generation.[21]

Drawing on Montessori's idea of the Casa dei Bambini as a surrogate home for children, and borrowing from American philosopher William James the concept of moral equivalency he put forward in his classic essay "The Moral Equivalent of War," I developed a conception of school as a moral equivalent of home. Consciously modeling what I called "the schoolhome" on an idealized vision of home and family, I envisioned an arena of gender equality so permeated by domestic affections that children would breathe the three Cs in with the air: a site where they would feel secure and at ease—that is to say, where they would feel at home.

Aware of the changes the U.S. population was undergoing as the twenty-first century drew near, I made it clear that the schoolhome was to be a place where *all* children, and not just a privileged few, would feel at home. Agreeing with Dewey about the need to educate "the whole child" and understanding that home was the educational agent whose job it had long been to induct children into human culture, I gave the schoolhome responsibility for educating heads, hearts, and hands simultaneously. Recognizing that teaching the next generation how to live together, both at home and in the world, was one of home's traditional educational functions, I insisted that the schoolhome transmit cultural assets that the two-sphere ideology assigns to the world of the private home and family, as well as those it assigns to the public world of work, politics, and the professions.

I revisit the idea of the schoolhome here because, at this writing, the violence in children's lives has not abated in my country[22] and the cultural assets whose fate concerned me are still at risk. Furthermore, a conception of school has, on occasion, been promoted that is the antithesis of the schoolhome and promises to turn school into an arena where children breathe in cultural stock that is inimical to democracy. I hasten to say that, in setting forth reasons why the schoolhome can fulfill the function of inducting children into democracy as a way of life, I do not mean to suggest that it is the only kind of school capable of doing so. For that matter, I do not mean to suggest that the schoolhome is the only kind of school in which all children can feel at home. A school can, for instance, share with the schoolhome the principle that children should breathe the three Cs of care, concern, and connectedness in with the air, but adopt a subject-based, rather than an activity-based, curriculum; or it can share that principle, yet think of itself as a model of social justice, rather than a moral equivalent of home.

Advocates of what may be called "the boot camp school" define good schools as ones whose students do well on standardized tests and are intent on improving the academic achievement of minority students. Thus, according to an observer, at one "high performing" school whose students were 99 percent African-American and Hispanic, a teacher stood before his math students "as tightly coiled as a drill sergeant. He issued instructions in a loud, slightly fearsome voice, without an extra word or gesture. 'Five minutes on the clock,' he told the 26 fifth graders, as they began a 'Do Now' review sheet on least common denominators." From there, he moved to a timed exercise of 60 multiplication problems in 60 seconds.

" 'Pencils down,' he ordered after the minute was up. 'Switch papers with your partner.' " After calling out the answers he ordered, "Hands on your head when you're done counting" and again started his digital Teacher Timer.[23]

The mission of raising the academic achievement of all children—and especially of minority children—is a relatively recent one in the U.S.[24] and I do not for a moment mean to suggest that it is not worthwhile. It is important to remember, however, that, from the standpoint of democracy, academic achievement is not school's only function. It is imperative, therefore, to ask if a school with a rigidly structured environment in which "everything is measured, everything is compared, graphed and displayed publicly"[25] and students are drilled not only in math but in posture, clear speaking, nodding for understanding, and tracking the speaker—aka the teacher—can induct a nation's young into democracy as a way of life. Indeed, it must be wondered if a school modeled on an institution that is notoriously authoritarian will not be miseducative rather than educative in respect to democratic citizenship.

The efficacy of the boot camp school in raising academic performance has by no means been established but that is not the issue here. For, supposing the model were to prevail, there would then be two vital educational functions in the U.S. that were not being met: home would still not be yoking its domestic curriculum to the capacities of the next generation and school would have fallen short in its citizen making responsibilities.

In a culture that distributes the function of citizen making across the whole range of its educational agents, this second educational gap might not matter. In a culture whose other educational agents are prepared to step into the breach and are equal to the task, the citizen-making gap can be quickly filled. When, however, school is a culture's one and only designated citizen maker, the desired kind of citizen is democratic, and democratic miseducation is rife in the cultural surround: a model that ignores school's citizen making function and adds democratic miseducation of its own to that already in the cultural surround puts democracy at risk.

It need hardly be said that many educational thinkers have stressed school's academic function without embracing the boot camp model. Nevertheless, it is all too easy when, in pursuit of academic achievement, to neglect school's democratic citizen making function. The deep structure of educational thought encourages the setting of standards and designing of programs that divorce mind from body, thought from action, and reason from feeling and emotion, thereby making it that much harder for school to be a place in which children breathe democracy in with the air. It also fosters the tendency to yoke to student capacities the knowledge that is deemed to be of most worth without attending to the fact that methods of teaching, ways of testing, techniques for maintaining order, and classroom atmospheres can themselves be the bearers of an undemocratic hidden curriculum.

If it were impossible for children to breathe democracy in with the air in school and also acquire the desired items of academic cultural stock, there might be some justification for sacrificing school's citizen making function. But the idea of the schoolhome and the practices of many existing democratic schools demonstrate that it is quite possible, and not so very difficult, for a school to carry out both functions. Indeed, it is no more difficult—and, quite possibly, much easier—for the cultural stock of reading, writing, mathematics, science, the social sciences, and the humanities to attach to individual capacities in friendly environments than in hostile ones; no more difficult—and, quite possibly, easier—for them to attach to individual capacities when children are interested in what they are doing and self-motivated than when they are subjected to a drill master.

The schoolhome's activity pattern of curriculum organization makes it relatively easy for it to be an arena in which democracy is experienced as a way of life, for one criterion for the selection of activities can be their capability or potential for yoking the cultural stock of democracy to children's capacities. In my initial formulation of the schoolhome, I placed theater and newspaper at the center of its curriculum proper. I selected these activities because of their ability to engage children's interest and yoke a wide range of cultural assets, including those associated with literacy, numeracy, the sciences, and the arts to their capacities. I made it clear, however, that an activity that one generation finds vibrant and meaningful may appear irrelevant or tedious to another generation. As it happens, both theater and newspaper are fruitful vehicles for yoking the cultural assets of democracy to individual capacities. Children can write their own plays about the unsung heroes and heroines of democracy and about critical events in democracy's history, or perform ones written by others. They can draft articles for the school newspaper on issues concerning democracy in the world outside school or within the schoolhome itself. Nonetheless, it is for the teachers in each schoolhome—or for the teachers and students together—to select activities that engage everyone's interest, channel their energies, and also serve as vehicles for the yoking of valuable cultural stock to individual capacities.

So far as education for democracy is concerned, a second mark in the schoolhome's favor is the inclusiveness of its curriculum proper.[26] Instead of representing the voices and perspectives of only one segment of the population, the schoolhome curriculum includes cultural stock authored by people across the whole range of humankind: women as well as men, people of color as well as whites, gays as well as heterosexuals, and so on. Rather than focusing solely on the deeds, experiences, and achievements of a select few, it again includes stock that represents the lives of people across the whole spectrum. When I first conceptualized the schoolhome, I did not consider the question of the representation of non-human animals in its curriculum. However, just as the schoolhome seeks to eliminate race, gender, class and other biases regarding humans from its curriculum proper, it can strive to eliminate speciesism: that is, strive to prevent the transmission of cultural stock that misrepresents and demeans non-human animals.

From the standpoint of transmitting democracy as a way of life, one more advantage of the schoolhome is that it is a place where children of all races, classes, genders, and so on do not merely congregate—as, for instance, they may do at a shopping mall. Rather, it is a place where all kinds of people live together and engage in joint enterprises whose success requires that they work cooperatively together. It has sometimes been suggested that "a pedagogy of discomfort" is required to dislodge racist, sexist, and homophobic beliefs, and that this pedagogy is incompatible with students feeling at home in school.[27] The history of schooling is replete with pedagogies that create discomfort, although they have usually been justified on other grounds, and the boot camp model would seem to preserve this tradition. In the schoolhome, however, it is the fact that children feel at home in school and think of themselves as a family that makes it relatively easy for them to learn to get along with and value people unlike themselves.

A caveat is necessary here: to say that children in a schoolhome feel at home and breathe the three Cs in with the air does not mean that they never experience discomfort.[28] When, for example, a young reporter writes an article for the school newspaper, a teacher—or, better still, other students—will then check its facts, its spelling and grammar, and the logic of its reasoning. If the article needs to be rewritten, the author may feel aggrieved at having to do more work or mortified at not having done the job right in the first place. Similarly, if a child says or does something that is—or is perceived to be—racist, sexist, or homophobic, other students or the teacher will intervene. Whether what ensues takes the form of a private meeting between teacher and student, whether an apology is made, whether the incident is turned into an occasion for an extended all-school discussion of the nation's history of race relations will depend on the circumstances. If everything goes as the teacher hopes, however, the student will feel ashamed of and rue what he or she has done; in other words, experience a degree of discomfort.

The schoolhome does not, however, approve of the use of methods of yoking cultural stock to its students' capacities that are specifically designed or known to cause physical or psychological pain or discomfort any more than it sanctions student behavior that is designed or known to do so.[29] As it happens, a school in which the three Cs are breathed in with the air is particularly well suited without such recourse to make and shape individuals who do not tolerate cultural liabilities such as racism, sexism, and homophobia. Because of its home-like atmosphere and its activity curriculum, it provides teachers with any number of opportunities to yoke the cultural stock of racial, gender, and other forms of equality to individual capacities, and to unyoke from them the stock of racism, sexism, and homophobia. The activities students engage in can, moreover, be vehicles for transmitting cultural stock relating to equality, and the everyday transactions of living can constitute educational encounters that do the same.

The question remains whether freedom of expression can thrive in an arena in which the three Cs are breathed in with the air or whether this central feature of democracy will be stifled in such an atmosphere. The answer depends on what is meant by freedom of expression. The schoolhome does not countenance speech and actions that constitute bullying, character assassination, or racial, sexist, and homophobic slurs.[30] It does, however, welcome disagreement about matters great and small and encourages discussion of controversial topics, including that of whether, in order to maintain democracy as a way of life, there must be some limitations on free speech. It also welcomes criticism of its own policies and practices, including those regarding bullying, character assassination, and the use of racist and other epithets.

4. Must School Mirror Its Cultural Surround?

Noting the energy and excitement in the atmosphere of a U.S. middle school located in "a tough urban environment," a visiting journalist asked a child why there were no fights in the school. "Because it's not allowed," replied the boy.[31] Surely, the youngster did not merely mean that the school had a rule against fighting. School rules are often broken. Nor, presumably, was he saying that the children were afraid to fight because their teachers were always watching them. Rather, he was making the point that, in the culture of his school, fighting was "not the thing to do;" indeed, that, in its culture, fighting was unthinkable. In addition to stating this obvious fact, the boy was proudly claiming membership in his school's culture.

In the schoolhome, fighting is not the thing to do. Neither is bullying. Nor is the harassment, ridicule, devaluation, and demeaning of others be they girls and women, racial and ethnic minorities, gays, lesbians, and the transgendered, the differently abled, or the poor and homeless. Believing that racism, sexism, classism, homophobia, and the like are stains on democracy and also realizing that the greater part of the schoolhome population will be at risk if these behaviors and practices are allowed to flourish, the teachers in the schoolhome are anxious to nip them in the bud.

Yet, how possibly can the schoolhome or any other form of schooling banish from its precincts behaviors and practices that commonly occur in the culture at large? Think how difficult it has proven to be to make the co-educational classroom climate girl- and woman-friendly. Is not school doomed to reproduce the social order? If the other educational agents in children's lives are eagerly transmitting the very liabilities that school would banish, are not its efforts bound to fail?

The stock of most, if not absolutely all, cultures includes practices such as murder, rape, torture, bribery, and extortion, yet these do not, for the most part, occur in their schools. The question is not: Can school be a harassment-, ridicule-, devaluation-, and demeaning-free zone within a larger culture in which these practices occur? The question is: *What does school have to do to become one?*

When the illusion reigns that school is an island entire to itself, courage is needed even to admit that sexist, racist, or otherwise objectionable behavior in a democracy has occurred in school's precincts, for it will be assumed that school bears full responsibility for the event. Supposing that the behavior is identified and named, it then requires courage for school to take positive action rather than to stand idly by, look the other way, or simply say, "This shocking behavior has never happened before," "Boys will be boys," or "Those children do not know what the words they uttered mean."

In at least some boot camp schools, teachers are free to repeat a math lesson if the students have not mastered the material.[32] In a school that wants all students to feel at home, teachers may have to stop short a math or science or reading lesson when an undesirable behavior occurs in order to name the offense, discuss its moral meaning, and work through its larger political and social implications.[33] They must also be vigilant lest their school's curriculum proper contributes to the harassment, ridicule, devaluation, and demeaning of girls or minority boys by ignoring or misrepresenting their lives and experiences.

The New York City school that did not allow fighting had a traditional subject-based curriculum. When the curriculum proper is organized around activities that engage the students' interests and require that they work together cooperatively with all deliberate speed, it would seem to be that much easier to create and sustain, not only a non-violent school culture, but also one that is friendly to all children. Still, vigilance is demanded lest the gender, race, and other relations in the student occupations mirror those in the workplace: lest the boys, for instance, end up performing those tasks traditionally considered masculine and, most important, while the girls play supporting roles and are harassed, just as women so often are in the workplace.

Be this as it may, a school that has the will to become a zone where harassment, ridicule, devaluing, and demeaning are not allowed must inevitably face up to the age-old re-entry problem. The SEED students returned to their homes and neighborhoods each weekend and on holidays. For the children in most schools, re-entry occurs every afternoon. Thus, to the extent that school's cultural surround is filled with race, gender, and other forms of miseducation, the immediate difficulty is that the very cultural liabilities school is trying to banish from its premises are being transmitted daily. Even as school tries to uncouple from children's capacities whichever of these items of cultural stock may previously have been yoked to them, the other educational agents in their lives may well be reinforcing those yokings.

If children have a sense of ownership in their school and are devoted to its culture, school can override, as it were, the miseducation they receive from the cultural surround. Yet, ironically, the very success of the endeavor to make school a place where everyone feels at home can generate a new difficulty. Some individuals can inhabit two cultures with contradictory belief systems relatively easily. On others, however, the culture clash can take a heavy toll. In response to culture conflicts that may arise when school is a non-racist, non-sexist zone, teachers can look the other way as their students struggle with having to lead a kind of double life. Or, acting on the assumption that knowledge is—or, at least, can be—power, they can raise the larger culture's hidden curricula in racism, sexism, homophobia, and so on to consciousness and bring these into the curriculum proper as objects of study.

In ways that are age-appropriate and, on occasions, that grow naturally out of daily school activities, children can learn in school about racial stereotyping, the oppression of girls and women across the world, and the struggles of women and minorities for political, economic, and educational equality. They can participate in a school-wide cultural bookkeeping project in which they identify educational agents in their own lives that engage in the various forms of miseducation and compile a record of the cultural stock in those agents' portfolios. In addition, they can learn how to mediate the potentially harmful messages transmitted by the media and the other educational agents in their lives so that they will do the least damage. And they can engage in ongoing discussions about what to believe and how to act when they see the very behaviors that are not allowed in school done hourly at home, in the neighborhood, and at the mall.

5. School as a Maker of Individuals and Cultures

A skeptic may, nonetheless, wonder if it is not hopelessly utopian to suppose that, in a culture in which the two-sphere ideology prevails, a co-educational school can create a friendly atmosphere for girls and women. If the dominant culture passes down the belief that the "private" world of home and family is inferior to the world of work, politics, and the professions, along with the belief that the former world is women's domain, will not this ideology inevitably be acted out in school? To make sure that girls and women feel at home in co-educational classrooms, do we not first have to transform the larger culture?

It is true that, to rid itself of the chilly classroom climate for girls and women, school may find it necessary to yoke to its students' capacities the beliefs that home and family are as important as politics and economics, and that the three Cs of care, concern, and connection to others should be practiced by boys as well as girls. As it happens, however, school is adept at transmitting items of cultural stock that run counter to the larger culture's mores.

In the nineteenth century, many girls and boys were required to enter school through different doors and were supposed to use different staircases. In the twentieth century, children lined up and walked through corridors by twos, sat silently at their desks until a bell rang, and were punished for helping a friend answer a question. School has easily managed the seemingly impossible feat of yoking items of stock to individual capacities that are not represented in the larger culture because it and other educational agents transmit to young and old alike the conviction that school is a zone in which any number of the beliefs and practices of the larger culture simply do not apply.[34] With this groundwork laid, school's way is clear to yoking all kinds of counter-cultural stock to its students' capacities, at least in the form of temporary assets to be used only during school hours, even if not as living legacies that the students carry with them into their futures.[35]

To be sure, if school transmitted all the items of stock in its portfolio as temporary assets, there would be little reason for it to exist—let alone to be the culture's designated educational agent. Granted, tales are told of boys and girls who receive 100 percent on arithmetic and spelling tests in school, yet, in later years, are unable to balance their checkbooks or spell the word "twelve." Nevertheless, the functions of citizen making, academic preparation, vocational training, and the like that cultures assign school all presuppose that it is a future-oriented institution. This is not to deny that school is a place in which living takes place "here and now," or that its quality of life matters. It is simply to say that school is a particular kind of place in which living occurs: one that expects those inhabitants it calls "students" to hold onto a goodly portion of the cultural assets that school yokes to their capacities.

If school had only short-term goals, its role as a maker and shaper of individuals and cultures would not have to be taken seriously. Since, however, school has long-term goals, the question that the influential teacher and scholar George Counts asked in a series of lectures he delivered to the U.S. Progressive Education Society in 1932 is pertinent.[36]

In those lectures, Counts, who is classified in textbooks as a "social reconstructionist,"[37] asked: "Dare the school build a new social order?" Like Spencer's question, Counts' question lives on. In comparison to the question "What knowledge is of most worth?" however, it has a distinctly radical ring. As it happens, Counts believed that the economic base of society should be transformed. But, although Counts' intent was radical, there is nothing radical about Counts' question, for what it dares school to do is something that school is already doing.

To dare a person or an institution X to do some action A entails that X could refrain from doing A. However, school must willy-nilly project some of the items of cultural stock in its portfolio into the future; hence it is inevitably in the business of making and shaping both individuals and cultures, and, therefore, in the business of making and shaping social orders. Furthermore, the stock in school's portfolio changes over time and, in addition, anything can happen when a given item of stock attaches to the capacities of an individual. Thus, it is almost guaranteed that the social orders school forms will be new in some respects. But, then, it is misleading in the extreme to ask if school *dare* build a new social order; indeed, it makes no sense to do so, for school has no choice in the matter. The question is not: Dare school build a new social order? It is: *What kind of order is school and should school be making and shaping?*

When Counts' question is abstracted from his lectures, it is misleading for another reason too. Just as Spencer's question "What knowledge is of most worth?" when taken out of its original context, reduces education to the getting of knowledge, Counts' question, when taken out of context, reduces education to schooling. Chiding the leaders of progressive education for having "an over-weening faith in the power of the school,"[38] Counts actually said that school is "but one formative agency among many, and certainly not the strongest."[39] When it is decontextualized, however, his question gives the distinct impression that school can single-handedly transform the world, if only it dare do so.

An "over-weening faith" in school's power is so deeply embedded in the collective consciousness that Counts' question may sound reasonable when it is taken out of context. Yet, school does not have the ability to build any particular social order single-handedly, and, given the existence of multiple educational agency, it cannot possibly attain it. Furthermore, despite its long-term goals, it is a short-term educational agency.

One of the great paradoxes of the deep structure of educational thought is that it awards a monopoly over educational agency to an institution that, from the standpoint of the individual, is relatively short-lived. It bids us think only about school, hold only school accountable for the next generation's learning, and pour all the resources we reserve for education into school alone, even though educational agents such as family, neighborhood, religion, government, corporations, the workplace, and the media are likely to yoke items of cultural stock to any given individual's capacities over the entire lifespan. Admittedly, school takes up a goodly portion of a child's time, but childhood represents a comparatively short period of a human life and, at its end, children leave school behind. No doubt, those who wish to transform society are well advised to enlist school's help. They are misguided, however, if they imagine that school can accomplish this task working alone.

6. Democracy's Joint Venture

It is naïve to suppose that school could accomplish the social and economic transformation that Counts desired on its own, and equally quixotic to expect it single-handedly to change a larger culture in which gender, race, or some other form of miseducation is rife into one in which everyone feels at home. This does not mean, however, that school's only course of action is to sit back and say, "Whatever will be, will be."

One challenge every democracy faces is to enlist as many of its educational agents as possible in the joint venture of making and shaping democratic citizens. Joint ventures in education are not new to school. Throughout its history, it has entered into them with governmental offices, religious bodies, corporations, families, the military, and the media. Some of these institutions have tried to impose their agendas on school, and school, in its turn, has often regarded other educational agents merely as means to its own ends. The challenge for democracy is to get non-school educational agents to acknowledge that they are education's agents and to take responsibility for transmitting cultural liabilities when they do so; to impress upon school that these other agents are its partners and not merely its humble servants in the educative process; and, of course, to see that one and all work cooperatively and not at cross-purposes.

What could school contribute to this joint venture in democratic citizen making? For schools that know how to make all kinds of children feel at home, several tasks and functions immediately come to mind. First and foremost is that of yoking the cultural stock that enables school to be a welcoming place to their students' capacities as living legacies that stay in their possession after graduation. In addition, such schools could try to transmit to their students both the belief that education is a gift that should be circulated to others and the specific desire to circulate the cultural assets of knowing how to live and work in the world with people very different from themselves.

Three attributes of the practice that anthropologists call "gift exchange" are particularly relevant to this discussion. One is that the gift always moves: whatever you are given is given away again; or else something of similar value is given. A second attribute is that the gift does not become another's capital; it is not used for profit. And a third is that the gift is not the giver's or the recipient's private property.[40] School learning is often conceptualized as the antithesis of a gift: the learning process is considered to be hard work and what is learned in school tends to be viewed as the student's private property.[41] Nevertheless, if children were to acquire in school the propensity to circulate the cultural assets that they breathe in with the air there, school might make a significant contribution to democracy's joint venture in citizen making.

In Chapter 1, I pointed out that amplification occurs in education as well as in biology. The example I gave was that a small change in the capacities of a single individual can lead to a radical change of self. But the process of amplification need not stop there. Indeed, when the gift of education is circulated, there is no telling where the change in a single individual may lead. Assume, for the sake of argument, that school's cultural surround is miseducative but that a number of schools, nonetheless, exist in which democracy is breathed in with the air. If the individuals who graduate from these schools were to circulate the cultural assets they had acquired; and if the recipients of those assets were, in their turn, to circulate the gift: some relatively large-scale changes in the miseducative cultural surround might eventually occur.

One more contribution school could make to a joint venture in making and shaping a democratic citizenry would be to serve as a kind of laboratory for democracy. The progressive schools that flourished in the U.S. in the first half of the twentieth century were viewed by others and themselves as experiments in education: places where non-traditional pedagogies and curricula were being tried out and their validity tested. Similarly, a democracy might well want to think of its schools as sites for trying out and testing ways for very different kinds of people to live and work together.

The full range of schools that managed to make all children feel at home could then be conceived of as experimental stations where ways of creating and maintaining a warm climate for people of all races, classes, genders, ethnicities, and so on were devised. Schools modeled on the idea of the schoolhome could, in turn, be seen as laboratories where one particular type of experiment was being conducted. Rejecting the ideology of two polar opposite genderized spheres; dedicated to the proposition that home and family are just as important as work, politics, and the professions; convinced that men and women have an equal responsibility for maintaining the well-being of both areas of life; and thinking of themselves as one large family governed by the three Cs of care, concern, and connection to others: they would be laboratories that tried out and tested ways of making and shaping boys and girls so that they could live and work together in the world as equals.

Schools that followed SEED's example and created a friendly atmosphere for inner-city students with the express purpose of preparing them for college would represent another type of experiment in living, and there could be many other experimental forms as well.[42] The temptations to impose uniformity on schooling are many. However, the theory of education as encounter resists the belief that there is one right way for school or any other education agent to proceed: one right curriculum to yoke to individual capacities, one right method of transmitting the culture's stock, one right way of organizing the learning environment.

Recognizing that education is everywhere, our theory affirms that each individual is bound to encounter different items of cultural stock; therefore—and as has long been known—a method that works for one individual may not work for another. In addition, it holds that the cultural stock that one individual lacks and sorely needs, another may already possess, and that, even if the same cultural stock were transmitted to everyone, it would attach to the capacities of different individuals in different ways; hence, a curriculum proper that suits one individual may not be appropriate for another. Thus, if a democracy were willing to think of its schools as laboratories from which it could learn, our theory would encourage a variety of experimental forms.

One last caveat is needed here. To suggest that school could serve as a laboratory for living in a democracy is not to say that school should, after all, be thought of as an island entire to itself.[43] To carry out its experiment in education, The Little Red School House in New York City needed the cooperation of the local community, the city's sanitation department, a New Jersey sugar refinery, and, of course, the children's homes and families. Similarly, to try out and test ways of living, a democracy's schools would need to work with families, religious institutions, the media—indeed, with the whole range of participants in democracy's joint venture.

Finally, John Donne's insight is apposite that, if no man is an island entire of itself, then "any man's death diminishes me, because I am involved in mankind." In a democracy, any educational agent's sin of omission or commission diminishes every other agent because they are all involved in the culture. School is no exception to this rule. It is diminished when talk radio hosts and political party members undermine its efforts to make democratic citizens by spewing hatred and bigotry; or, for that matter, when the entertainment media and the news media subvert its academic mission by deriding intellectuals and substituting gossip for serious discussions of world problems. And school, in turn, diminishes its brother and sister educational agents when, for example, it becomes so consumed with yoking concepts belonging to the various academic disciplines to children's capacities that it neglects its citizen making function.

CONCLUSION

Education is one of the most powerful and least understood forces in human society. Trivialized, even by those who are proud to call themselves educators, the labor that education performs is ignored by the very social commentators who note its large-scale effects. Reconfiguring education as an interaction between an individual and a culture in which both parties change, the theory of education as encounter shows, not only why education is too important to be left to the professionals, but also why the failure to acknowledge its workings can place a nation or a culture at risk.

It goes without saying that every theory leaves some questions hanging, and the theory of education as encounter is no exception. Nevertheless, it offers a viable alternative to the view of education that now prevails and is so narrow as to conceal its subject's importance. My theory also has the decided advantage of including not only all learning but also all cultural transmission in its embrace.

Invoking the optical illusion of the duck–rabbit, Thomas Kuhn said that, when a scientific revolution occurs, what were ducks in the scientist's world are now rabbits.[1] Kuhn believed that his account applied only to the natural sciences, yet one who looks through the lens of the theory of education as encounter will see things differently: what were simply groups and institutions are now educational agents; what were habitual practices are now cultural assets and liabilities. The duck–rabbit image relates to our theory in another way as well. The stereoscopic vision it provides shows every educational event to be both a case of learning and an instance of cultural transmission.

In applying the theory of education as encounter to three pressing educational problems, I hope to have demonstrated the value of looking at education simultaneously from the perspectives of the individual and the culture. Of course, other long-established problems could have been selected instead, and here, again, the duck-rabbit is relevant. When education is reconfigured, phenomena that were assumed to have little, if anything, to do with education may emerge as the most pressing educational issues of the day.

In closing, let me emphasize what perhaps I should have reiterated on every page: namely, that a basic teaching of the theory of education as encounter is that not a single individual stands outside the educational process. Because my theory identifies groups and institutions, rather than individuals, as a culture's educational agents, it is easy, yet fundamentally mistaken, to conclude that only institutions and the like can and should be held accountable when miseducation is rife in a culture—or, for that matter, when a culture is genuinely educative. Those myriad educational agents are not abstract philosophical entities. They are made up of flesh-and-blood individuals. Thus, the fact that groups and institutions are the agents that yoke cultural stock to individual capacities does not absolve us humans of all responsibility. I leave it to others to decide what the position of non-human animals may be in this regard. If, however, education is to form the best individuals and cultures it can: we human animals in our everyday capacities of family members, worshippers, breadwinners, consumers, sports fans, and the rest have to try to ensure that the groups and institutions to which we belong work together to maximize the transmission of cultural assets, and minimize the transmission of cultural liabilities. I do not say that this will always be easy to do. But, if education is too important to be left to the experts, and it is: then we must take charge.

NOTES

Introduction

1 Because I call my theory "education as encounter" it may be thought that I downplay the element of change, but I ask readers to regard this name as shorthand for the more cumbersome title, "education as encounter that produces change."

2 That research was first written up in Jane Roland Martin, "Sophie and Emile: A Case Study of Sex Bias in the History of Educational Thought," *Harvard Educational Review*, 1981, 51 (3), pp. 357–372; "The Ideal of the Educated Person," *Educational Theory*, 1981, 31 (2), pp. 97–109; "Excluding Women from the Educational Realm," *Harvard Educational Review*, 1982, 52 (2), pp. 138–148; "Sex Equality and Education in Plato's Just State" in Mary Vetterling-Braggin Ed., *"Femininity," "Masculinity," and "Androgyny"* (Totowa, NJ: Littlefield Adams, 1982), pp. 279–300. It was then pulled together in Jane Roland Martin, *Reclaiming a Conversation* (New Haven, CT: Yale University Press, 1985). "Excluding Women," "Sophie and Emile," and "The Ideal of the Educated Person" are reprinted in Jane Roland Martin, *Changing the Educational Landscape* (New York: Routledge, 1994), Chs. 1–3. See D.G. Mulcahy, *Knowledge, Gender, and Schooling: The Feminist Educational Thought of Jane Roland Martin* (Westport, CT: Bergin & Garvey, 2002) for an interpretation of my work that attempts to synthesize this research, my earlier papers, and two books that followed.

3 For a full development of the cultural wealth perspective, see Jane Roland Martin, *Cultural Miseducation* (New York: Teachers College Press, 2002). I first distinguished the two standpoints and formulated the cultural wealth perspective in the DeGarmo Lecture I presented at the 1995 national meeting of the American Educational Research Association: "There's Too Much to Teach: Cultural Wealth in an Age of Scarcity," *Educational Researcher*, 1996, 25 (2), pp. 4–10, 16.

4 Interestingly enough, in the introduction to a book of readings I edited in 1970, I wrote: "Insofar as a curriculum is for someone, is it necessarily for people, or can there be a curriculum for, say, circus animals or Seeing Eye dogs?" Jane Roland Martin, *Readings in the Philosophy of Education* (Boston: Allyn & Bacon, 1970), p. 1.

5 These are written up and analyzed in Jane Roland Martin, *Educational Metamorphoses* (Lanham, MD: Rowman & Littlefield, 2007).

6 Jess Stein Ed., *The Random House Dictionary* (New York: Ballantine Books, 1980).

7 John Dewey, *The School and Society* (Chicago: University of Chicago Press, 1915/1956), p. 7.
8 "There is in all cultures ongoing education for everyone. It is virtually as ubiquitous as the air we breathe," say John I. Goodlad et al., *Education for Everyone* (San Francisco: Jossey-Bass, 2004), p. 6.

Chapter 1

1 Martin Luther, "Letters to the Mayors and Aldermen of All the Cities of Germany in Behalf of Christian Schools" in Robert Ulich Ed., *Three Thousand Years of Educational Wisdom* (Cambridge, MA: Harvard University Press, 1947), p. 225, emphasis added.
2 John Locke, "Some Thoughts Concerning Education" in *On Politics and Education* (New York: Walter J. Black, 1947), p. 209.
3 William K. Frankena, "A Model for Analyzing a Philosophy of Education" in Jane Roland Martin Ed., *Readings in the Philosophy of Education* (Boston, MA: Allyn & Bacon, 1970), p. 16, emphasis added.
4 Mortimer J. Adler, *The Paideia Proposal* (New York: Macmillan, 1982), p. 10.
5 Steven M. Cahn, *Education and the Democratic Ideal* (Chicago: Nelson-Hall, 1979), p. 1.
6 John Dewey, *Democracy and Education* (New York: Macmillan, 1916/1961), p. 10.
7 Michael Oakeshott, "The Study of 'Politics' in a University" in Jane Roland Martin Ed., *Readings in the Philosophy of Education*, p. 41.
8 Theodore Brameld, *Cultural Foundations of Education* (New York: Harper & Brothers, 1957), pp. 148–149.
9 Ibid., p. 6.
10 Bernard Bailyn, *Education in the Forming of American Society* (New York: Vintage, 1960), p. 14.
11 For further discussion of the concept of cultural stock in particular and the cultural perspective on education in general, see Jane Roland Martin, *Cultural Miseducation* (New York: Teachers College Press, 2002).
12 For example, see Brian Greene, *The Elegant Universe* (New York: Norton, 2003). But see also Peter Woit, *Not Even Wrong: The Failure of String Theory and the Search for Unity in Physical Law* (New York: Basic Books, 2006); Lee Smolin, *The Trouble with Physics* (Boston, MA: Houghton Mifflin, 2006).
13 Susan Blackmore, *The Meme Machine* (Oxford: Oxford University Press, 1999); Richard Dawkins, *The Selfish Gene* (Oxford: Oxford University Press, 1976); Daniel Dennett, *Consciousness Explained* (Boston, MA: Little, Brown, 1991). Viewing cognition as embodied action, Francisco J. Varela et al. put forward an enactive approach to mind in which an individual's sensorimotor capacities are "embedded in a more encompassing biological, psychological, and cultural context" in *The Embodied Mind* (Cambridge, MA: MIT Press, 1993), p. 173. But although it may seem to capture our two perspectives, their theory is, at present, at such a high level of abstraction that it cannot provide the kind of illumination of education that is being sought here.
14 Blackmore, *The Meme Machine*, p. 15.
15 Ibid., p. 17. The other objects are things such as books.
16 For extended discussions of the cases cited here, see Jane Roland Martin, *Educational Metamorphoses* (Lanham, MD: Rowman & Littlefield, 2007).
17 Some might want to insist that they can become yoked before birth.
18 My discussion of Victor is based on Harlan Lane, *The Wild Boy of Aveyron* (Cambridge, MA: Harvard University Press, 1976).
19 Some might want to call birth our first metamorphosis, but it is not, strictly speaking, one that is due to education.

20 My discussion of Minik is based on Kenn Harper, *Give Me My Father's Body* (New York: Washington Square Press, 2000).

21 My discussion of Rodriguez is based on Richard Rodriguez, *Hunger of Memory* (Boston, MA: David R. Godine, 1982).

22 It should be noted that what is considered a cultural whole will be dependent on the context. Thus, for some purposes the Mexican-American culture that Rodriguez crossed out of can itself be considered a cultural whole. In addition, it should be pointed out that culture crossings such as Minik's into an American boy may be called "external" and ones such as Rodriguez's into an educated man "internal." (For more on this issue see Martin, *Educational Metamorphoses*.) The external/internal distinction leaves many questions hanging, among them: Are external crossings more difficult to make than internal ones? Do those who make external crossings find it harder to go home again? Are there other kinds of culture crossings? The point at issue here does not, however, turn on the answers to queries such as these.

23 Because the first great metamorphosis brings an individual into human culture from the "outside," it does not, strictly speaking, qualify as a culture crossing.

24 Jean-Jacques Rousseau, trans. Allan Bloom, *Emile* (New York: Basic Books, 1979/1762), p. 38.

25 Edward O. Wilson, *Naturalist* (Washington D.C.: Island Press, 1994), p. 5.

26 Transcript, Daughter of Danang, American Experience, Public Broadcasting System.

27 See, for example, Theodora Kroeber, *Ishi in Two Worlds: A Biography of the Last Wild Indian in North America* (Berkeley: University of California Press, 1976); "Hundreds of Languages Face Extinction," *The Boston Globe*, February 20, 2009.

28 William R. Miller and Janet C'de Baca, *Quantum Change* (New York: Guilford Press, 2001).

29 Rather than supposing that educational metamorphoses are reducible to a series of deliberate, discrete educational events or episodes, some might be inclined to say cases of learning that appear to be incremental are actually instances of metamorphoses. But even if there is a gap between, for example, a young boy learning how to write each letter of his name and knowing how to write his name, this will not, in most cases, amount to a whole-person transformation.

30 See James Gleick, *Chaos* (New York: Penguin Books, 1988); see also Varela et al.'s account of emergent properties, Ch. 5; cf. Bert Hölldobler and E.O. Wilson, *The Superorganism* (New York: Norton, 2008), p. 58.

31 Malcolm X, *The Autobiography of Malcolm X* (New York: Grove Press, 1965), p. 36, emphasis in original.

32 Rodriguez, *Hunger of Memory*, pp. 20–21.

33 Hölldobler and Wilson, *The Superorganism*, p. 77.

34 Thus, for example, Wilson's studies of ants and social insects more generally changed the field of biology, and his eventual turn to environmental activism led to the establishment in 2008 of the Encyclopedia of Life.

35 Ralph Linton, *The Study of Man* (New York: Appleton-Century-Crofts, 1936), pp. 348–353; see B. Othanel Smith et al., *Fundamentals of Curriculum Development* (New York: Harcourt, Brace & World, 1957), Ch. 1 for an interesting discussion of this example.

36 This example is taken from Paul Starr, *The Creation of the Media* (New York: Basic Books, 2004), Ch. 6.

Chapter 2

1 See, for example, S.B. Sarason, *The Culture of the School and the Problem of Change* (Boston, MA: Allyn & Bacon, 2nd ed., 1982); David Tyack and William Tobin, "The 'Grammar' of Schooling: Why Has it Been so Hard to Change?" *American Educational*

Research Journal, Fall, 2004, 31 (3), pp. 453–479; Barbara Benham Tye, *Hard Truths* (New York: Teachers College Press, 2000).

2 Willard Van Orman Quine, *From a Logical Point of View* (Cambridge, MA: Harvard University Press, 1953), p. 43; cf. Larry Laudan, *Progress and Its Problems* (Berkeley: University of California Press, 1977), p. 267.

3 Quine, *From a Logical Point of View*, p. 42.

4 It is appropriate to use the pronoun "he" and the noun "man" here rather than gender-neutral terms such as "they" and "human being" because the literature on this subject is by no means gender neutral. Many of those theorists who have seen fit to place man apart from and above the animals have gone out of their way to argue that women do not possess a full complement of whatever is presumed to be man's distinctive virtue. For the moment, however, I bracket the "woman question" lest the nature/culture split be lost to view.

5 It should also be noted that, even if a mind/body dualism were an unchallenged philosophical doctrine, in principle it would still be legitimate for education to value the body as much as, or more than, the mind. There is, after all, no logical barrier to education's joining together what philosophy tears apart.

6 Virginia Woolf, *Three Guineas* (New York: Harcourt Brace, 1938), p. 18.

7 See, for example, Judith Butler, *Gender Trouble* (New York: Routledge, 1990); Nancy Fraser and Linda J. Nicholson, "Social Criticism Without Philosophy: An Encounter between Feminism and Postmodernism" in Linda J. Nicholson Ed., *Feminism/Postmodernism* (New York: Routledge, 1990), pp. 19–38; Denise Riley, *Am I That Name?* (Minneapolis: University of Minnesota Press, 1988).

8 Even women who went out to work as domestics were expected to meet these expectations when they got home each evening.

9 For example, Sherry Ortner, "Is Female to Male as Nature is to Culture?" in Michelle Zimbalist Rosaldo and Louise Lamphere Eds., *Women, Culture, and Society* (Palo Alto, CA: Stanford University Press, 1974), pp. 67–87.

10 Indeed, in the U.S. home economics was officially classified as vocational education for girls, even though the job of homemaker for which it trained them was unpaid.

11 Henry Adams, *The Education of Henry Adams* (New York: The Book League of America, 1928), for example, p. 96.

12 Malcolm X, *The Autobiography of Malcolm X* (New York: Grove Press, 1966), p. 282.

13 Interestingly enough, even as R.S. Peters was urging philosophers of education to embrace his narrow, school-based concept of education, Bernard Bailyn was criticizing historians of education for reducing education to the part of the educational process carried on in formal institutions of instruction. In Bailyn's view, educational historians were motivated by the desire to raise the field's status, yet, as a result of the reductionism, the field had become isolated and parochial.

14 R.S. Peters, "Education and the Educated Man" in R.F. Dearden, P.H. Hirst, and R.S. Peters Eds., *A Critique of Current Educational Aims* (London: Routledge & Kegan Paul, 1972), p. 6.

15 Ibid., pp. 13, 8.

16 Ibid., p. 7.

17 Ibid., p. 9.

18 Ibid.

19 R.S. Peters, "What Is an Educational Process?" in R.S. Peters Ed., *The Concept of Education* (New York: Humanities Press, 1967), p. 3.

20 Peters, "Education and the Educated Man," p. 8.

21 The concept of the intentional fallacy is usually attributed to William K. Wimsatt and Monroe C. Beardsley, "The Intentional Fallacy," *Sewanee Review*, 1946, 54, pp. 468–488; cf. Wimsatt and Beardsley, *The Verbal Icon: Studies in the Meaning of Poetry* (Lexington: University of Kentucky Press, 1954). For an application of the concept to

another discipline, see Steve W. Dykstra, "The Artist's Intentions and the Intentional Fallacy in Fine Arts Conservation," *Journal of the American Institute for Conservation*, 1996, 35 (3), pp. 197–218.

22 As John I. Goodlad et al. say in *Education for Everyone* (San Francisco: Jossey-Bass), p. 84: "Education is . . . value neutral in that it can be positive, put to constructive ends, made useful or otherwise good; or it can be negative and of a destructive nature. In some extreme cases, education can actually be extremely dangerous."

23 John Dewey, *Democracy and Education* (New York: Macmillan, 1916/1961), p. 4.

24 Bernard Bailyn, *Education in the Forming of American Society* (New York: Vintage, 1960), pp. 17–18.

25 Lawrence Cremin, *The Transformation of the School* (New York: Vintage, 1961); *The Genius of American Education* (New York: Vintage, 1965).

26 Ivan Illich, *Deschooling Society* (New York: Harper & Row, 1970).

27 According to Patricia Albjerg Graham, *Schooling America* (Oxford: Oxford University Press, 2005), p. 6: "Certainly school can be influential, but even more significant in youths' development is the education they receive in their homes, their communities, and through the media. Those influences, while more important, are much more difficult for a society to regulate, and thus our attention remains upon the educational institutions, whose policies we can regulate but whose practices are vastly more difficult to change."

28 Once again, a caveat may be in order. Although philosophers often use the terms "agent" and "agency" in their intentional sense, no such assumption is being made here. Rather, these terms are used in the neutral dictionary sense of a means or instrumentality.

29 John Dewey, *The School and Society* (Chicago: University of Chicago Press, 1915/1956), p. 12.

30 Jane Roland Martin, *The Schoolhome* (Cambridge, MA: Harvard University Press, 1992).

31 To be sure, some school programs aimed at the reduction of violent behavior do exist. Yet these are likely to be considered therapeutic rather than educational. Moreover, the fact that, in an age of violence, they tend to be few and far between suggests that they are not consonant with, but run counter to, education's deep structure. Because not everyone in Western culture is guided by that set of premises, it is to be expected that some programs will defy one or more of them. If enough such programs are instituted, the deep structure will presumably change. At this writing, however, violence continues to be a neglected educational issue.

32 Bernard Bailyn, *Education in the Forming of American Society* (New York: Vintage, 1960), p. 9.

33 For more on this point, see Jane Roland Martin, *The Schoolhome*.

34 See Chapter 8 for a discussion of the post-feminist version of this ideology.

35 Jean-Jacques Rousseau, trans. Allan Bloom, *Emile* (New York: Basic Books, 1979), p. 363.

36 Benjamin Barber in a panel discussion, "Education for Civility and Civitas," in John I. Goodlad and Timothy J. McMannon Eds., *The Public Purpose of Education and Schooling* (San Francisco: Jossey-Bass, 1997), p. 103.

Chapter 3

1 Jane Roland Martin, "Sophie and Emile: A Case Study of Sex Bias in the History of Educational Thought," *Harvard Educational Review*, 1981, 51 (3), pp. 357–372; "Excluding Women from the Educational Realm," *Harvard Educational Review*, 1982, 52 (2), pp. 133–148; "The Ideal of the Educated Person," *Educational Theory*, 1981, 31 (2), pp. 97–109; *Reclaiming a Conversation* (New Haven, CT: Yale University Press, 1985). See also Jane Roland Martin, *Changing the Educational Landscape* (New York: Routledge, 1994), Chs. 1–6.

2 Lorenne M.G. Clark, "The Rights of Women: The Theory and Practice of the Ideology of Male Supremacy" in William R. Shea and John King-Farlow Eds., *Contemporary Issues in Political Philosophy* (New York: Science History Publications, 1976), pp. 49–65.

3 For further discussion of this point, see Jane Roland Martin, "Feminism" in Randall Curran Ed., *A Companion to the Philosophy of Education* (Oxford: Blackwell, 2003), pp. 192–205.

4 For an extended discussion of this example, see Jane Roland Martin, "Sophie and Emile" and *Reclaiming a Conversation*, Ch. 3.

5 See, however, Jane Roland Martin, *Reclaiming a Conversation*, Ch.6.

6 Whether it is so must be decided on a case-by-case basis. For an extended discussion of the issues raised in this section and the next, see Jane Roland Martin, "Methodological Essentialism, False Difference, and Other Dangerous Traps," *Signs*, Spring 1994, 19 (3), pp. 630–657; *Coming of Age in Academe* (New York: Routledge, 2000).

7 One important exception is Marvin Lazerson and W. Norton Grubb Eds., *American Education and Vocationalism* (New York: Teachers College Press, 1974).

8 See, for example, Stephen Jay Gould, *The Mismeasure of Man* (New York: Norton, 1981).

9 Ibid.; Tommy L. Lott, *The Invention of Race* (Malden, MA: Blackwell, 1999).

10 On this and related issues see, for example, Bernard Boxill Ed., *Race and Racism* (Oxford: Oxford University Press, 2001); Cornell West, *Race Matters* (New York: Vintage, 1993); Tommy L. Lott, *The Invention of Race*.

11 For two interesting discussions of disabilities, see Eva Feder Kittay, *Love's Labor* (New York: Routledge, 1998); Martha C. Nussbaum, *Frontiers of Justice* (Cambridge, MA: Harvard University Press, 2006).

12 I first made this point in Jane Roland Martin, "The Ideal of the Educated Person."

13 For more on this movement, see Lazerson and Grubb, *American Education and Vocationalism*.

14 Howard Gardner, *Frames of Mind* (New York: Basic Books, 1983).

15 John Dewey, *Democracy and Education* (New York: Macmillan, 1916/1961), p. 141. Dewey rejected the philosophical doctrine of mind/body dualism but it is not necessary to do so to agree with this sentiment.

16 Jean-Jacques Rousseau, trans. Allan Bloom, *Emile* (New York: Basic Books, 1762/1979), p. 38.

17 R.S. Peters, "Education and the Educated Man" in R.F. Dearden et al. Eds., *A Critique of Current Educational Aims* (London: Routledge & Kegan Paul, 1972), p. 6.

18 Peter Singer, *Animal Liberation* (New York: HarperCollins, 2002), p. 7, emphasis in original.

19 Olivia Judson, "The Wild Side," October 6, 2009, NYTimes.com.; Nicholas Wade, "Chimps and Monkeys Could Talk. Why Don't They?" *New York Times*, January 12, 2010, p. D1, 4.

20 American Kennel Club. "AKC's Canine Good Citizen® Program," January 8, 2009, www.akc.org/events/cgc/imdex.cfm, emphasis added.

21 My discussion of Nim is based on Elizabeth Hess, *Nim Chimpsky* (New York: Bantam, 2008).

22 Natalie Angier, "Pigs Prove to Be Smart, if Not Vain," *New York Times*, November 10, 2009, p. D1; cf. Jeffrey Kluger, "Inside the Minds of Animals," *Time*, August 16, 2010, pp. 36–43.

23 It might also be expected that Nim's learning to sign would weaken the belief held by many linguists and psychologists that language is a uniquely human ability or characteristic. The head of "Project Nim" publicly announced, however, that Nim's signing did not constitute language and this belief may have at least temporarily been given a new lease on life.

24 Singer, *Animal Liberation*, p. 6.

25 See, for example, James Rachels, "Drawing Lines" in Cass R. Sunstein and Martha C. Nussbaum Eds., *Animal Rights* (Oxford: Oxford University Press, 2004).

26 See Peter Singer, *Animal Liberation*, Ch. 1, for an interesting discussion of animal rights, and also Sunstein and Nussbaum Eds., *Animal Rights*.

27 Interestingly, although Michael Oakeshott did not reduce what he called "civilization" to high culture, he rejected the view that it is "a stock of things like books, pictures, musical instruments and compositions, buildings, cities, landscapes, inventions, devices, machines and so on—in short, as the results of mankind having impressed itself upon a 'natural' world," and he said instead that it is composed of "a stock of emotions, beliefs, images, ideas, manners of thinking, languages, skills, practices, and manners of activity out of which these 'things' are generated." Michael Oakeshott, "The Study of 'Politics' in a University" in Jane R. Martin Ed., *Readings in the Philosophy of Education* (Boston, MA: Allyn & Bacon, 1970), p. 41.

28 See Kwame Anthony Appiah, *Cosmopolitanism* (New York: Norton, 2006) for an interesting discussion of this thesis.

29 "Hustler" is Malcolm X's term. See Jane Roland Martin, *Educational Metamorphoses* (Lanham, MD: Rowman & Littlefield, 2007), Ch. 3, for a discussion of Malcolm's numerous metamorphoses.

30 If this was indeed the case, then what I have called his first great metamorphosis may well have been his second—his first one being a transformation from a human newborn into a member of animal culture.

31 A commentator on Cardinal Newman's philosophy of liberal education has said that, on Newman's view, "The personal intermediacy of the teacher between the students and the body of knowledge contained in the various sciences" is fundamental to the very idea of the university and to liberal education. See D.G. Mulcahy, *The Educated Person* (Lanhan, MD: Rowman & Littlefield, 2008), p. 45. But supposing that Newman's characterizations of both the university and liberal education are correct, it remains the case that a relatively small proportion of the yokings of stock and capacities that occur in this world are carried out by teachers.

32 Similarly, the individuation of items of cultural stock will depend on the interests and purposes of the inquiry.

33 Instances of what is often called self-education should not be confused with encounters in which an educator yokes some items of cultural stock to the capacities of other individuals and, in the process, learns something. For an example of the latter, think of a schoolteacher who is trying to yoke some mathematical knowledge to students' capacities and, while doing so, gains insight into their cognitive development.

34 E. O. Wilson, *Naturalist* (Washington D.C.: Island Press, 1994), p. 52.

35 Bert Hölldobler and E.O. Wilson, *The Superorganism* (New York: Norton, 2008), p. xviii, say: "The modern insect societies have a vast amount to teach us today."

36 See, for example, Steven Pinker, *The Language Instinct* (New York: Summit Books, 1995).

37 Stanley Milgram, *Obedience to Authority* (New York: Harper & Row, 1974).

38 Bernard Bailyn, *Education in the Forming of American Society* (New York: Vintage, 1960), p. 16.

39 John Dewey, *Democracy and Education*, p. 3.

Chapter 4

1 See, for example, Nelson Goodman, *Fact, Fiction, and Forecast* (Cambridge, MA: Harvard University Press, 1955); John Rawls, *A Theory of Justice* (Cambridge, MA: Harvard University Press, 1971); Martha C. Nussbaum, *Frontiers of Justice* (Cambridge, MA: Harvard University Press, 2006). See Nussbaum, p. 352ff. for a fascinating discussion

of the problem the inclusion of non-human animals in the realm of justice raises for the idea of reflective equilibrium.

2 For a fuller discussion of Plato's version, see Jane Roland Martin, *Reclaiming a Conversation* (New Haven, CT: Yale University Press, 1985); for a fuller discussion of Ovid's, see Jane Roland Martin *Educational Metamorphoses* (Lanham, MD: Rowman & Littlefield, 2007).

3 Elwood Cubberley, quoted in Jonathan Kozol, *The Shame of the Nation* (New York: Three Rivers Press, 2005), p. 210.

4 See, for example, Benson R. Snyder, *The Hidden Curriculum* (New York: Alfred A. Knopf, 1971), p. 106.

5 Jane Roland Martin, *Reclaiming a Conversation*, Ch. 3. In *Knowledge, Gender, and Schooling* (Westport, CT: Bergin & Garvey, 2002), p. 46, D.G. Mulcahy has said that, since education is a cultural phenomenon, it is "little more than a tautology" to call something a production model of education. Thus, supposing Mulcahy is correct, and I am not convinced that he is, because the growth model is so often contrasted with the idea of education as production, it nevertheless seems important to show, not only that there can be different kinds of production models, but also that the growth model is a production model in disguise.

6 In the Just State envisioned by Socrates, women, as well as men, can be rulers and the institutions of private home and family are abolished.

7 For an excellent account of the British open-classroom schools, see, for example, Lydia A.H. Smith, *Activity and Experience* (New York: Agathon Press, 1976).

8 Even so-called "free schools" such as Summerhill in England and the Sudbury Valley School in the U.S. do not want cultural stock such as rape and murder to attach to their students' capacities. Nor would they consider it acceptable if the students did not learn to read and write, add and subtract, and acquire at least a smattering of knowledge of science, history, literature, and so on.

9 Russ Rymer, *Genie* (New York: HarperCollins, 1993).

10 John Stuart Mill, *The Subjection of Women* (Cambridge, MA: MIT Press, 1869/1970), p. 22.

11 Still, whenever the subject is Rousseau, it is well to remember that contradictions and paradoxes were his delight.

12 Charlotte Perkins Gilman, *Herland* (New York: Pantheon, 1979), p. 59. For discussions of Gilman's educational philosophy, see Jane Roland Martin, *Reclaiming a Conversation*, Ch. 6; Karen Mahoney, "Charlotte Perkins Gilman: The Origin of Education is Maternal" in Connie Titone and Karen E. Maloney, Eds. *Women's Philosophies of Education* (Upper Saddle River, NJ: Prentice-Hall, 1999), Ch. 5; Susan Laird, "Rethinking Coeducation" in James Garrison, Ed. *The New Scholarship on Dewey* (Dordrecht, Netherlands: Kluwer Academic Publishers, 1995), pp. 193–210.

13 Gilman, *Herland*, p. 107.

14 Ibid., p. 98.

15 Ibid., p. 107.

16 Ibid., p. 100.

17 Jared Diamond, *Collapse* (New York: Viking, 2005). See Malcolm Gladwell, "The Vanishing," *The New Yorker*, January 3, 2005, pp. 70–73, for a perceptive review of Diamond's book.

18 Diamond, *Collapse*, pp. 200ff. If it were to turn out that Diamond is mistaken in the details of his case studies, the point at issue here would not be affected. For, if in fact different beliefs, skills, attitudes, and values were at stake than the ones I cite, their yoking to capacities would still mean that education is a shaper of culture.

19 Ibid., p. 201.

20 Ibid., Ch. 8.

21 For example, Japan and the Dominican Republic.

22 Karl R. Popper, *The Poverty of Historicism* (Boston, MA: Beacon Press, 1957).

23 Ibid., p. 87.

24 Ibid., p. 65.

25 Ibid., pp. 83–84.

26 Ibid., p. 61.

27 For a very different view of engineering, see, for example, David P. Billington, "One Bridge Doesn't Fit All," *New York Times*, August 18, 2007, p. A23.

28 John Dewey, *The School and Society* (Chicago: University of Chicago Press, 1915/1956), p. 12. As Bernard Bailyn has shown, this was not the first transformation of home in American history that had radical implications. See Bernard Bailyn, *Education in the Forming of American Society* (New York: Vintage, 1960).

29 Maria Montessori, *The Montessori Method* (New York: Schocken Books, 1964), p. 52.

30 For an extended discussion of Montessori's conception of school see Jane Roland Martin, *The Schoolhome* (Cambridge, MA: Harvard University Press, 1992). The idea of school I developed in *The Schoolhome* is discussed in Chapter 9 of this volume.

31 I do not for a moment want to deny that engineering itself requires these other traits. Popper's account masks this fact, however.

32 For school to undertake "foreign" practices was not something new. "Schools and formal schooling had acquired a new importance. They had assumed cultural burdens they had not borne before," wrote Bailyn about the American colonial period. Bailyn, *Education in the Forming of American Society*, p. 21.

33 Diamond, *Collapse*, Chs. 7, 8.

Chapter 5

1 Eva Hoffman, *Lost in Translation* (New York: Penguin, 1989), p. 29.

2 Ibid., p. 30.

3 Ibid., p. 74.

4 Annie Dillard, *An American Childhood* (New York: Harper & Row, 1987), pp. 252–253.

5 Mark Mathabane, *Kaffir Boy* (New York: Simon & Schuster, 1986), p. 29.

6 Michael Oakeshott, "The Study of 'Politics' in a University" in Jane R. Martin, Ed. *Readings in the Philosophy of Education* (Boston, MA: Allyn & Bacon, 1970), p. 42.

7 Herbert Spencer, "What Knowledge Is of Most Worth?" in *Education* (New York: D. Appleton, 1860).

8 Jonathan Turner, "Herbert Spencer" in J.J. Chambliss, Ed. *Philosophy of Education: An Encyclopedia* (New York: Garland, 1996), pp. 623–626.

9 William K. Frankena, "A Model for Analyzing a Philosophy of Education" in Jane Roland Martin, Ed. *Readings in the Philosophy of Education* (Boston, MA: Allyn & Bacon, 1970), p. 19.

10 "Epistemological fallacy" is my term, not Frankena's. Jane Roland Martin, "Needed: A New Paradigm for Liberal Education" in Jonas P. Soltis, Ed. *Philosophy of Education: Eightieth Yearbook of the National Society for the Study of Education* (Chicago: University of Chicago Press, 1981), pp. 37–59.

11 See Jane Roland Martin, "What Should We Do with a Hidden Curriculum When We Find One?" *Curriculum Inquiry*, 1976, 6 (2), pp. 135–151.

12 M. Elaine Mar, *Paper Daughter* (New York: HarperCollins, 2000), p. 72.

13 Edward Humes, *School of Dreams* (Orlando, FL: Harcourt, 2003); cf. Alexandra Robbins, *The Overachievers* (New York: Hyperion, 2006).

14 Yale Sustainable Food Project, *Annual Report*, 2005.

15 A reviewer of a biography of the great baseball player Willie Mays wrote that, in Fairfield, Alabama, "Young Willie learned to hit and run and slide and catch and throw. The full curriculum. Most important, he learned the rules of the game." Pete Hamill, "Say Hey," *New York Times Magazine*, February 28, 2010, p. 8.

16 Charles R. Keller, "Needed: Revolution in the Social Studies" in Byron G. Massialas and Andreas M. Kazemias, Eds. *Crucial Issues in the Teaching of Social Studies* (Englewood-Cliffs, NJ: Prentice-Hall, 1964), p. 38.

17 For more on school subjects, see Jane Roland Martin, "The Disciplines and the Curriculum," *Educational Theory and Philosophy*, 1969, 1; "The Anatomy of a Subject," *Educational Theory*, Spring 1977, 27 (2), pp. 85–95; "Two Dogmas of Curriculum," *Synthese*, April 1982, 51 (1), pp. 5–20.

18 I initially called this a subject-entity. See Jane Roland Martin, "Two Dogmas of Curriculum."

19 Ibid.

20 See, for example, Hilda Taba, *Curriculum Development* (New York: Harcourt, Brace, and World, 1962), p. 393.

21 John Dewey, *Experience and Education* (New York: Macmillan, 1938/1963), pp. 26–27.

22 Matt Richtel, "Thou Shalt Not Kill, Except in a Game at Church," *New York Times*, October 7, 2007, pp. A1, 20.

23 Dewey, *Experience and Education*, p. 49.

24 For a fuller discussion of such a project, see Jane Roland Martin, *Cultural Miseducation* (New York: Teachers College Press, 2002).

25 Edward O. Wilson, *The Future of Life* (New York: Vintage, 2002), p. 15.

26 Ibid., p. 21.

27 *EOL Newsletter*, Issue 1, www.EOL.org.

28 Thus, for example, although it may seem that, only yesterday, bookmobiles were common sights in Massachusetts towns and cities, in 2007 they were rapidly becoming extinct. Anna Badkhen, "A Few Libraries, Drivers Refuse to Give up on Relic of Days Gone By," *Boston Globe*, October 2, 2007.

29 See, for example, Robert D. Putnam, *Bowling Alone* (New York: Simon & Schuster, 2000).

30 Tara Parker-Pope, "For Clues on Teenage Sex, Experts Look to Hip-Hop," *New York Times*, November 6, 2007, pp. D 5, 8.

31 See transcript of Bill Moyers, *Journal*, November 23, 2007, www.pbs.org; cf. Philip Dray, "Noose," *The Boston Globe*, December 2, 2007; Elissa Gootman, "For Scholar of Race, Noose Case Draws Spotlight," *New York Times*, October 12, 2007, p. A 23.

32 Carl Becker, "Everyman His Own Historian," *American Historical Review*, 37 (2), pp. 221–236; www.Historians.org/info, p. 2.

33 This example is adapted from Sandra Lee Bartky, *Femininity and Domination* (New York: Routledge, 1990), Ch. 1.

Chapter 6

1 John Rawls, *A Theory of Justice* (Cambridge, MA: Harvard University Press, 1971), pp. 3, 6.

2 See Michael Martin and Lee C. McIntyre, Eds., *Readings in the Philosophy of Social Science* (Cambridge, MA: MIT Press, 1994), Part IV, for discussions of reductionism, individualism, and holism.

3 Karl Mannheim, "The Problem of Generations" in P. Keckskemti, Ed. *Essays in the Sociology of Knowledge* (London: Routledge & Kegan Paul, 1952), pp. 276–320.

4 For a fuller discussion of the educational problem of generations, see Jane Roland Martin, *Cultural Miseducation* (New York: Teachers College Press, 2002).

5 See, for example, John A. Hostetler, *Amish Society* (Baltimore, MD: The John Hopkins University Press, 1993, fourth ed.).

6 Actually, the boy Emile does occasionally venture into the world outside.

7 Jean-Jacques Rousseau, trans. Allan Bloom. *Emile* (New York: Basic Books, 1979), p. 178.

8 Ibid., p. 188.

9 Hostetler, *Amish Society*, p. 247.
10 Rousseau, *Emile*, p. 184.
11 Hostetler, *Amish Society*, p. 362.
12 Plato, trans. G.M.A. Grube, *Republic* (Indianapolis, IN: Hackett, 1974), p. 377b. Experts disagree over whether the Socrates of the *Republic* represents the historical Socrates or simply Plato's own prejudices. I bracket this question here. Thus, when, for instance, I say, "Socrates believed . . ." I am using shorthand for "the Socrates of the *Republic* believed . . ." It is worth noting that Rousseau, who admired the *Republic* immensely, wrote: "The most dangerous period of human life is that from birth to the age of twelve. This is the time when errors and vices germinate without one's yet having any instrument for destroying them; and by the time the instrument comes, the roots are so deep that it is too late to rip them out." *Emile*, p. 93.
13 Plato, *Republic*, p. 378e.
14 Sisela Bok, *Mayhem* (Reading, MA: Addison-Wesley, 1998).
15 Ibid., p. 62.
16 Ibid.
17 Jane Mayer, "Whatever It Takes," *The New Yorker*, February 19, 2007, p. 4.
18 Ibid., p. 5.
19 Transcript of "Is Torture on Hit Fox TV Show '24' Encouraging US Soldiers to Abuse Detainees?" *Democracy Now! The War and Peace Report*, www.democracynow.org/2007/2/22/is_torture_on_hit_fox_tv, p. 5.
20 Mayer, "Whatever It Takes," p. 5.
21 Whether the critics themselves are objective is a question in its own right. If nothing else, they hold the studies on harm to children to a higher standard of proof than seems reasonable; seldom, if ever, mention the most egregious cases of violence in the electronic media, let alone cases of racism, sexism, and the like; and tend to give the benefit of the doubt to the catharsis model, according to which one who sees violence is less likely to commit violence. Indeed, the critics of the research seem as intent on demonstrating the evils of the blue-pencil strategy as the advocates are eager to show that it is necessary. Thus, for example, after claiming that studies fail to show that television violence has "model effects," one critic blithely affirmed that censorship may teach "authoritarianism, intolerance for unpopular opinions, erotophobia, and sexual guilt" without ever examining the evidence in support of her case. Marjorie Heins, *Not in Front of the Children* (New York: Hill & Wang, 2001), p. 257.
22 Leo Tolstoy, trans. Constance Garnett. *War and Peace* (New York: Modern Library, 1994), p. 611.
23 John Stuart Mill, *On Liberty* (Indianapolis: Bobs-Merrill, 1859/1956), p. 21.
24 Ibid.
25 Ibid., p. 13.
26 Ibid.
27 On this subject, see, for example, Jarlan Coben, "The Undercover Parent," *New York Times*, March 16, 2008, p. WK 14.
28 Actually, Plato's blue-pencil strategy can, in its turn, be seen as an instance of the immunization strategy, one in which a wall of separation is built between a whole state and the rest of the world. In Rousseau's case, the wall separates children—or rather boys, for Rousseau makes it clear that Emile is meant to represent Everyboy, not Everychild—from the larger culture into which they are born. In the Amish case, it separates one religious group from the culture of the nation to which the group belongs. In Plato's case, the wall separates a whole state from the other states in the world.
29 See Alison Lurie, "The Royal Family," *New York Review of Books*, December 16, 2004, p. 6; Edward Rothstein, "All About Mr. Elephant, in His Becoming Green Suit," *New York Times*, September 22, 2008, pp. B 1, 5.
30 Stephen Armstrong, "Rough Justice," *Newstatesman*, March 19, 2007.

31 Martin Miller, "'24' and 'Lost' Get Symposium on Torture," *Seattle Times*, February 14, 2007.
32 Barry Bergman, "Prime-Time Torture Gets a Reality Check," *Berkeleyan*, March 5, 2008, p. 2.
33 Marianne Lavelle, "Can Industry Spread Its Green Fever?" *US News & World Report*, June 6, 2005, p. 49.
34 Mayer, "Whatever It Takes," p. 6.
35 Bernard Bailyn, *Education in the Forming of American Society* (New York: Vintage, 1960), p. 26.
36 Ibid., p. 27.
37 And it is what I did when I developed my idea of a schoolhome; see Jane Roland Martin, *The Schoolhome* (Cambridge, MA: Harvard University Press, 1992).
38 It should be noted that the Morrill Act itself did not define "the people," and what came to be called the Land Grant colleges and universities did not at the beginning include African-American men or women of any color in their definitions. Nevertheless, by naming white men *of all classes* the designated beneficiaries of that portion of the culture's stock known as the liberal arts and sciences, this legislation transformed higher education in the U.S.
39 There is more to this story. As early as the turn of the twentieth century, it was realized that adults in the farming community often resisted the new knowledge but that young people did not. It was also noticed that, when the children acquired the new knowledge, their elders soon followed suit. And so, clubs for rural boys and girls were established whose aim was not only to provide the children with first hand farm experience but also, through them, to introduce new ideas to their parents. These clubs were included in the charter of the Extension Service and, in 1924, became what has since been known as the 4-H Clubs.
40 Jared Diamond, *Collapse* (New York: Viking, 2005), p. 213.
41 Edmund V. White, "Sons and Brothers," *New York Review of Books*, October 11, 2007, pp. 47–48.
42 The very first kindergarten in the U.S. was, however, German speaking and was founded in 1856 by Margarethe Meyer Schurz, a German immigrant who had met Froebel when she was young, studied his methods, and taught in the kindergarten her sister and brother-in-law established in England.
43 "The isolated home . . . may do for babies, but every mother and nurse knows how hard it is to meet the demands of a young child too young to be taught to read, but whose opening intelligence and irrepressible bodily activity are so hard to be met by an adult, however genial and active." Mary Peabody Mann and Elizabeth Peabody, *Moral Culture of Infancy and Kindergarten Guide* (Boston, MA: T.O.H.P. Burnham, 1864), p. 12.

Chapter 7

1 Thomas Jefferson, "Notes on Virginia" in Adrienne Koch and William Peden, Eds., *The Life and Selected Writings of Thomas Jefferson* (New York: Modern Library, 1944), p. 265.
2 John Dewey, *Democracy and Education* (New York: Macmillan, 1916/1961), p. 87.
3 Amy Guttman and Dennis Thompson, *Why Deliberative Democracy?* (Princeton, NJ: Princeton University Press, 2004), p. 35.
4 Steven M. Cahn, *Education and the Democratic Ideal* (Chicago: Nelson-Hall, 1979), p. 1.
5 Benjamin Barber, *Strong Democracy* (Berkeley: University of California Press, 1984), p. 234.
6 For other lists see, for example, C.B. Macpherson, *The Life and Times of Liberal Democracy* (Oxford: Oxford University Press, 1976); Barber, *Strong Democracy*; Gutmann and

Thompson, *Why Deliberative Democracy?*; Ian Shapiro, *The State of Democratic Theory* (Princeton, NJ: Princeton University Press, 2003).

7 I derive the phrase "the cultural surround" from John I. Goodlad, *In Praise of Education* (New York: Teachers College Press, 1997), p. 23, and John I. Goodlad et al., *Education for Everyone* (San Francisco: Jossey-Bass, 2004), pp. 33–34.

8 M. Elaine Mar, *Paper Tiger* (New York: HarperCollins, 2000), p. 8.

9 Ibid., p. 23.

10 Ibid., p. 9.

11 Ibid., p. 228.

12 Ibid., p. 23.

13 Frank McCourt, *Teacher Man* (New York: Scribner, 2005), pp. 91–92; cf. the home life of A.P. Frank in Alexandra Robbins, *The Overachievers* (New York: Hyperion, 2006).

14 www.crin.org.

15 Jennifer Wedekind, "The Children's Crusade," *In These Times*, June 3, 2005, www.inthesetimes.com/article/2136.

16 Anthony Swofford, *Jarhead* (New York: Scribner, 2003), p. 28.

17 Louis Uchitelle, *The Disposable American* (New York: Alfred A. Knopf, 2006), p. 101.

18 Ibid., p. 34.

19 Bethany McLean and Peter Elkind, *The Smartest Guys in the Room* (New York: Penguin Group, 2003).

20 This is not to say that a single individual who possesses the Enron package of traits poses a threat to democracy. My point is simply that, from the standpoint of democracy, Enron's culture was seriously miseducative.

21 Bob Herbert, "Coming Late to the Table," *New York Times*, May 31, 2008, p. A 27.

22 See, for example, Jimmy Carter's speech to the Parliament of the World's Religions, December 3, 2009, Melbourne, Australia, in which he documented the violence against women that occurs every day, and the Southern Baptist Convention's ruling that women must be subservient to their husbands and cannot serve as deacons, pastors, chaplains in the military or teachers of men; cf. Nicholas D. Kristof, "Religion and Women," *New York Times*, January 10, 2010, p. WK 11.

23 Uchitelle, *The Disposable American*, pp. 187–188.

24 Quoted in John Nichols and Robert W. McChesney, *Tragedy & Farce* (New York: The New Press, 2005), p. 1.

25 Dewey, *Democracy and Education*, p. 87.

26 Cahn, *Education and the Democratic Ideal*, p. 5.

27 Goodlad et al., *Education for Everyone*, p. 82.

28 Bill Moyers, *Journal*, Public Broadcasting System, July 24, 2009.

29 Gutmann and Thompson, *Why Deliberative Democracy?*, p. 61.

30 Patricia White, *Civic Virtues and Public Schooling* (New York: Teachers College Press, 1996), p. 3ff.

31 Martha C. Nussbaum, *Cultivating Humanity* (Cambridge, MA: Harvard University Press, 1997), p. 9.

32 Ibid., pp. 9–10; see also Martha C. Nussbaum, *Poetic Justice* (Boston, MA: Beacon Press, 1995).

33 I am not ruling out here that some children may have learned all this at home or in their communities.

34 Gutmann and Thompson, *Why Deliberative Democracy?*, p. 7.

35 However, see Michael Walzer, "Deliberation, and What Else?" in Stephen Macedo, Ed., *Deliberative Politics* (New York: Oxford University Press, 1999), p. 67, for a discussion of whether it should be considered an independent aspect of democracy.

36 Nussbaum, *Cultivating Humanity*, p. 295.

37 Michael W. Apple and James A. Beane, Eds., *Democratic Schools* (Portsmouth, NH: Heinemann, 2007, second ed.), p. 8, say schools "as a common experience of virtually

all young people, have a moral obligation to bring the democratic way of life in the culture and the curriculum of the school."

38 Linda Darling-Hammond, "Education for Civility and Civitas" in John I. Goodlad and Timothy J. McMannon, Eds., *The Public Purpose of Education and Schooling* (San Francisco: Jossey-Bass, 1997), p. 111. Apple and Bean, *Democratic Schools*, p. 13, in turn, call school a "remarkably undemocratic institution."

39 Following tradition, I will henceforth call them "democratic schools," although my assumption throughout will be that they are simply schools whose cultures are democratic.

40 Interestingly enough, these are the ones frequently held up to ridicule. See, for example, Josephine Tey, *Brat Farrar* (New York: Scribner, 1997), p. 138.

41 See, for example, Deborah Meier and Paul Schwartz, "Central Park East Secondary School" in Apple and Beane, Eds., *Democratic Schools*, pp. 130–149; Eugene F. Provenza, Jr., "An Adventure with Children" in Susan F. Semel and Alan R. Sadovnik, Eds., *"Schools of Tomorrow," Schools of Today* (New York: Peter Lang, 1999), pp. 103–120.

42 Agnes De Lima, *The Little Red School House* (New York: Macmillan, 1942), p. 112. Written in collaboration with the school's director, Elisabeth Irwin, its 14 teachers, and one parent, and containing an introduction by John Dewey, this book offers a vivid picture of the democratic schooling of approximately 350 children, ages 4 to 13, and of the philosophy behind it at a perilous moment in the history of democracy. In the interests of full disclosure, let it be known that I attended The Little Red School House from 1939 to 1943 and graduated from its high school, Elisabeth Irwin, in 1947.

43 Ibid., p. 23.

44 Ibid.

45 Ibid.

46 Ibid., p. 24.

47 These functioned as what have sometimes been called "central subjects" and there tended to be just one such subject per class per school year.

48 For example, Meier, "Central Park East;" Provenza, "An Adventure with Children."

49 De Lima, *The Little Red School House*, p. 234.

50 Ibid., p. 98.

51 Ibid., p. 99.

52 Ibid., p. 113.

53 Ibid., p. 114.

54 Ibid., p. 115.

55 Other observers have insisted that it is acceptable for school to teach children *about* values—for instance, honesty, courage, and respect for others—but not to instill values in children.

56 See, for example, Patricia Albjerg Graham, *Schooling America* (Oxford: Oxford University Press, 2005).

57 This does not mean that every single educational agent must cooperate. In a democracy, there will always be room for some institutions that, intentionally or unintentionally, promote democratic miseducation. When, however, democratic miseducation becomes an obstacle to the achievement of education for democratic citizenship, it is time to be concerned.

58 James Risen, "Electrical Risks Worse Than Said at Bases in Iraq," *New York Times*, July 18, 2008, pp. A 1, 10; cf. Robert Reich, *Supercapitalism* (New York: Knopf, 2007).

59 Shapiro, *The State of Democratic Theory*, p. 80; "The Debate About the Social Responsibilities of Companies is Heating up Again," *The Economist*, September 8, 2007, pp. 65–66.

Chapter 8

1 At the end of the last century, economist Amartya Sen brought to light the worldwide phenomenon of "Missing Women." Documenting the excess mortality and artificially lower survival rates of women in many countries of the world, Sen calculated that, in China alone, the number of missing women would be more than 50 million and estimated that, in the world at large, there would be more than 100 million (see "More Than 100 Million Women Are Missing," *New York Review of Books*, December 20, 1990). He later refined that analysis by adding a discussion of the emergence of the statistically significant phenomenon of sex selective abortion (Amartya Sen, "Missing Women—Revisited," *British Medical Journal*, December 6, 2003, p. 1,297). The disappearance of women in higher education is not as troubling as the disappearances that Sen detailed. Nevertheless, an understanding of the worldwide status of women can be enhanced by expanding Sen's concept of the missing women so as to include women's disappearances at other stages of the life cycle. I first identified the problem of the missing women in higher education in Jane Roland Martin, "In Search of Equality: The Missing Women in Higher Education," *Gender Law and Policy Annual Review*, 2004, 2, pp. 133–146. I introduced a two-culture analysis into my discussion of the problem in Jane Roland Martin, "The Missing Women in Higher Education: A Case Study of Culture Crossing" in Ann Mari May, Ed., *The "Woman Question" and Higher Education* (Cheltenham, UK: Edward Elgar, 2008), pp. 77–92.
2 Malcolm Scully, "Women Account for Half of College Enrollment in US, 3 Other Nations," *Chronicle of Higher Education*, September 17, 1986, 33 (3), pp. 1, 42.
3 "Doctoral Recipients from United States Universities," United States Department of Education, National Center for Educational Statistics, 1987.
4 "Digest of Education Statistics," United States Department of Education, 2008, Table 291.
5 This is not to say that the theory of education as encounter assumes that the so-called "hard" curriculum areas of science, technology, engineering, and mathematics and the like are superior to the "soft" ones, or that occupations in engineering, science, and the like are superior to ones in social work, nursing, and teaching. It is merely to take note of the facts. For further discussion of this point, see Jane Roland Martin, *The Schoolhome* (Cambridge, MA: Harvard University Press, 1992) and *Coming of Age in Academe* (New York: Routledge, 2000).
6 See Pamela Stone, *Opting Out?* (Berkeley: University of California Press, 2007), Ch. 5, for an interesting discussion of choice rhetoric; cf. Sandra Tsing Loh, "I Choose My Choice!" *The Atlantic*, July/August 2008, pp. 125–133.
7 Cf. Susan J. Douglas and Meredith W. Michaels, *The Mommy Myth* (New York: Free Press, 2004), p. 108; Joan Williams, *Unbending Gender* (Oxford: Oxford University Press, 2000) p. 39; Ann Crittendon, *The Price of Motherhood* (New York: Holt, 2001), p. 234ff.
8 Cf. Rachel Donadio, "Betty Friedan's Enduring 'Mystique'," *New York Times Book Review*, February 26, 2006, p. 23.
9 "The big problem with the rhetoric of choice is that it leaves out power," Crittendon, *The Price of Motherhood*, p. 234.
10 See, for example, Roberta M. Hall and Bernice Resnick Sandler, *The Classroom Climate: A Chilly One for Women* (Washington D.C.: Association of Women's Colleges, 1982); Bernice Resnick Sandler et al., *The Chilly Classroom Climate: A Guide to Improve the Education of Women* (Washington D.C.: National Association for Women in Education, 1996); Constance Backhouse et al., *The Chilly Climate for Faculty Women at UWO: Postscript to the Backhouse Report* (London, Ontario: University of Western Ontario, 1989); Linda Briskin, "Negotiating Power in the Classroom," *York Gazette*, September 13, 2000; Lani Guinier et al., *Becoming Gentlemen* (Boston, MA: Beacon Press, 1997); Mona Harrington, *Women Lawyers* (New York: Penguin, 1995); VèVè Clark et al., Eds., *Anti-Feminism in the Academy* (New York: Routledge, 1996); Peggy Orenstein, *School Girls* (New York: Doubleday, 1994); Myra Sadker and David Sadker, *Failing at Fairness* (New York: Touchstone, 1995); Nan Stein and Lisa Sjpostrom, *Flirting or Hurting?*

(Washington D.C.: National Education Association, 1994). This is not to say that all boys and men, or all girls and women, are treated alike regardless of their race, class, ethnicity, and so on.

11 Guinier et al., *Becoming Gentlemen*, p. 48.

12 Hall and Sandler, *The Classroom Climate*, p. 3.

13 Sandler et al., *The Chilly Classroom*, p. 33.

14 "Digest of Education Statistics," 2008, Tables 186, 249.

15 "Digest of Education Statistics," United States Department of Education, 2008, Table 275.

16 Marciella Bombardieri, "MIT Set to Pick Its First Female President," *Boston Globe*, August 26, 2004, p. A 26.

17 "Developing a Diverse Faculty," *Harvard Magazine*, September–October, 2006, p. 77.

18 Annette Kolodny, "Paying the Price of Anti-Feminist Intellectual Harassment" in Clark et al., *Anti-Feminism in the Academy*, p. 24.

19 Referring to the field of law, Crittendon, *The Price of Motherhood*, p. 39, says, "A selection process that winnows women out of this stream has the effect of keeping a disproportionate number of qualified women out of top government jobs, off the bench, and out of the loop for corporate directorships and other leadership position."

20 See, for example, Kristen Monroe et al., "Gender Equity in Academia: Bad News from the Trenches, and Some Possible Solutions," *Perspectives on Politics*, June 2008, 6 (2), pp. 215–233, for a qualitative study that uncovered a wide array of overt and covert inequities.

21 Greta Gaard, "Anti-Lesbian Intellectual Harassment in the Academy" in Clark et al., *Anti-Feminism in the Academy*, pp. 115–140.

22 Backhouse et al., *Chilly Climate*, p. 26.

23 For example, Anita Palepu and Carol P. Herbert, "Medical Women in Academia: The Silences We Keep," *JAMC*, October 15, 2002, 167 (8), pp. 877–879; "Women Medical School Faculty Perceive Gender Bias, Sexual Harassment," June 6, 2000, http://mgh.harvard.edu/pubaffairs. See also Jennifer Freyd and J.Q. Johnson, "References on Chilly Climate for Women Faculty in Academe," http://dynamic.uoregon.edu.

24 Kenji Yoshino, *Covering* (New York: Random House, 2006), p. 162.

25 Maike Ingrid Philipsen, *Challenges of the Faculty Career for Women* (San Francisco: Jossey-Bass, 2008).

26 Although supporters of the two strategies for radical curricular change sometimes gave the impression that the two approaches were mutually exclusive, these were—and still are—complementary policies.

27 "A Harvard Magazine Roundtable: The Future of the Research University," *Harvard Magazine*, October, 2000, pp. 46–57.

28 See, for example, Harrington, *Women Lawyers*, p. 67; Meg Lovejoy, " 'You Can't Go Home Again': The Impact of Women's Studies on Intellectual and Personal Development," *National Women's Studies Association Journal*, 1998, 10 (1), pp. 119–138.

29 Whether or not they do is another matter.

30 Immanuel Kant, trans. J.T. Goldthwait, *Observations on the Feeling of the Beautiful and Sublime* (Berkeley: University of California Press, 1960), p. 78.

31 John Stuart Mill, *The Subjection of Women* (Cambridge, MA: MIT Press, 1869/1970), p. 29.

32 See Philipsen, *Challenges of the Faculty Career for Women*, p. 196, for an example of sexual harassment that results, says an interviewee, "because I am an academic woman who does her nails, and wears low-cut shirts, and make-up, whatever, you know."

33 See, for example, Kathryn Joyce, *Quiverfull* (Boston, MA: Beacon Press, 2009). Indeed, the Christian patriarchy movement goes so far as to attach to its members' capacities the belief that, because women's place is the home and their lot is to be submissive to men, they should not attend college.

34 Lawrence Summers, "Remarks at NBER Conference on Diversifying the Science and Engineering Workforce," January 14, 2005, www president.harvard.edu/speeches, p. 2.

35 Adrienne Rich, *Of Woman Born* (New York: Bantam, 1977), p. 3.
36 Douglas and Michaels, *The Mommy Myth*. Stone, *Opting Out?*, calls it "intensive mothering;" see also Crittendon, *The Price of Motherhood*, p. 20, on the shift from "having babies" to "raising children."
37 For more on this, see Leslie Bennetts, *The Feminine Mistake* (New York: Hyperion, 2007). It is not known just how many women and men believe in the new momism, but Crittendon, *The Price of Motherhood*, p. 213, says: "A huge segment of the [U.S.] population worries that care by anyone other than a mother herself is not only not optimal but downright harmful to children."
38 Amartya Sen, *Identity and Violence* (New York: Norton, 2006), p. xii.
39 Douglas and Michaels, *The Mommy Myth*, p. 22.
40 Williams, *Unbending Gender*, p. 76.
41 "I had to get divorced before I was able to find a healthy balance in my life, because then I started having my children only half of the time. My former husband and I share custody and care." Philipsen, *Challenges of the Faculty Career for Women*, p. 13. Feeling torn apart is not unique to faculty women; see, for example, Stone, *The Feminine Mistake*.
42 Martin, *Coming of Age in Academe*, p. 52ff. Exceptions to this principle can, of course, be adduced. For instance, E.O. Wilson's standing in the academic world is exceptionally high, whereas the status in the culture at large of the ants he studies is fairly low. The guilt by association principle comes with an "other things being equal clause," however, and, in Wilson's case, his interest in the "lowly" ants is far outweighed by his contributions to the very shape and form of the field of Evolutionary Biology.
43 Martha C. Nussbaum, *Cultivating Humanity* (Cambridge, MA: Harvard University Press, 1997), p. 33.
44 Ibid., p. 66.
45 Ibid., p. xvi.
46 See, for example, Benjamin Barber, *Strong Democracy* (Berkeley: University of California Press, 1984), p. 34; Amy Guttman and Dennis Thompson, *Why Deliberative Democracy?* (Princeton, NJ: Princeton University Press, 2004), Ch. 1; Patricia White, *Civic Virtues and Public Schooling* (New York: Teachers College Press, 1996).
47 Kwame Anthony Appiah, *Cosmopolitanism* (New York: Norton, 2006), p. 4.
48 Philip Hallie, *Lest Innocent Blood Be Shed* (New York: Harper & Row, 1979).
49 For two examples of more far-reaching changes, see Rich, *Of Woman Born*, p. 148ff, and Crittendon, *The Price of Motherhood*, p. 256ff.
50 Thomas S. Kuhn, *The Structure of Scientific Revolutions* (Chicago: University of Chicago Press, 1970 second ed.), p. 53.
51 Ibid., p. 52.
52 Philipsen, *Challenges*, p. 263, points out that women are haunted by anxiety that the benefits of these "come with a price tag."
53 According to an acclaimed sociological study, "most working fathers who fully share the emotional responsibility and physical care of children and do half the housework face great difficulty." Arlie Russell Hochschild, *The Second Shift* (New York: Penguin, 2003), p. 33. No doubt one reason why is that they are doing work and exhibiting traits that are genderized in favor of females, and another is that the work they are doing is devalued. In addition, women whose identity is defined solely by motherhood often feel threatened when men attempt to share the work and responsibilities, and they can even respond by sabotaging their efforts. The sociological study reported that some women "didn't make room for their husband's hand at home; they played expert with the baby, the dinner, the social schedule. Something in their tone of voice said, 'This is my domain.'" (Ibid., pp. 271–272). Following 100 new parents for 5 years, another study "found the problem of maternal sabotage to be nearly universal." Susan Maushart, *The Mask of Motherhood* (New York: Penguin, 2000), p. 194.
54 C.P. Snow, *The Two Cultures* (Cambridge: Cambridge University Press, 1998), p. 4.

55 Ibid.
56 Ibid., p. 9.
57 Ibid., p. 64.
58 It should be noted that it is possible to speak of "the culture" of home and family without being committed to essentialism. Just as it is legitimate to refer to the culture of school or of symphony orchestras or of football without attributing a small set of necessary and immutable characteristics to school, symphony orchestras, or football teams, it is legitimate to say that the world of the private home and family has a culture of its own. This is quite compatible, moreover, with affirming that every home is unique; indeed, with saying that every home has its own culture. It is also consistent with the thesis that the cultures of particular homes differ according to the race, class, or ethnicity of their members. Furthermore, to speak of "the" culture of home and family allows for exceptions. Just as some schools possess so few of the attributes of "the" culture of school that it can truly be said that they do not share it, there can also be homes that do not partake of "the" home culture.
59 Snow, *The Two Cultures*, p. 16.
60 Ibid., pp. 33, 61.
61 For a discussion of higher education's devotion to "aerial distance" from real-life problems, see Martin, *Coming of Age in Academe*, Ch. 2.
62 For instance, Antioch College in the U.S.
63 On this point see, for example, Derek Bok, *Our Underachieving Colleges* (Princeton, NJ: Princeton University Press, 2006), p. 59ff.

Chapter 9

1 Amartya Sen, *Development as Freedom* (New York: Knopf, 1999), p. 142.
2 Robert Redfield, "The Little Community" in *The Little Community and Peasant Society and Culture* (Chicago: University of Chicago Press, 1989), p. 19.
3 This is the way I proceeded in Jane Roland Martin, *The Schoolhome* (Cambridge, MA: Harvard University Press, 1992); *Cultural Miseducation* (New York: Teachers College Press, 2002).
4 Bernard Bailyn, *Education in the Forming of American Society* (New York: Vintage, 1960), p. 26.
5 Ibid., p. 31.
6 Actually, Adam Smith believed that, because of the workings of "an invisible hand," people are likely to promote the interest of society when they act out of self-interest. Adam Smith, *An Inquiry into the Nature and Causes of the Wealth of Nations* (Chicago: University of Chicago Press, 1776/1976), pp. 477–478.
7 Emile Durkheim, *The Division of Labor in Society* (New York: Free Press, 1997), p. 210, remarked, "As they perform different services they can perform them in harmony. However, the closer the functions are to one another . . . the more they tend to conflict."
8 Ibid., p. 218.
9 "Electric Car Dreams," *NOW*, Public Broadcasting System, October 30, 2009.
10 Maggie Jones, "A Different Kind of Prep School," *New York Times Magazine*, September 27, 2009, pp. 43–45, 57.
11 Historian Patricia Albjerg Graham, *Schooling America* (Oxford: Oxford University Press, 2005), p. 1, says, "Schools in American have danced to different drummers during their long history. Sometimes the drumbeat demanded rigidity in all programs; sometimes it wanted academic learning for only a few. Sometimes it encouraged unleashing children's creativity, not teaching them facts. Sometimes it wanted children to solve the social problems, such as racial segregation, adults could not handle. Sometimes it tacitly supported some schools as warehouses, not instructional facilities. Sometimes it sought schooling to be the equalizer in a society in which the gap between rich and

poor was growing. Sometimes the principal purpose of schooling seemed to be teaching citizenship and developing habits of work appropriate for a democratic society, while at other times its purpose seemed to be preparation for employment . . ."

12 *Urban Dictionary*, www.urbandictionary.com.

13 See, for example, Jane Roland Martin, *Educational Metamorphoses* (Lanham, MD: Rowman & Littlefield, 2007).

14 Lawrence Cremin, *The Transformation of the School* (New York: Vintage, 1961), p. 18. For a summary of Harris's views on the school curriculum, see Herbert M. Kleibard, *Forging the American Curriculum* (New York: Routledge, 1992), Ch. 1.

15 Mary Tripsas, "When Names Change to Protect the Future," *New York Times*, November 29, 2009, p. BU 3.

16 Patricia Graham's insightful history of schooling in the U.S., *Schooling America*, can be read as an account of school's changing "nature."

17 Lawrence Cremin, *The Genius of American Education* (New York: Vintage, 1965), p. 8.

18 Ibid., p. 9.

19 For further discussion of this point see Martin, *Cultural Miseducation*.

20 Bailyn, *Education in the Forming of American Society*, p. 27.

21 D.G. Mulcahy, *Knowledge, Gender, and Schooling* (Westport, CT: Bergin & Garvey, 2002), p. 67, speaks of my "desire to give over to the school the task of education for domesticity" but, in *The Schoolhome*, I propose that school *share* responsibility for that task with home, not that school take over the whole thing.

22 See, for example, Tracey Jan, "Spike in Violence in Middle Schools Raises Concerns," *The Boston Globe*, October 2, 2007, www.boston.com; Damien Cave, "Eight Teenagers Charged in Internet Beating Have Their Day on the Web," *New York Times*, April 12, 2008, pp. A 10–11; Derrick Z. Jackson, "Still Blind to Swastikas in School," *Boston Globe*, October 22, 2004, p. A19; Christopher Maag, "Short but Troubled Life of a High School Student Ended in Shooting and Suicide," *New York Times*, October 12, 2007, p. A 21; Jon Hurdle and Ian Urbina, "Boy Held in Plot to Open Fire at Pennsylvania School," *New York Times*, October 12, 2007, p. A 21; Bob Herbert, "Cops Vs. Kids," *New York Times*, March 6, 2010, p. A 19; Bob Herbert, "Bloody Urban Landscapes," *New York Times*, May 8, 2010, p. A19; Bob Herbert, "Too Long Ignored," *New York Times*, August 21, 2010, p. A 17.

23 Trip Gabriel, "Many Charter Schools, Varied Grades," *New York Times*, May 2, 2010, p. 22.

24 Graham, *Schooling America*.

25 Gabriel, "Many Charter Schools, Varied Grades," p. 22.

26 This would, of course, count in any other kind of school's favor as well.

27 For an interesting discussion of this topic, see Helen Anderson, "Renovating the Schoolhome," *Philosophy of Education 2006* (Urbana, IL: Philosophy of Education Society, 2007), pp. 236–244.

28 As philosopher of education Ann Diller says: "Not to make appropriate demands, not to expect and require adherence to standards is to confuse nurturance with neglect, to conflate care and indulgence." See Ann Diller, "Is Rapprochement Possible Between Educational Criticism and Nurturance?" in Ann Diller et al., *The Gender Question in Education* (Boulder, CO: Westview Press, 1996), p. 136.

29 It should perhaps be added that the schoolhome does not tolerate the sexual abuse of students either.

30 See, for example, Kevin Cullen, "Too Little, Too Late Against Bully Tactic," *Boston Globe*, January 31, 2010, www.boston.com; Sophia Yan, "Anonymous Gossip Sites," *Time*, December 7, 2009, pp. 97–98.

31 Bob Herbert, "Where the Bar Ought to Be," *New York Times*, February 23, 2010, p. A 23.

32 Gabriel, "Many Charter Schools, Varied Grades," p. 22.

33 The moral meaning and larger implications of the offense will depend on the name given it and, for better or worse, one and the same action or set of behaviors can be assigned different labels, all of which are correct. For example, some behavior that, at this writing, is called "bullying" can also be called "sexual harassment" and some of it "homophobic." See Jane Roland Martin, "Gender in the Classroom: Now You See It, Now You Don't," *Democracy and Education*, 1999, 9 (3), pp. 9–13.

34 In Montessori's Casa dei Bambini, boys served the soup at mealtime, something they and their fathers definitely did not do in the world of the private home.

35 This is not to deny that the school practices can have analogs in the larger culture or that instilling them may be thought to have disciplinary value.

36 George S. Counts, *Dare the School Build a New Social Order?* (Carbondale, IL: Southern Illinois University Press, 1932/1978).

37 See, for example, David Miller Sadker and Karen R. Zittleman, *Teachers, Schools, and Society* (New York: McGraw-Hill, 2007), p. 210.

38 Counts, *Dare The School Build a New Social Order?*, p. 20.

39 Ibid., p. 21.

40 Lewis Hyde, *The Gift* (New York: Vintage, 1979).

41 For more on learning as gift, see Jane Roland Martin, *Cultural Miseducation* (New York: Teachers College Press, 2002) and *Educational Metamorphoses*.

42 To cite just one example, the Thurgood Marshall Magnet School in Bridgeport, CT calls itself a "model for social justice."

43 Mulcahy, *Knowledge, Gender, and Schooling*, p. 146, suggests that, despite my acknowledgement of multiple educational agency, because I call the schoolhome a "surrogate home," I give it a near monopoly over education, and regard it as *the* educational agent. I hope this discussion has made it clear that this is not so.

Conclusion

1 Thomas Kuhn, *The Structure of Scientific Revolutions* (Chicago: University of Chicago Press, 1962), p. 111.

REFERENCES

"A Harvard Magazine Roundtable: The Future of the Research University," *Harvard Magazine*, October, 2000, pp. 46–57.

Adams, Henry. *The Education of Henry Adams* (New York: The Book League of America, 1928).

Adler, Mortimer J. *The Paideia Proposal* (New York: Macmillan, 1982).

American Kennel Club. "AKC's Canine Good Citizen® (CGC) Program," January 8, 2009, www.akc.org/events/cgc/index.cfm.

Anderson, Helen. "Renovating the Schoolhome," *Philosophy of Education 2006* (Urbana, IL: Philosophy of Education Society, 2007), pp. 236–244.

Angier, Natalie. "Pigs Prove to Be Smart, if Not Vain," *New York Times*, November 10, 2009, p. D1.

Appiah, Kwame Anthony. *Cosmopolitanism* (New York: Norton, 2006).

Apple, Michael W. and James A. Beane, Eds. *Democratic Schools* (Portsmouth, NH: Heinemann, 2007, second ed.).

Armstrong, Stephen. "Rough Justice," *Newstatesman*, March 19, 2007.

Backhouse, Constance, Roma Harris, Gillian Mitchell, and Alison Wylie. *The Chilly Climate for Faculty Women at UWO: Postscript to the Backhouse Report* (London, Ontario: University of Western Ontario, 1989).

Badkhen, Anna. "A Few Libraries, Drivers Refuse to Give up on Relic of Days Gone By," *Boston Globe*, October 2, 2007.

Bailyn, Bernard. *Education in the Forming of American Society* (New York: Vintage, 1960).

Barber, Benjamin. *Strong Democracy* (Berkeley: University of California Press, 1984).

——. "Education for Civility and Civitas," in John I. Goodlad and Timothy J. McMannon, Eds. *The Public Purpose of Education and Schooling* (San Francisco: Jossey-Bass, 1997), p. 103.

Bartky, Sandra Lee. *Femininity and Domination* (New York: Routledge, 1990).

Becker, Carl. "Everyman His Own Historian," *American Historical Review*, 37 (2), pp. 221–236.

Bennetts, Leslie. *The Feminine Mistake* (New York: Hyperion, 2007).

Bergman, Barry. "Prime-Time Torture Gets a Reality Check," *Berkeleyan*, March 5, 2008, p. 2.

Billington, David P. "One Bridge Doesn't Fit All," *New York Times*, August 18, 2007, p. A23.

Blackmore, Susan. *The Meme Machine* (Oxford: Oxford University Press, 1999).

Bok, Derek. *Our Underachieving Colleges* (Princeton, NJ: Princeton University Press, 2006).

Bok, Sisela. *Mayhem* (Reading, MA: Addison-Wesley, 1998).

Bombardieri, Marciella. "MIT Set to Pick Its First Female President," *Boston Globe*, August 26, 2004, p. A 26.

Boxill, Bernard, Ed. *Race and Racism* (Oxford: Oxford University Press, 2001).

Brameld, Theodore. *Cultural Foundations of Education* (New York: Harper & Brothers, 1957).

Briskin, Linda. "Negotiating Power in the Classroom," *York Gazette*, September 13, 2000.

Butler, Judith. *Gender Trouble* (New York: Routledge, 1990).

Cahn, Steven M. *Education and the Democratic Ideal* (Chicago: Nelson-Hall, 1979).

Cave, Damien. "Eight Teenagers Charged in Internet Beating Have Their Day on the Web," *New York Times*, April 12, 2008, pp. A 10–11.

Clark, Lorenne M.G. "The Rights of Women: The Theory and Practice of the Ideology of Male Supremacy" in William R. Shea and John King-Farlow, Eds. *Contemporary Issues in Political Philosophy* (New York: Science History Publications, 1976), pp. 49–65.

Clark, VèVè, Shirley Nelson Garner, Margaret Higonnet, and Ketu H. Katrak, Eds. *Anti-Feminism in the Academy* (New York: Routledge, 1996).

Coben, Jarlan. "The Undercover Parent," *New York Times*, March 16, 2008, p. WK 14.

Counts, George S. *Dare the School Build a New Social Order?* (Carbondale, IL: Southern Illinois University Press, 1932/1978).

Cremin, Lawrence. *The Transformation of the School* (New York: Vintage, 1961).

———. *The Genius of American Education* (New York: Vintage, 1965).

Crittendon, Ann. *The Price of Motherhood* (New York: Holt, 2001).

Cullen, Kevin. "Too Little, Too Late Against Bully Tactic," *Boston Globe*, January 31, 2010, www.boston.com.

Darling-Hammond, Linda. "Education for Civility and Civitas" in John I. Goodlad and Timothy J. McMannon, Eds. *The Public Purpose of Education and Schooling* (San Francisco: Jossey-Bass, 1997), pp. 41–54.

Dawkins, Richard. *The Selfish Gene* (Oxford: Oxford University Press, 1976).

De Lima, Agnes. *The Little Red School House* (New York: Macmillan, 1942).

Dennett, Daniel. *Consciousness Explained* (Boston, MA: Little, Brown, 1991).

"Developing a Diverse Faculty," *Harvard Magazine*, September–October, 2006.

Dewey, John. *The School and Society* (Chicago: University of Chicago Press, 1915/1956).

———. *Democracy and Education* (New York: Macmillan, 1916/1961).

———. *Experience and Education* (New York: Macmillan, 1938/1963).

Diamond, Jared. *Collapse* (New York: Viking, 2005).

"Digest of Education Statistics," 2008, Table 275, Washington D.C.: U.S. Department of Education, National Center for Educational Statistics.

"Digest of Education Statistics," 2009, Tables 186, 291, 249, Washington D.C.: U.S. Department of Education, National Center for Educational Statistics.

Dillard, Annie. *An American Childhood* (New York: Harper & Row, 1987).

Diller, Ann. "Is Rapprochement Possible Between Educational Criticism and Nurturance?" in Ann Diller, Barbara Houston, Kathryn Pauly Morgan, and Maryann Ayim, *The Gender Question in Education* (Boulder, CO: Westview Press, 1996), pp. 135–143.

"Doctoral Recipients from United States Universities," 1987, Washington, D.C.: U.S. Department of Education, National Center for Educational Statistics.

Donadio, Rachel. "Betty Friedan's Enduring 'Mystique'," *New York Times Book Review*, February 26, 2006, p. 23.

Douglas, Susan J. and Meredith W. Michaels, *The Mommy Myth* (New York: Free Press, 2004).

Dray, Philip. "Noose," *The Boston Globe*, December 2, 2007.

Durkheim, Emile. *The Division of Labor in Society* (New York: Free Press, 1997).

Dykstra, Steve W. "The Artist's Intentions and the Intentional Fallacy in Fine Arts Conservation," *Journal of the American Institute for Fine Arts Conservation*, 1996, 35 (3), pp. 197–218.

"Electric Car Dreams," *NOW*, Public Broadcasting System, October 30, 2009.

EOL Newsletter, Issue 1, www. EOL.org.

Frankena, William K. "A Model for Analyzing a Philosophy of Education" in Jane Roland Martin, Ed. *Readings in the Philosophy of Education* (Boston, MA: Allyn & Bacon, 1970), pp. 15–22.

Fraser, Nancy and Linda J. Nicholson. "Social Criticism without Philosophy: An Encounter between Feminism and Postmodernism" in Linda J. Nicholson, Ed. *Feminism/Postmodernism* (New York: Routledge, 1990), pp. 19–38.

Freyd, Jennifer and J.Q. Johnson. "References on Chilly Climate for Women Faculty in Academe," http://dynamic.uoregon.edu.

Gaard, Greta. "Anti-Lesbian Intellectual Harassment in the Academy" in VèVè Clark, Shirley Nelson Garner, Margaret Higonnet, and Ketu H. Katrak, Eds. *Anti-Feminism in the Academy* (New York: Routledge, 1996), pp. 115–140.

Gabriel, Trip. "Many Charter Schools, Varied Grades," *New York Times*, May 2, 2010, p. 22.

Gardner, Howard. *Frames of Mind* (New York: Basic Books, 1983).

Gilman, Charlotte Perkins. *Herland* (New York: Pantheon, 1979).

Gladwell, Malcolm. "The Vanishing," *The New Yorker*, January 3, 2005, pp. 70–73.

Gleick, James. *Chaos* (New York, Penguin Books, 1988).

Goodlad, John I. *In Praise of Education* (New York: Teachers College Press, 1997).

Goodlad, John I. and Timothy J. McMannon, Eds. *The Public Purpose of Education and Schooling* (San Francisco: Jossey-Bass, 1997).

Goodlad, John I., Corinne Mantle-Bromley, and Stephen John Goodlad. *Education for Everyone* (San Francisco: Jossey-Bass, 2004).

Goodman, Nelson. *Fact, Fiction, and Forecast* (Cambridge, MA: Harvard University Press, 1955).

Gootman, Elissa. "For Scholar of Race, Noose Case Draws Spotlight," *New York Times*, October 12, 2007, p. A 23.

Gould, Stephen Jay. *The Mismeasure of Man* (New York: Norton, 1981).

Graham, Patricia Albjerg. *Schooling America* (Oxford: Oxford University Press, 2005).

Greene, Brian. *The Elegant Universe* (New York: Norton, 2003).

Guinier, Lani, Michelle Fine, and Jane Balin. *Becoming Gentlemen* (Boston, MA: Beacon Press, 1997).

Guttman, Amy and Dennis Thompson. *Why Deliberative Democracy?* (Princeton, NJ: Princeton University Press, 2004).

Hall, Roberta M. and Bernice Resnick Sandler. *The Classroom Climate: A Chilly One for Women* (Washington D.C.: Association of Women's Colleges, 1982).

Hallie, Philip. *Lest Innocent Blood Be Shed* (New York: Harper & Rowe, 1979).

Hamill, Pete. "Say Hey," *New York Times Magazine*, February 28, 2010, pp. 1, 8–9.

Harper, Kenn. *Give Me My Father's Body* (New York: Washington Square Press, 2000).

Harrington, Mona. *Women Lawyers* (New York: Penguin, 1995).

Heins, Marjorie. *Not in Front of the Children* (New York: Hill & Wang, 2001).

Herbert, Bob. "Coming Late to the Table," *New York Times*, May 31, 2008, p. A 27.

———. "Where the Bar Ought to Be," *New York Times*, February 23, 2010, p. A 23.

———. "Cops Vs. Kids," *New York Times*, March 6, 2010, p. A 19.

———. "Bloody Urban Landscapes," *New York Times*, May 8, 2010, p. A 19.

———. "Too Long Ignored," *New York Times*, August 21, 2010, p. A 17.

Hess, Elizabeth. *Nim Chimpsky* (New York: Bantam, 2008).

Hochschild, Arlie Russell. *The Second Shift* (New York: Penguin, 2003).

Hoffman, Eva. *Lost in Translation* (New York: Penguin, 1989).

Hölldobler, Bert and E.O. Wilson. *The Superorganism* (New York: Norton, 2008).

Hostetler, John A. *Amish Society* (Baltimore, MD: The John Hopkins University Press, 1993, fourth ed.).

Humes, Edward. *School of Dreams* (Orlando, FL: Harcourt, 2003).

"Hundreds of Languages Face Extinction," *The Boston Globe*, February 20, 2009.

Hurdle, Jon and Ian Urbina. "Boy Held in Plot to Open Fire at Pennsylvania School," *New York Times*, October 12, 2007, p. A 21.

Hyde, Lewis. *The Gift* (New York: Vintage, 1979).

Illich, Ivan. *Deschooling Society* (New York: Harper & Row, 1970).

Jackson, Derrick Z. "Still Blind to Swastikas in School," *Boston Globe*, October 22, 2004, p. A 19.

Jan, Tracey. "Spike in Violence in Middle Schools Raises Concerns," *The Boston Globe*, October 2, 2007, www.boston.com.

Jefferson, Thomas. "Notes on Virginia" in Adrienne Koch and William Peden, Eds. *The Life and Selected Writings of Thomas Jefferson* (New York: Modern Library, 1994), pp. 187–292.

Jones, Maggie. "A Different Kind of Prep School," *New York Times Magazine*, September 27, 2009, pp. 43–45, 57.

Joyce, Kathryn. *Quiverfull* (Boston, MA: Beacon Press, 2009).

Judson, Olivia. "The Wild Side," NYTimes.com, October 6, 2009.

Kant, Immanuel, trans. J.T. Goldthwait. *Observations on the Feeling of the Beautiful and Sublime* (Berkeley: University of California Press, 1960).

Keller, Charles R. "Needed: Revolution in the Social Studies" in Byron G. Massialas and Andreas M. Kazemias, Eds. *Crucial Issues in the Teaching of Social Studies* (Englewood-Cliffs, NJ: Prentice-Hall, 1964), pp. 38–45.

Kittay, Eva Feder. *Love's Labor* (New York: Routledge, 1998).

Kleibard, Herbert M. *Forging the American Curriculum* (New York: Routledge, 1992).

Kluger, Jeffrey. "Inside the Minds of Animals," *Time*, August 16, 2010, pp. 36–43.

Kolodny, Annette. "Paying the Price of Anti-Feminist Intellectual Harassment" in VèVè Clark, Shirley Nelson Garner, Margaret Higonnet, and Ketu H. Katrak, Eds. *Anti-Feminism in the Academy* (New York: Routledge, 1996), pp. 3–34.

Kozol, Jonathan. *The Shame of the Nation* (New York: Three Rivers Press, 2005).

Kristof, Nicholas D. "Religion and Women," *New York Times*, January 10, 2010, p. WK 11.

Kroeber, Theodora. *Ishi in Two Worlds: A Biography of the Last Wild Indian in North America* (Berkeley: University of California Press, 1976).

Kuhn, Thomas S. *The Structure of Scientific Revolutions* (Chicago: University of Chicago Press, 1970, second ed.).

Laird, Susan. "Rethinking Coeducation" in James Garrison, Ed. *The New Scholarship on Dewey* (Dordrecht, Netherlands: Kluwer Academic Publishers, 1995), pp. 193–210.

Lane, Harlan. *The Wild Boy Of Aveyron* (Cambridge, MA: Harvard University Press, 1976).

Laudan, Larry. *Progress and Its Problems* (Berkeley: University of California Press, 1977).

Lavelle, Marianne. "Can Industry Spread Its Green Fever?" *U.S. News and World Report*, June 6, 2005.

Lazerson, Marvin and W. Norton Grubb, Eds. *American Education and Vocationalism* (New York: Teachers College Press, 1974).

Linton, Ralph. *The Study of Man* (New York: Appleton-Century-Crofts, 1936).

Locke, John. "Some Thoughts Concerning Education" in *On Politics and Education* (New York: Walter J. Black, 1947), pp. 205–388.

Loh, Sandra Tsing. "I Choose My Choice!" *The Atlantic*, July/August 2008, pp. 125–133.

Lott, Tommy L. *The Invention of Race* (Malden, MA: Blackwell, 1999).

Lovejoy, Meg. "'You Can't Go Home Again': The Impact of Women's Studies on Intellectual and Personal Development," *National Women's Studies Association Journal*, 10 (1), pp. 119–138.

Lurie, Alison. "The Royal Family," *New York Review of Books*, December 16, 2004, volume 51, no. 20.

Luther, Martin. "Letters to the Mayors and Aldermen of All the Cities of Germany in Behalf of Christian School" in Robert Ulich, Ed. *Three Thousand Years Of Educational Wisdom* (Cambridge, MA: Harvard University Press, 1947), pp. 218–238.

Maag, Christopher. "Short but Troubled Life of a High School Student Ended in a Shooting and Suicide," *New York Times*, October 12, 2007, p. A 21.

Macpherson, C.B. *The Life and Times of Liberal Democracy* (Oxford: Oxford University Press, 1976).

Mahoney, Karen. "Charlotte Perkins Gilman: The Origin of Education is Maternal" in Connie Titone and Karen E. Maloney, Eds. *Women's Philosophies of Education* (Upper Saddle River, NJ: Prentice-Hall, 1999), Ch. 5.

Malcolm X. *The Autobiography of Malcolm X* (New York: Grove Press, 1965).

Mann, Mary Peabody and Elizabeth Peabody. *Moral Culture of Infancy and Kindergarten Guide* (Boston, MA: T.O.H.P. Burnham, 1864).

Mannheim, Karl. "The Problem of Generations" in P. Keckskemti, Ed. *Essays in the Sociology of Knowledge* (London: Routledge & Kegan Paul, 1952), pp. 276–320.

Mar, M. Elaine. *Paper Daughter* (New York: HarperCollins, 2000).

Martin, Jane Roland. "The Disciplines and the Curriculum," *Educational Theory and Philosophy*, 1969, 1.

——, Ed. *Readings in the Philosophy of Education* (Boston, MA: Allyn & Bacon, 1970).

——. "What Should We Do with a Hidden Curriculum When We Find One?" *Curriculum Inquiry*, 1976, 6 (2), pp. 135–151.

——. "The Anatomy of Subject," *Educational Theory*, Spring 1977, 27 (2), pp. 85–95.

——. "Sophie and Emile: A Case Study of Sex Bias in the History of Educational Thought," *Harvard Educational Review*, 1981, 51 (3), pp. 357–372.

——. "The Ideal of the Educated Person," *Educational Theory*, 1981, 31 (2), pp. 97–109.

——. "Needed: A New Paradigm for Liberal Education" in Jonas P. Soltis, Ed. *Philosophy of Education: Eightieth Yearbook of the National Society for the Study of Education* (Chicago: University of Chicago Press, 1981), pp. 37–59.

——. "Two Dogmas of Curriculum," *Synthese*, April 1982, 51 (1), pp. 5–20.

——. "Excluding Women from the Educational Realm," *Harvard Educational Review*, 1982, 52 (2), pp. 138–148.

——. "Sex Equality and Education in Plato's Just State" in Mary Vetterling-Braggin, Ed. *"Femininity," "Masculinity," and "Androgyny"* (Totowa, NJ: Littlefield Adams, 1982), pp. 279–300.

——. *Reclaiming a Conversation* (New Haven, CT: Yale University Press, 1985).

——. *The Schoolhome* (Cambridge, MA: Harvard University Press, 1992).

——. *Changing the Educational Landscape* (New York: Routledge, 1994).

——. "Methodological Essentialism, False Difference, and Other Dangerous Traps," *Signs*, Spring 1994, 19 (3), pp. 630–657.

——. "There's Too Much to Teach: Cultural Wealth in an Age of Scarcity," *Educational Researcher*, 1996, 25 (2), pp. 4–10, 16.

——. "Gender in the Classroom: Now You See It, Now You Don't," *Democracy and Education*, 1999, 9 (3), pp. 9–13.

——. *Coming of Age in Academe* (New York: Routledge, 2000).

——. *Cultural Miseducation* (New York: Teachers College Press, 2002).

——. "Feminism" in Randall Curran, Ed. *A Companion to the Philosophy of Education* (Oxford: Blackwell, 2003), pp. 192–205.

——. "In Search of Equality: The Missing Women in Higher Education," *Gender Law and Policy Annual Review*, 2004, 2, pp. 133–146.

——. *Educational Metamorphoses* (Lanham, MD: Rowman & Littlefield, 2007).

——. "The Missing Women in Higher Education: A Case Study of Culture Crossing" in Ann Mari May, Ed. *The "Woman Question" and Higher Education* (Cheltenham, UK: Edward Elgar, 2008), pp. 77–92.

Martin, Michael and Lee C. McIntyre, Eds. *Readings in the Philosophy of Social Science* (Cambridge, MA: MIT Press, 1994).

Mathabane, Mark. *Kaffir Boy* (New York: Simon & Schuster, 1986).

Maushart, Susan. *The Mask of Motherhood* (New York: Penguin, 2000)

Mayer, Jane. "Whatever It Takes," *The New Yorker*, February 19, 2007.

McCourt, Frank. *Teacher Man* (New York: Scribner, 2005).

McLean, Bethany and Peter Elkind. *The Smartest Guys in the Room* (New York: Penguin Group, 2003).

Meier, Deborah and Paul Schwartz, "Central Park East Secondary School" in Michael W. Apple and James A. Bean, Eds. *Democratic Schools* (Portsmouth, NH: Heinemann, 2007, second ed.), pp. 130–149.

Milgram, Stanley. *Obedience to Authority* (New York: Harper & Row, 1974).

Mill, John Stuart. *On Liberty* (Indianapolis: Bobs-Merrill, 1859/1956).

——. *The Subjection of Women* (Cambridge, MA: MIT Press, 1869/1970).

Miller, Martin. "'24' and 'Lost' Get Symposium on Torture," *Seattle Times*, February 14, 2007.

Miller, William R. and Janet C'de Baca. *Quantum Change* (New York: Guilford Press, 2001).

Monroe, Kristen, Saba Ozyurt, Ted Wrigley, and Amy Alexander. "Gender Equity in Academia: Bad News from the Trenches, and Some Possible Solutions," *Perspectives on Politics*, June 2008, 6 (2), pp. 215–233.

Montessori, Maria. *The Montessori Method* (New York: Schocken Books, 1964).

Moyers, Bill. *Journal*, Public Broadcasting System, November 23, 2007.

——. *Journal*, Public Broadcasting System, July 24, 2009.

Mulcahy, D.G. *Knowledge, Gender, and Schooling* (Westport, CT: Bergin & Garvey, 2002).

——. *The Educated Person* (Lanham, MD: Rowman & Littlefield, 2008).

Nichols, John and Robert W. McChesney. *Tragedy & Farce* (New York: The New Press, 2005).

Nussbaum, Martha C. *Poetic Justice* (Boston, MA: Beacon Press, 1995).

——. *Cultivating Humanity* (Cambridge, MA: Harvard University Press, 1997).

——. *Frontiers of Justice* (Cambridge, MA: Harvard University Press, 2006).

Oakeshott, Michael. "The Study of 'Politics' in a University" in Jane Roland Martin, Ed. *Readings in the Philosophy of Education* (Boston, MA: Allyn & Bacon, 1970), pp. 30–64.

Orenstein, Peggy. *School Girls* (New York: Doubleday, 1994).

Ortner, Sherry. "Is Female to Male as Nature is to Culture?" in Michelle Zimbalist Rosaldo and Louise Lamphere, Eds. *Women, Culture, and Society* (Palo Alto, CA: Stanford University Press, 1974), pp. 67–87.

Palepu, Anita and Carol P. Herbert. "Medical Women in Academia: The Silences We Keep," *JAMC*, October 15, 2002, 167 (8), pp. 877–879.

Parker-Pope, Tara. "For Clues on Teenage Sex, Experts Look to Hip-Hop," *New York Times*, November 6, 2007, pp. D. 5, 8.

Peters, R.S. "Education and the Educated Man" in R.F. Dearden, P.H. Hirst, and R.S. Peters, Eds. *A Critique of Current Educational Aims* (London: Routledge & Kegan Paul, 1972), pp. 1–16.

——. "What Is an Educational Process?" in R.S. Peters, Ed. *The Concept of Education* (New York: Humanities Press, 1967), pp. 1–23.

Philipsen, Maike Ingrid. *Challenges of the Faculty Career for Women* (San Francisco: Jossey-Bass, 2008).

Pinker, Steven. *The Language Instinct* (New York: Summit Books, 1995).

Plato, trans. G.M.A. Grube. *Republic* (Indianapolis, IN: Hackett, 1974).

Popper, Karl R. *The Poverty Of Historicism* (Boston, MA: Beacon Press, 1957).

Provenza, Eugene F., Jr. "An Adventure with Children" in Susan F. Semel and Alan R. Sadovnik, Eds. *"Schools of Tomorrow," Schools of Today* (New York: Peter Lang, 1999), pp. 103–120.

Putnam, Robert D. *Bowling Alone* (New York: Simon & Schuster, 2000).

Quine, Willard Van Orman. *From a Logical Point of View* (Cambridge, MA: Harvard University Press, 1953).

Rachels, James. "Drawing Lines" in Cass R. Sunstein and Martha C. Nussbaum, Eds. *Animal Rights* (Oxford: Oxford University Press, 2004).

Rawls, John. *A Theory of Justice* (Cambridge, MA: Harvard University Press, 1971).

Redfield, Robert. "The Little Community" in *The Little Community and Peasant Society and Culture* (Chicago: University of Chicago Press, 1989).

Reich, Robert. *Supercapitalism* (New York: Knopf, 2007).

Rich, Adrienne. *Of Woman Born* (New York: Bantam, 1977).

Richtel, Matt. "Thou Shallt Not Kill, Except in a Game at Church," *New York Times*, October 7, 2007, pp. A 1, 20.

Riley, Denise. *Am I That Name?* (Minneapolis: University of Minnesota Press, 1988).

Risen, James. "Electrical Risks Worse than Said at Bases in Iraq," *New York Times*, July 18, 2008, pp. A 1, 10.

Robbins, Alexandra. *The Overachievers* (New York: Hyperion, 2006).

Rodriguez, Richard. *Hunger of Memory* (Boston, MA: David R. Godine, 1982).

Rothstein, Edward. "All About Mr. Elephant, in His Becoming Green Suit," *New York Times*, September 22, 2008, pp. B 1, 5.

Rousseau, Jean-Jacques, trans. Allan Bloom. *Emile* (New York: Basic Books, 1762/1979).

Rymer, Russ. *Genie* (New York: HarperCollins, 1993).

Sadker, David Miller and Karen R. Zittleman. *Teachers, Schools, and Society* (New York: McGraw-Hill, 2007).

Sadker, Myra and David Sadker. *Failing at Fairness* (New York: Touchstone, 1995).

Sandler, Bernice Resnick, Lisa A. Silverberg, and Roberta M. Hall. *The Chilly Classroom Climate: A Guide to Improve the Education of Women* (Washington D.C.: National Association for Women in Education, 1996).

Sarason, S.B. *The Culture of the School and the Problem of Change* (Boston, MA: Allyn & Bacon, 2nd ed., 1982).

Sen, Amartya. "More Than 100 Million Women Are Missing," *New York Review of Books*, December 20, 1990.

——. *Development as Freedom* (New York: Knopf, 1999).

——. "Missing Women—Revisited," *British Medical Journal*, December 6, 2003, p. 1,297.

——. *Identity and Violence* (New York: Norton, 2006).

Shapiro, Ian. *The State of Democratic Theory* (Princeton, NJ: Princeton University Press, 2003).

Singer, Peter. *Animal Liberation* (New York: HarperCollins, 2002).

Smith, Adam. *An Inquiry into the Nature and Causes of the Wealth of Nations* (Chicago: University of Chicago Press, 1776/1976).

Smith, B. Othanel, William O. Stanley, and J. Harlan Shores, *Fundamentals of Curriculum Development* (New York: Harcourt, Brace & World, 1957).

Smith, Lydia A.H. *Activity and Experience* (New York: Agathon Press, 1976).

Smolin, Lee. *The Trouble with Physics* (Boston, MA: Houghton Mifflin, 2006).

Snow, C.P. *The Two Cultures* (Cambridge: Cambridge University Press, 1998).

Snyder, Benson R. *The Hidden Curriculum* (New York: Alfred A. Knopf, 1971).

Spencer, Herbert. "What Knowledge Is of Most Worth?" in *Education* (New York: D. Appleton, 1860).

Starr, Paul. *The Creation of the Media* (New York: Basic Books, 2004).

Stein, Jess, Ed. *The Random House Dictionary* (New York: Ballantine Books, 1980).

Stein, Nan and Lisa Sjpostrom. *Flirting or Hurting?* (Washington D.C.: National Education Association, 1994).

Stone, Pamela. *Opting Out?* (Berkeley: University of California Press, 2007).

Summers, Lawrence. "Remarks at NBER Conference on Diversifying the Science and Engineering Workforce," January 14, 2005, www.president.harvard.edu/speeches, p. 2.

Swofford, Anthony. *Jarhead* (New York: Scribner, 2003).

Taba, Hilda. *Curriculum Development* (New York: Harcourt, Brace, and World, 1962).

Tey, Josephine. *Brat Farrar* (New York: Scribner, 1997).

"The Debate About the Social Responsibilities of Companies Is Heating up Again," *The Economist*, September 8, 2007, pp. 65–66.

Tolstoy, Leo, trans. Constance Garnett. *War and Peace* (New York Modern Library, 1994).

Transcript, Daughter of Danang, American Experience, Public Broadcasting System.

Tripsas, Mary. "When Names Change to Protect the Future," *New York Times*, November 29, 2009, p. BU 3.

Turner, Jonathan. "Herbert Spencer" in J.J. Chambliess, Ed. *Philosophy of Education: An Encyclopedia* (New York: Garland, 1996), pp. 623–626.

Tyack, David and William Tobin. "The 'Grammar' of Schooling: Why Has it Been so Hard to Change?" *American Educational Research Journal*, Fall 2004, 31 (3), pp. 453–479.

Tye, Barbara Benham. *Hard Truths* (New York: Teachers College Press, 2000).

Uchitelle, Louis. *The Disposable American* (New York: Alfred A. Knopf, 2006).

Urban Dictionary, www.urbandictionary.com.

Varela, Francisco J., Evan Thompson, and Eleanor Rosch. *The Embodied Mind* (Cambridge, MA: MIT Press, 1993).

Wade, Nicholas. "Chimps and Monkeys Could Talk. Why Don't They?" *New York Times*, January 12, 2010, pp. D1, 4.

Walzer, Michael. "Deliberation, and What Else?" in Stephen Macedo, Ed., *Deliberative Politics* (New York: Oxford University Press, 1999), pp. 58–69.

Wedekind, Jennifer. "The Children's Crusade," *In These Times*, June 3, 2005, www.inthesetimes.com/article/2136.

West, Cornell. *Race Matters* (New York: Vintage, 1993).

White, Edmund V. "Sons and Brothers," *New York Review of Books*, October 11, 2007, pp. 47–48.

White, Patricia. *Civic Virtues and Public Schooling* (New York: Teachers College Press, 1996).

Williams, Joan. *Unbending Gender* (Oxford: Oxford University Press, 2000).

Wilson, Edward O. *Naturalist* (Washington D.C.: Island Press, 1994).

———. *The Future of Life* (New York: Vintage, 2002).

Wimsatt, William K. and Monroe C. Beardsley. "The Intentional Fallacy," *Sewanee Review*, 1946, 54, pp. 468–488

———. *The Verbal Icon: Studies in the Meaning of Poetry* (Lexington: University of Kentucky Press, 1954).

Woit, Peter. *Not Even Wrong: The Failure of String Theory and the Search for Unity in Physical Law* (New York: Basic Books, 2006).

"Women Account for Half of College Enrollment in US," 1986.

"Women Medical School Faculty Perceive Gender Bias, Sexual Harassment," June 6, 2000, http://mgh.harvard.edu/pubaffairs.

Woolf, Virginia. *Three Guineas* (New York: Harcourt Brace, 1938).

Yale Sustainable Food Project. *Annual Report*, 2005.

Yan, Sophia. "Anonymous Gossip Sites," *Time*, December 7, 2009, pp. 97–98.

Yoshino, Kenji. *Covering* (New York: Random House, 2006).

INDEX